Narrative

Designed to meet the complex needs of patients with psychosis, *Narrative CBT for Psychosis* combines narrative and solution-focused therapy with established techniques from CBT (cognitive behaviour therapy) into one integrated flexible approach.

In this book John Rhodes and Simon Jakes bring the practitioner up to date, as treatment and practice evolve to draw on other therapeutic approaches, creating an approach which is client centred and non-confrontational. The book contains many tried and tested practical ideas for helping clients, with several chapters including detailed and illuminating case studies.

Areas of discussion include:

- how to work with delusions, voices and visions
- working with core beliefs
- an exploration of narratives of past difficulties and traumas
- recovery and ending therapy.

Narrative CBT for Psychosis will be essential reading for all mental health professionals who deal with psychosis who wish to learn a new approach.

John Rhodes is a Consultant Clinical Psychologist in the Department of Psychology, Brent (CNWL Trust), Lecturer on Clinical Psychology at the University of Hertfordshire and Honorary Lecturer at University College London.

Simon Jakes is a Senior Clinical Psychologist on the Sub-acute Mental Health Unit at Campbelltown Hospital, South West Sydney, an Honorary Fellow at Wollongong University and an Honorary Associate at the University of Sydney.

Narrative CBT for Psychosis

John Rhodes and Simon Jakes

Routledge
Taylor & Francis Group

LONDON AND NEW YORK

First published 2009
by Routledge
27 Church Road, Hove, East Sussex BN3 2FA

Simultaneously published in the USA and Canada
by Routledge
270 Madison Avenue, New York, NY 10016

Routledge is an imprint of the Taylor & Francis Group, an informa business

Copyright © 2009 John Rhodes and Simon Jakes

Typeset in Times by Garfield Morgan, Swansea, West Glamorgan
Printed and bound in Great Britain by T J International Ltd, Padstow,
Cornwall
Paperback cover design by Lisa Dynan

This publication has been produced with paper manufactured to strict
environmental standards and with pulp derived from sustainable forests.

British Library Cataloguing in Publication Data
A catalogue record for this book is available from the British Library

Library of Congress Cataloging-in-Publication Data
Rhodes, John, 1955–
    Narrative CBT for psychosis / John Rhodes & Simon Jakes.
        p. ; cm.
    Includes bibliographical references.
    ISBN 978-0-415-40730-4 (hbk) – ISBN 978-0-415-47572-3 (pbk.)
    1. Psychoses—Treatment. 2. Cognitive therapy. 3. Narrative therapy. I.
Jakes, Simon, 1956– II. Title.
    [DNLM: 1. Cognitive Therapy—methods. 2. Narration. 3. Psychological
Theory. 4. Psychotic Disorders—psychology. 5. Psychotic Disorders—
therapy. WM 425.5.C6 R476n 2009]
    RC512.R65 2009
    616.89—dc22
                                                            2008032724

ISBN: 978-0-415-40730-4 (hbk)
ISBN: 978-0-415-47572-3 (pbk)

Contents

Acknowledgements

We would both like to acknowledge the cooperation of our patients in helping us develop our work.

John Rhodes: I would like thank Natan, my circle of friends, and my parents for support and much else over many years.

Simon Jakes: I would like to thank Soraya, Ben, Joseph, Sam, and Luke for their support and patience while writing the book. Also thanks to Charles, Ruth, and Ian Jakes for everything.

Chapter 1

Narrative CBT for psychosis

INTRODUCTION

Over several years we have developed a way of working with psychosis that for convenience might be termed narrative cognitive behaviour therapy (NCBT). In this chapter we discuss the origins of these ideas and practices. We will also look at what might justify adopting such an approach, and how it fits into wider theories of mental life.

Solution focused therapy

Solution focused therapy (SFT) developed from systemic family therapy by a process of observing what appeared to work, that is, what aspects of therapy seemed to help clients to make desired changes (de Shazer, 1985, 1988): it was not developed from any 'grand theory', psychological or otherwise (de Shazer et al., 2007). It is essentially a practice, a way of working with people. It aims to solve problems by helping clients to describe situations in which the problem does not occur, that is, when there are exceptions to the problem pattern. Exceptions might occur spontaneously, or might involve deliberate activities by the client. By knowing more about exceptions and by thinking together how these might be augmented, it is hoped that the client can begin to solve the presenting problem.

Another essential strand of SFT is to clarify with clients what their goals are, and in particular, to help clients describe how they would know in detail how they are making progress. Many therapies use the idea of 'goal' to some extent: SFT, however, is explicit in making this a central focus and in emphasising what might be thought of as the 'phenomenology' of a goal for a person, that is, how the achievement of a goal might appear in experience, how this specific client would know that specific goals were being achieved. It is not assumed that all clients arrive knowing their goals: often it is part of the therapy to articulate and to construct possible goals and this can be aided by focus on a picture of the future.

In line with systemic therapy, there is an attempt to understand problems and solutions within their interpersonal context. It is also explicit in emphasising not only that must one know a client's goals, but also that one needs to understand how a client's goals might or might not conflict with the goals of other persons involved in the client's network or social system.

Narrative therapy

A central claim of narrative therapy (NT) is that we 'narrate' our lives: that we form narratives of the past and future, and that these not only describe our lives but might also influence our lives. For example, after a psychotic breakdown, a person may form a narrative idea such as, 'All I did led me to this collapse . . . I must be weak': believing such a narrative to be the case might then influence the person to give up college, for example.

The concept of narrative needs to be understood in its wider sense, that is, to potentially include descriptions of events, characterisations, metaphor, metonymy, and diverse forms of discourse. Furthermore, these aspects of narrative are not understood as first occurring in literature and then borrowed for use in everyday life. In fact the reverse: narrative might be considered to occur naturally in human experience and that literature borrows from this intrinsic phenomenon (Turner, 1996).

White and Epston (1990) argue that clients have 'problem-saturated stories' and the aim of their work is both to articulate the negative story and its effects upon the person and then to move on to constructing an alternative and preferred narrative with the client. The latter may be constructed in many ways, but often involves locating events or characteristics that somehow do not fit the negative story. White has called these 'unique outcomes', but recently termed them 'initiatives' (White, 2004).

NT suggests that it is sometimes useful to investigate the origins of these narratives. For example, a person might think that he or she is not a 'success'. The therapist might discuss with the client how such ideas or discourses entered into the person's life. NT considers a narrative to be constructed within a social and sociological context; for example, there are collective discourses about being a 'success' and these might influence people to choose certain goals and live certain lifestyles. Psychiatric patients, however, besides their immediate suffering, also suffer the consequences of being narrated as 'outsiders' and as not as 'rational' as others (Foucault, 1965; Harper, 2004).

NT has very strong overlaps with SFT, and many writers fuse the two traditions and borrow aspects from both (for example Eron and Lund, 1996). To contrast these two therapies one might say that it is typical of narrative therapy to narrate the negative story and move on to the preferred positive story, whereas solution focused therapy tends to concentrate where possible on constructing a positive narrative, and asks only the minimum concerning the presenting negative story. We will return to this topic in the chapter on solution focused approaches. Given the profound conceptual and procedural overlap of these therapies, we will refer to them when thinking of them collectively as narrative solution focused therapies (NSFT).

Unlike de Shazer, who did not use a theory as such to justify SFT, White and Epston from the beginning have always used ideas about narrative drawn from Bruner and ideas about the formative influence of discourse taken from Foucault. Like de Shazer, they developed their approach from a version of systemic therapy (Cecchin, 1987). We will return to the possible justification of NSFT in a later section.

Cognitive behaviour therapy

We draw upon a very wide range of approaches found in the general field of cognitive behaviour therapy (CBT): from work in which the main focus is changing daily behaviour patterns such as the 'behavioural activation' of Martell, Addis, and Jacobson (2001) or from coping enhancement strategy (Tarrier, 2002), to types of cognitive challenges as outlined by Beck, Rush, Shaw, and Emery (1979) for depression. We also use cognitive techniques adapted for psychosis (Chadwick and Lowe, 1990; Nelson, 2005; Fowler, Garety, and Kuipers, 1995; Kingdon and Turkington, 2004).

One approach we have adapted and use with most clients is taken from Padesky (1994). Clients are asked to state any negative beliefs they have about themselves, others, and the world, and then are asked to describe how they would prefer all these things to be. For example, a client might say 'I'm horrible' and would prefer 'I'm pleasant'. Several techniques are used to build upon the preferred option, for example asking the client to collect any evidence of being pleasant. As this example indicates, there are clear parallels between this approach and the practice of narrative solution focused therapy to the extent that both aim to construct something useful and positive for the person.

We usually carry out a Padesky-style focus on preferred core beliefs about self and others without first examining 'cognitions' as has been traditionally recommended for conventional mood disorders (Beck et al., 1979). We agree with Lee (2005) that for some clients, usually those with complex and severe presentations, conventional cognitive challenging often does not seem to work as a first strategy. If conventional 'challenging' of cognitions is used, then we tend to do this in a penultimate stage of therapy and normally where there is pretty good evidence that various changes in emotional and social functioning have already occurred. Furthermore, as will be illustrated later, we tend to use very 'gentle' approaches; for example, we do not set out to prove that a specific 'thought' is false but rather that another perspective, another narrative, is possible.

When working with hallucinations, in particular, we tend to mix ideas and practices from both SFT and 'coping enhancement strategy' (CES) as developed by Tarrier (2002). SFT is certainly not just about coping, but can be used for that purpose, and as such blends coherently with CES. SF questions can be used to explore goals and what works, while CES introduces the idea of systematic 'experimenting' and consistent use.

If solution focused questions do not generate ideas of 'what works', we might then describe to the client certain techniques as outlined by Nelson (2005). In this book she lists some simple approaches, for example that some people have found the use of headphones helpful. We leave it up to the client to choose which to try out.

Each client is unique and if appropriate we might borrow any aspects from the full range of CBT techniques to construct a specific approach for an individual. We sometimes focus specifically on depression and use behavioural activation (Martell et al., 2001). For the fear of leaving the house, we might attempt adaptations of graded exposure therapy (Hawton, Salkovskis, Kirk, and Clark, 1989).

We have made extensive use of 'narrative exposure therapy' (Neuner, Schauer, Roth, Elbert, 2002), combined with narrative therapy ideas in general, for working with those clients who have described difficult, if not abusive, events in childhood. That is, in one phase of work we attempt to put into a narrative the often disjointed memories of traumatic events, but also consider the history of a person's strengths and ways of coping.

All the above CBT approaches can be, and often are, combined with ideas from the practice of NSFT. So, for example, if we were working with a specific phobia using exposure we would do this with an additional focus of looking for exceptions, that is, times when the person has coped with the phobia.

We borrow techniques and approaches from both NSFT and CBT, producing what we believe to be a coherent and useful practice. We have carried out research that suggests that this combined approach may be effective for some cases (Jakes and Rhodes, 2003). While we borrow techniques and therapeutic practices from both of these types of therapy, we are not, however, wholly convinced by several of the theories or parts of theories involved in CBT nor those used by White and Epston. Like de Shazer, we tend to be more convinced of evidence that certain approaches work, help clients, than by the abstract theories which are supposed to justify these practices. Brewin (2006) has argued that the theories to explain CBT are not yet wholly convincing (we return to this later).

Some key features of our approach

The approach we use, NCBT, has the following key features:

1 There is a very strong emphasis on constructing or building something new, or alternatively, strengthening an under-used strength or resource of the person. This emphasis is present in SFT, NT, and Padesky's work. This might be thought of as being 'constructional' and has also emerged in other areas of CBT, for example: Hall and Tarrier (2003), Hackman (2005). Hackman explores the possibility of building new benign imagery to help with difficulties involving negative images from the past.

2 Like most CBT, our work also involves the exploration and the emotional expression of experienced difficulties. Our commitment to being constructional does not take away recognition of the usefulness of expression of difficulties and the new understandings that might emerge. In fact, we tend to agree with Greenberg (2002) that in many cases it may be the case that a person first needs to attend to and articulate what the problem is, before they can move towards building solutions. The attempt to 'put into words' is a central part of narrative therapy (White, 2007).

3 Our work combines the notion of understanding problems within their context, as in behaviour therapy (Martell et al., 2001), but also within a 'system' or 'network' of others (Hedges, 2005). To this extent, we see our approach as systemic.

4 Our work is narrative in that it pays attention to a client's use of language, metaphor, and complex characterisations of self and other. It is also narrative in the sense of seeking an understanding of how problems are seen to develop over time. Our assessment of delusions, for example, spends considerable time on the period of onset, on the time before onset, and how things developed over the months and years.

5 There is a movement in our work towards being 'phenomenological'. Here phenomenology is to be understood as the attempt via our interaction and dialogue to grasp, to conceive, the 'lived' world of the other person, the world as experienced by the client. In SFT, in particular, there is an attempt to, as it were, go with the client, to work on 'goals', what is desired, what is hoped for, as presented by the client and in the language actually used. We very rarely take up an 'educational' stance as is sometimes suggested in some CBT (Hawton et al., 1989). We think this can be unhelpful by setting up a 'passive pupil' role. If giving information, we would tend to do that in later stages, and normally only if sought by the client. One other major consequence of taking a phenomenological stance is that we tend not to use simple linear models of explanation, for example that an automatic thought might lead directly to a response. Rather, to explain a response, one needs to consider a holistic range of simultaneous influences. This aspect is wholly consistent with a narrative emphasis, but is better illumined by a model of mental experience to be described later (in particular one based on the concept of intentionality).

6   Our approach might be thought of as cautious in seeking to make change, somewhat as Nelson advocates when she discusses how just a partial change in someone's belief system might be helpful, but we also 'go slow' as outlined by Lipchick (2002). This contribution of being cautious, staying with a client's concerns and goals, and not seeking to prove to clients that they have made errors all helps, we believe, in building a therapeutic alliance and therapeutic cooperation.

WHY NOT JUST USE CBT?

We think there are several reasons why NCBT is a useful modification of CBT. First and foremost is that it allows a therapist to work in a very flexible way; in particular, it outlines ways of working with clients other than just challenging beliefs. The therapist can accept the presentation as given, if this is useful, and then work within the world view of the client. Using NCBT one can in fact delay or avoid giving a formulation which, however careful, is understood by clients as rejecting their beliefs.

NCBT is also useful in complex situations and for presentations where it is difficult to think how to proceed, and where there might not be well practised ways of working: it is extremely flexible and of course uses the ingenuity of the client to generate solutions.

NCBT is useful for very challenging cases, that is, where any progress at all is difficult to achieve. For such cases often one has to aim for small steps or improvements over long periods of time: working in this way is intrinsic to a solution orientation.

NCBT is systemic, that is, it naturally leads to considering problems in their context: this is crucial when working with serious mental health since such difficulties inevitably occur in the context of psychiatric teams, hospital, and of course, often in the context of a family or social relations. We have developed our way of working in real situations of routine practice and believe there lies its greatest strength. We are not claiming that it would be superior at changing specific symptoms, but do believe it has allowed our work to be more pragmatic and allowed greater client cooperation.

ARGUMENTS IN SUPPORT OF NARRATIVE CBT

Our therapy has a strong emphasis on building or rediscovering resources in the life of the person and simultaneously building solutions, benign ideas, and narratives of self and the person's world. What might justify this constructional orientation? In this section we first examine possible support based mainly on theory and then consider more direct empirical evidence.

Building resources

One major reason for being constructional in therapy is that positive and negative experiences do not form two ends of one single all-encompassing dimension, but rather, there are many areas of a person's life, and each can be separately experienced as positive or as negative (MacLeod and Moore, 2000). Put simply, one person may receive a lot of bad news concerning one area of life such as work, yet at the same time continue to have several close positive relationships. However, another person might receive the same bad news concerning work, but has no relief or satisfaction in other areas of life such as relations, hobbies, and so forth. Furthermore, some people not only experience negative events, they also have no ways of understanding, conceptualising and thus retaining any positive events that do occur to them.

MacLeod and Moore (2000) review several studies that suggest that areas of 'strength' and 'resource' may buffer or prevent conditions such as depression occurring and may prevent relapse. Cohen and McKay (1985) described in particular the 'stress-buffering' effect of social support. Much of MacLeod and Moore's arguments concerned mood disorders, but given that mood disorder is common in psychosis, and that emotion might have a central role in manifestations of psychosis (Freeman and Garety, 2003), then we believe the same arguments may apply to psychosis.

As well as therapists working in the solution focused tradition, several other authors have argued that it may be a useful therapeutic strategy to focus on positive changes rather than problems (Padesky, 1994; Fava, Rafanelli, Cazzaro, Conti, and Grandi, 1998; Seligman, Steen, Park, and Peterson, 2005). We are in broad agreement with this. The word 'positive' may have unhelpful connotations of being bright and optimistic in spite of all, and perhaps even an attitude of ignoring certain truths. A better phrase might be 'resource-building'.

The implications of MacLeod and Moore's review might be that therapy should aim at helping a person to notice and conceptualise any area of strength or positive information, but also to engage in long-term activities which yield a sense of satisfaction, achievement, and so on. The constructional parts of our therapy, and the therapies we borrow from have, we believe, those aims.

The retrieval of positive representations as a model for CBT

Brewin (2006) has recently published an article reviewing theories about the causal process of change in CBT, that is, what might make it an effective therapy. It has been traditionally suggested or assumed that CBT might help people to recover by changing negative ideas, cognitions, and emotional reactions such that these are transformed and permanently altered. So, for example, a person might no longer hold the belief that 'people don't like me', this being replaced with 'some people do like me'. Another person, for example someone with a spider phobia, might after therapy no longer have a tendency or disposition to react to spiders with fear. These changes, Brewin argues, are supposed to be due to a transformation of the relevant negative representations, for example the relevant meaning found either in explicit ideas or in those meanings or other types of feature, accessible or otherwise, that form part of an emotional reaction.

Considerable empirical evidence, however, suggests that the above claims are unlikely to be an adequate explanation. There is considerable evidence, reviewed by Brewin, that even after successful therapy, in certain extreme conditions, some clients are likely to revert to the negative thoughts and reactions they had before therapy.

Given these sorts of observations, Brewin has suggested the following alternative explanation. Successful therapy might work by strengthening a person's capacity to retrieve positive representations. He suggests we could conceive of a sort of competition for retrieval between negative and positive representations, and successful therapy gives positive representations greater likelihood of winning any such competition.

He speculates on what might increase the likelihood of a representation winning a retrieval competition. He suggests that this may be influenced by, features such as being distinctive, being well rehearsed, or being significant.

Brewin argues that the theory of enhanced positive representations can explain what might be considered traditional CBT, but might also be a good explanation of various recent developments in CBT, which, on the whole, involve an orientation towards being constructional, namely Padesky (1994) on the idea of a preferred self, Hackman (2005) on imagery, but also Gilbert's (2005) ideas on compassion therapy where there is an explicit effort to build an attitude of compassion to oneself.

Brewin considers it possible that his theory of positive representations might also help to explain therapies outside traditional CBT, and mentions, in particular, White and Epston's narrative therapy with its aim of constructing a benign narrative.

The possibility is considered that representations might change not just because of rational arguments using evidence for and against a negative cognition but that change might also involve processes of 'associative' thinking as might be found in types of imagination and imagery work. Such approaches are a central feature of narrative therapy.

It is fascinating to note how Brewin, working from a cognitive psychology and neuro-psychological perspective, has developed a model that might yield a unified and convincing explanation for the practice of CBT and therapies which involve an emphasis on building things in a person's life such as narrative therapy and, we suggest, solution focused therapy.

Representations and resources

The ideas of Brewin and those of MacLeod and Moore are different but overlap. Their combination, we suggest, might yield the following conceptualisation. A therapy produces benign changes for a person when:

1   there is an increase in the retrieval of positive representations and a person's available concepts for making sense of the 'positive', and
2   a person changes their habits, aspects of the self, ways of living, and external environment such that more positive events occur in the person's life.

We are emphasising here not only representations but also that which is represented be it external properties of the person's environment or properties of the self, that is, things which could be thought of as resources for the person. These resources, we believe, are essential since positive representations are hard to sustain in the long run without 'input' to work on. In line with this conception it is interesting to note that 'fresh starts' (Brown, Adler, and Bifulco, 1988), that is, some unexpected good news for a person, have powerful effects in encouraging the retrieval of positive representations. Finally, thinking about how to change the social systems and environment of a person is often an effective way of working.

We deliberately added the concept of 'habit' to the above statements since we are not at all sure that all psychological features do in fact include or work using 'representations'. For example, we clearly have procedural memory for a skill such as driving and it is still a matter of debate whether these types of memory involve any conscious or unconscious 'representations' (Searle, 1992). Physical exercise appears to have a benign effect on mood, yet it seems doubtful that this effect could be explained solely by a theory of representations.

Research supporting SFT and NT

There is a great deal of evidence supporting the effectiveness of CBT in psychosis (Garety et al., 1997; Sensky et al., 2000). There is, however, also some evidence supporting SFT and NT. A database compiled by Gingerich and Eisengart (2000) suggests that SFT yields results comparable to other therapies. Eakes et al. (1997) compared SFT for patients with schizophrenia and their families to a control group and demonstrated positive results. We ourselves have published three articles (Jakes, Rhodes, and Turner, 1999; Rhodes and Jakes, 2002; Jakes and Rhodes, 2003) specifically using SFT in combination with CBT.

For narrative therapy there is also a small but growing body of evidence. France and Uhlin (2006) review several uses of narrative in therapy. In the area of psychosis, narrative is a central part of the 'open dialogue' approach of Seikkula and associates (Seikkula, Alakare, and Aaltonen, 2001). Several detailed studies have been published by Lysaker and colleagues (Lysaker, Lancaster, and Lysaker, 2003). Roberts has described the importance of narrative in helping patients, particularly those with severe and chronic psychotic symptoms, to make sense of their lives. He also emphasises how a clinician might be able to draw upon both narrative approaches and evidenced based science (Roberts, 1999). Thornhill, Clare, and May (2004) found diverse styles of narrative in those recovering from psychosis, for example complex narratives of 'escape', or 'enlightenment'.

HOW NCBT FITS WIDER THEORIES OF MENTAL LIFE

In this chapter we have so far focused on therapeutic practices and theories that might begin to explain what these practices are and how they work. For the rest of the chapter we now wish to discuss certain wider theories, that is, theories not only of therapy, but of psychology in general. These theories are part of our therapeutic practice and thinking, but also have relevance to other issues such as understanding pathology and understanding behaviour in general. The topics we will consider are the constructivist framework, the concept of narrative, and finally a model of the mind developed in philosophy.

Constructivism

We wish to argue in this section that besides any specific empirical evidence, and specific ideas on the role of building resources in therapy, our approach fits in and is supported by a more general model within the social sciences. The model or framework we have adapted for our practice and thinking is 'constructivist' (Mahoney, 1991, 2003). As is often the case, a word or key term in psychology seems to acquire many meanings and this seems to be the case for 'constructivist'. To avoid ambiguity, we will present an outline of what we mean by a constructivist framework, which may or may not overlap with the ones given by other writers.

A constructivist theory or practice, we suggest, might be thought of as combining, to some degree, the following three major ideas.

First, psychological phenomena need to be described and understood in their 'naturalistic' form, that is, exactly as they occur in all their complexity. For example, a person does not simply have a negative idea or representation of himself or herself, rather over time a person elaborates complex ideas, stories, pictures, and metaphors of the self. Any part of a person's system of meanings will interconnect to other parts (Searle, 1992). The content and form of thinking is complex and interconnected; it involves imagination and elaborate combinations or 'blending' of ideas (Fauconnier and Turner, 2002). Experience may lead a person to develop complex 'stories' and 'characterisations' but these in turn influence experience and how a person lives (Bruner, 1986; White and Epston, 1990). Both language (Potter and Whetherell, 1987) and complex conceptualisation (Lakoff and Johnson, 1980; Fauconnier and Turner, 2002) are realities of human experience. Such complexity can be revealed if we attempt to describe social events as might a novelist or anthropologist. When we try to understand people in naturalistic contexts, the home, the school, it becomes apparent that human reality involves meaning, interpretation, culture: in line with constructivism we believe these are fundamental and must form part of a comprehensive science of persons (Henriques, 2003).

Second, psychological phenomena need to be understood in their context, in particular, their social and developmental contexts. This may seem obvious for social phenomena such as relationships and personality features, yet a constructivist perspective can also be extended to cognitive processes such as memory: Edwards and Potter (1992) point out how specific versions of 'what happened' can be the focus of argument between people and that these arguments involve complex social and linguistic practices. Some would also argue, for example Freeman (1995), that even in neurology one needs to take into consideration a 'society of brains', and recently Bentall (2003) has emphasised the social aspect of brain function, that is, that how the brain develops and changes over time is influenced by social processes.

Third, psychological phenomena cannot be understood as just passive reactions; rather, psychological processes are active. Bartlett (1932) suggested that the act of remembering is not just the reproduction of something fixed from the past; rather it involves the active construction of an account of events. Kelly (1955) emphasised that people actively 'construe' or anticipate future events: he underlined how this was an active process, something done by the person, not just something done to the person. The work of Kelly is strongly linked to the development of constructivist therapies (Winter and Viney, 2005).

The theory of Bartlett (1932), mentioned above, is perhaps a perfect illustration of a constructivist perspective. Not only did he explore how memories are actively reconstituted, he suggested that over time memories tend to become more 'conventional', that is, conform to social contexts and norms. It is also interesting to note that a central part of his research involved the telling and retelling of narratives.

We do not regard 'constructivism' as a theory of any one specific psychological or social phenomenon: rather, it is a framework and set of requirements for an adequate description and theory of social and psychological phenomena in general. Different writers are constructivist to varying degrees and in different ways. While Bartlett may well be a prototypical example of a constructivist, others would include: Piaget, Mead, Allport, Adler, Kelly, Bruner, Vygotsky, Harré, and discourse analysts such as Potter and Whetherall (1987) and Edwards and Potter (1992) on memory.

In a review of constructivist therapy, Neimeyer (1993) suggested as principal examples the work of Kelly (1955), Guidano (1991), Mahoney (1991), White and Epston (1990), and the constructivist systemic therapy of Boscolo, Cecchin, Hoffman, and Penn (1987). Several cognitive behaviour therapists, in addition to Mahoney, have also, to varying degrees, placed their work in a constructivist frame and these would include Russell (1991) and Gonçalves (1994). Greenberg (2002) writing on emotions also draws on constructivism in his theory of how a person needs to put feelings into words: for therapy he employs ideas from the experiential tradition such as Rogers, Gendlin, and Perls, but also uses aspects of CBT.

As stated, one might think of constructivism as an integrated and holistic framework for understanding persons and yet one that is open to the consideration of many types of theory and evidence. If we wish to understand persons, we need to use and consider any theories that are empirically supported and appear to illuminate the person at hand. We obviously need to draw upon many types of knowledge: for example, phenomenological descriptions, social psychology, neurobiology. An explanatory model needs, perhaps essentially, to be 'open'. It needs to be 'open' to many 'levels' of explanation, and diverse findings within any level: we discuss this further in Chapter 2.

The concept of narrative

We have introduced in this chapter the notion of narrative mainly as demonstrated in the therapy of White and Epston (1990). Many theorists in many diverse ways have developed or employed the concept of narration and its associated ideas of figuration (that is, use of metaphors, analogy, etc.), discourse, and so forth. From a literary linguistics point of view, Toolan (1988) has written an excellent introduction. He outlines the major contributions of the twentieth century to thinking about narrative in writers such as Propp, Barthes, and Greimas. He also presents Labov's work on how narrative is used in everyday situations. In psychology, several writers have used the concept of narration, in particular Bruner (1986, 1987). Bruner argued that cognitive science, in a sense, lost its way as it moved towards 'information processing' models.

Recently, some psychologists have examined narrative in the light of the unconscious: Talvitie and Tiitinen (2006) suggest there are various types of non-conscious processes and one type may be the 'unnarrated', that is, those parts of our experiences which have not entered a conscious deliberate narration of events and of personality over time. For example, a person might think of himself or herself as being close to one parent and that this had been true in childhood, and yet this story does not include information about life-long conflicts. The conflicts do not form part of that person's narrative of what has happened. It is important to emphasise that these ideas of pre-narrative non-conscious processes do not commit one to present-day psychodynamic ideas of motivation or development. The concept of the unnarrated is relevant for our work, as many clients do not seem to see connections between various areas of their lives. There are, sometimes, in fact, quite shocking disconnections, for example where the theme of a voice is so similar to themes of suffering, or where conviction in a delusional account so clearly increases after a personal problem. We return to these issues in the relevant chapters.

Closely linked to ideas on narrative are the developing theories of metaphor, or figuration in general (Lakoff and Johnson, 1980). A central claim is that our thoughts, our basic conceptions of the world, are themselves composed of mixtures of literal statements, metaphors, metonymies, and schematic images (Lakoff, 1987). For many concepts it is not the case that 'pure' literal thought is sometimes put into a metaphor. Rather, our concepts, for example of an emotion, almost always involve a metaphor. For example, Lakoff argues that anger is often thought of as a substance under pressure in a container. We talk of the mind as if it were a space, 'filling' with emotion and thoughts.

Fauconnier and Turner (2002), as a development of the above, have elaborated a model of 'conceptual blends': specific metaphors are but one type of blend, whereas conceptual blends are also seen to explain what might be thought of as complex imaginative scenarios used in everyday contexts and as well as those in literary contexts. A person might use a 'scenario' in talking with colleagues, for example 'if I were king', and then elaborate the changes, might joke about how modest he would be, how he would treat his old boss and so forth. We believe metaphors and blends are powerful ways of expressing and accessing ideas and emotions and think it a central part of a narrative therapeutic approach. We return to this topic in a later chapter.

MacIntyre (1981) used the idea of narrative as central to social science, but also emphasised how learning childhood narratives is one way we learn the moral codes of a society. Kashima (1997) in a similar vein suggested that the narratives that are available in a society might influence a person's motivations since stories told in a society often indicate goals that are pursued or should be pursued, for example love or honour.

Goldie (2004) has recently given a fascinating analysis of narrative with regard to personality. He suggests that people can take up two quite contrasting perspectives on themselves. One he terms 'Woolfian', that is, a perspective as found in Virginia Woolf's stream of consciousness novel. In this perspective we see details, moments, indeterminacy, impulses: we are aware of the particulars of the moment, we do not see long-term patterns.

In contrast, in the Augustinian perspective, a person forms a complex coherent story of self: the self is represented as a character, as an identity over time, and this identity is the object of reflection. The person might, for example, at certain moments in life judge himself or herself as living a worthwhile life or not and these moments can be turning points, moments when the person begins a new way of living. We form a story of the past, but also think of our identity in the future. Sluzki (1992) argued that one comes across both over-fixed and rigid stories and stories which seem too loose, too disconnected: both extremes might create difficulties for a person.

Goldie points out that narrative can influence the real life of the person: he emphasises, however, that our actual lives have structures, patterns, and can be compared to a tragedy or triumph and so on. But he emphasises that real lives are not themselves 'narratives' or 'histories': rather, our constructed verbal narratives are life-like, that is, the narrative mimics the real. We agree strongly with this point: we suggest that most artistic practices and forms are developed in cultures from pre-existing patterns and features of life itself. Furthermore, it is for this reason that the use of visual arts, narrative, and even simple metaphors can be so powerful in helping people to express their experiences and emotions.

MacIntyre (1981) has emphasised that to understand any 'action' it is not enough, as is typical in much of psychology, to atomise the event by considering it as an isolated fragment. Actions and social events occur in a context and as part of a person's history, these in turn ultimately connecting to the history of the surrounding society.

That a person might have a personal narrative, or perhaps, a repertoire of both feared and desired narratives, appears to us to be a far richer and more accurate representation of our mental experience than the more simple notions of self-concept or self-belief. We certainly do use the latter concepts, but ultimately try to remember that any specific belief is part of a wider 'story' of self.

Critical realism

While we have emphasised a constructivist frame, we see ourselves, as did Mahoney (1991), as critical constructivists. We tend to agree with a 'critical realist' (Bhaskar, 1989; Greenwood, 1994) view of social science and knowledge in general, that is, while any science or knowledge is influenced by history or culture, to some degree or other, knowledge at least might correspond to, is about, a mind-independent reality (Searle, 1992). For example, while 'marriage' is a social institution varying in form according to culture, there are 'external' or objective features of 'marriage' external to any particular viewpoint upon marriage. Some constructivists at least appear in their writings to reject the possibility of objective knowledge and an external reality. We disagree with these philosophical claims and see nothing within constructivism as such that necessitates an 'anti-realist' position. In fact, the very opposite is required when we state that human processes are complex, social, cultural, and generative, that is, to make a claim reflecting the real nature of the mind. A major upshot of this critical constructivist outlook is that in thinking about a person we are cautious about any hypothesis we generate. We draw upon behavioural explanations, consider the influence of meaning in its multiple forms, and speculate about the effects of early experience on subsequent development. However, the formulations we generate are taken to be speculative: we accept that sometimes, if not often, one just cannot know. We do not accept, as some CBT texts seem to imply, that one always gets a clear data-based formulation that fully explains a person's symptoms. Great caution, if not outright rejection, towards any specific hypothesis about a person was also a strong mark of de Shazer's work (1988, 1991) and of narrative therapy in general.

Construction: the real and the imaginary

We have argued that we believe there is a mind-independent reality, and hence disagree with some versions of constructivism. However, what we are in agreement with, and it is something many constructivist writers have emphasised, is that to understand a person one needs to attempt to grasp how the other 'sees things', and further, that in a sense a person lives in a sort of personal 'construction', 'system', or 'world view'. For example, to understand why a person works so hard in an office, we might need to understand how that person has daydreams of success, how a whole future scenario is constructed in imagination. These 'scenarios' may contain everyday literal ideas such as 'I will have a lot of money', but also contain symbolic images and metaphors, to be, as Tom Wolf put it in his novel when describing New York financial workers, a 'master of the universe'. Our personal constructions of the world seem to be a fascinating mixture of literal and symbolic imagery. We live in what may be thought of as a real concrete world but a world that at least in part is made from human imagination. A version of this idea was given by Adler (Oberst and Stewart, 2003) when he spoke of 'fictions' and that these fictions actually influence how a person lives. The role of imagination and conceptual construction is clearly part of Lakoff and Johnson's work on thought and language. There are aspects of this in Allport's (1955) idea of how a person is motivated by ideas of the future, that is, by imagining what it will be like.

Our 'internal world' is a mixture of the 'real' and the 'imaginary', but likewise so is the mind-independent world. We live, as Baudelaire said, in a 'forest of symbols', but at the same time as being made of 'symbols', the world is made of solid wood, earth, and plants. To emphasise again, our personal 'worlds' are constructed, and the external real, one's surrounding culture, is also to some extent constructed, yet neither of these claims necessitate an anti-realist philosophy. The performance of a play involves imagination, yet it is a real event that a play has taken place or not. On this topic we are trying to explicitly maintain a sort of middle position between those who think only hard biology or physics is relevant and those constructivists who seem to suggest that there is nothing real, only perspectives, only fictions, only talk.

Intentionality: a key model of the mind

In addition to the more general requirements suggested by constructivism, we believe a coherent model of the mind, of mental phenomena, and one that points to what might be indispensable, is needed. The model we have found to be most convincing has been developed within philosophy: there is no specific name for this approach, except that it makes the claim that the mental life of persons involves the feature of being 'intentional', that is, that phenomena which we pick out as mental have the feature of being 'about' something (Searle, 1983; Lyons, 1995).

As an alternative way of making the same point, Goldie (2000) suggests that it has the feature of being 'directed' towards something. The idea of intentionality is said to have come into modern philosophy in the theories of Brentano (Moran, 2000), who traced the notion back to medieval philosophy and ultimately Aristotle. The idea played an important role in continental phenomenology (Moran, 2000), for example in the writings of Husserl and Heidegger; however, for our thinking about the mind we have tended to use the ideas of writers such as Nagel (1979), Davidson (1980), Searle (1992), McGinn (1999), and Goldie (2000). These writers might and do disagree on specific points, but on the whole argue that mental phenomena cannot be described or understood just in terms of behaviour, or in terms of the mind being just language.

The above writers also argue for an additional but linked hypothesis that we cannot 'reduce' basic mental features such as belief, desire, awareness, and so forth to something else. For example, we could not replace an explanation about someone's beliefs with an explanation about that person's biochemistry: something would be lost. These writers, however, are not Cartesians; that is, they do not believe the 'mind' is a separate substance from the body. Rather, they argue that we might have to approach the brain and consciousness in different ways, yet assume they are ultimately unified. Sometimes this is called dual-aspect perspective, though not all the theorists (for example Searle) accept this way of putting the argument. We return to this topic in Chapter 2.

Accepting the concept of intentionality has implications for how one might think about the person or mind in doing psychology.

First, it suggests, that the 'common-sense' or 'folk' model of the mind, that is, the way we talk about everyday beliefs, wants, feelings, resolve, noticing, and so on, is a perfectly good model of the mind, and one well able to make everyday predictions (Davidson, 1980; Fodor, 1987). Psychology, while 'refining' or critiquing these notions, at its centre still uses this model, this way of describing the mind. For example, if we take a CBT formulation using concepts such as 'cognition', 'attribution', etc., this is easily translated back into intentional concepts. We argue, in fact, that cognitive formulations would make no sense at all if we did not already have a folk model of the mind using intentionality.

Different cultures might well have different folk or philosophical models of the mind: and it has been recently argued that children may learn to think in terms of intentionality, for example when trying to understand the actions of others, by first learning simple narrative explanations (Hutto, 2008). That is to say, that these ways of thinking are to some extent fostered by culture. Given this is the case, we believe it useful that as psychologists we attempt to become aware of the model that is being used by ourselves and clients, that is, that we should take up a critical realist reflexive stance towards our taken-for-granted models.

Second, it is an assumption of the intentionality model that diverse mental features are relevant to any specific phenomena, or, to put this in other words, if we are attempting, for example, to explain a person's actions, then we might need, simultaneously, to consider a person's beliefs, desires, intentions, acts of willing, feelings, and so forth. We need to take a holistic perspective. In Beck's original theory of 1967, it was suggested that emotions were the consequence of thoughts, but likewise, so were actions and motivations. This original theory of Beck's is 'linear' and not holistic as described above. By 1995 Beck had radically changed his theory: in that later article he suggests the mind works by the person noticing something (an 'orientating schema'), which then triggers simultaneously schemas for thought, emotion, and motivation. This later idea is more in line with intentionality theory.

When we explain a psychosocial event using ideas from intentionality then, as argued, a wide range of features are of immediate relevance. The model, however, also underlines the fact that each feature we call upon will be embedded in a sort of 'network' of other beliefs or assumptions (Searle, 1983).

Goldie writing on emotion uses the concept of intentionality and emphasises how in order to understand an emotion we need to see how it emerges in the 'history' of the person. In a later book on personality Goldie (2004) suggests that by 'history' here he means not only the actual sequence of life-events in time, but also the person's attempts to construct a narrative. We live our lives and narrate our lives simultaneously, and both influence each other.

Third, some writers on intentionality have argued that not only are there intentional states, such as desiring, believing, etc., that occur as part of consciousness, there is in addition a sense of a continuous self (Searle, 2001). Whether there exists a 'self', and what it might be, is much debated in philosophy and not of direct relevance here (Zahavi, 2000). That there is a 'lived' sense of a self, a phenomenology of a self, however, is crucial to a psychology of persons, and does form part of our attempt to understand the experiences of psychosis for patients. We return to this concept of self in the next chapter.

We believe a notion of intentionality is crucial for a psychology of persons, and in this we are in line with the ideas of Allport (1955) and more recently Bolton and Hill (1997). Not all who might be described as constructivist are explicitly sympathetic to ideas of intentionality and consciousness, for example those theorists who argue that language practices are the fundamental reality of persons. Some constructivists, however, clearly do use concepts of intentionality, and our position is similar to these theorists. Greenberg's approach to emotion and therapy, for example, shows, we believe, thinking compatible with constructivism and intentionality. He assumes notions such as 'felt sense' and that a person needs to 'construct' the meaning of these feelings, that is, the person struggles to build an image, a metaphor, a statement. We are in agreement with this conception and see the effort to articulate, name, and narrate as an ongoing repeated process of work in NCBT for psychosis.

Our general theoretical orientation might be thought of as a sort of 'constructivist phenomenology', that is, the conscious person constructs meaning from mental states, and meaning has many manifestations. Smith (2004) in arguing for an interpretative phenomenological methodology is, we believe, proposing a similar model.

What are the implications of the theory of intentionality for our theorising and therapeutic practice? They are, in sum, as follows: (1) we think it provides an indispensable part of understanding of persons and states of suffering; (2) it is central to any person-specific case conceptualisation; (3) it emphasises 'holistic' explanations and the need to consider history and the social context.

A summary of how NCBT differs from CBT

In this chapter we have introduced the notion of NCBT, and here wish to summarise the differences between the original model of CBT and NCBT. These differences are displayed in Table 1.1. Of course, there are several variations of CBT and so any generalisations concerning CBT are only approximate. Likewise, the version of NCBT we present is one example from a group of possible constructivist approaches that use some aspects of CBT (Guidano, 1991; Mahoney, 2003).

The most striking difference is, of course, the emphasis on client constructed ideas, that is, on solutions, resources, and benign narration. This

Table 1.1 Differences between NCBT/constructivist approaches and CBT

CBT	NCBT
Focus on problems	Focus on solutions, resources, strengths
Tends to provide interventions from pre-established set	Prefers solutions generated by clients and client creativity
Exceptions not usually investigated	Prolonged investigation of exceptions, unique outcomes
Focus on specific cognition and on behaviour	Assumes a network of influences and relevance of history and context
Might use diagnostic DSM labels	Prefers to use non-technical terms for difficulties
No explicit emphasis on language, but used sometimes	Great emphasis on language, metaphor, narration, discourse
Uses specific behaviouristic and/or cognitive theories (e.g. of emotion)	Open to many theories: neurology, phenomenology, developmental theory, anthropology
No explicit focus on construction	Explicit focus on construction
Attempts to educate the client	No or little attempt to educate
Building a picture of the future is not usually used	Strong use of imagination to build a full picture of the preferred future
Distinct phases of assessment and intervention	Assessment and intervention can be combined
Formulation often based on linear causation (A causes B)	No explicit focus or holistic model of causation
Uses technical concepts rather than folk psychology	Some use versions of intentionality, i.e. concepts of belief, desire, feeling, etc.
Often draws on results from experiments or statistics and assumes these to be most important	Often draws on case studies, phenomenology, hermeneutics, ethnography, discourse analysis

focus is certainly now found in some key CBT figures such as Padesky (for example, in recent workshops she has termed her approach as resource based), but has its longest association with the various more constructivist approaches such as those found in de Shazer and White. We hope this book contributes to a fruitful dialogue between these traditions.

OVERVIEW

In this chapter we have outlined how we draw upon narrative solution focused therapeutic practices and upon cognitive behaviour therapy. We have argued that there are cogent reasons for combination in that these approaches aim at building resources, amplifying the accessibility of benign meaning, taking steps towards constructive actions, and allowing a review of negative meaning. Furthermore, at most stages in our work there is a concern with narration. Solution focused work aims at building a story of a preferred future, while White's approach is more general and flexible; it looks in detail at the past and then moves to a narrative of the future. There is also a central concern with narrative in Padesky's work in that a preferred self-characterisation is crucial and normally this work involves a focused review of the past. If we use more conventional cognitive challenging, then our preference is for building an alternative and better account, an alternative possible story, rather than attempting to show the illogicality of a person's claims.

We have emphasised, unlike many constructivists, that we believe there is a mind-independent reality. So, for example, even if the practice of 'marriage' is a cultural creation, it is still the case that in this society the existence of marriage is independent of any one person's thinking. We believe a certain concern and commitment to the truth of the claim or situation is, in fact, essential when working with clients suffering psychosis.

In the next chapter we outline a brief selection of research findings concerning psychosis which have had an impact upon our thinking and therapeutic practice. The rest of the book will then turn to engagement with the client, assessment, and the possible stages of our typical therapeutic practice, that is, beginning in the present, moving to an exploration of the past, then returning to the present and looking to the future.

Chapter 2

Understanding psychosis and implications for therapy

In this chapter we will present some key findings and theories concerning psychosis, present a basic model of onset and maintenance, and conclude with the therapeutic implications of these findings and ideas. The chapter is not a comprehensive review of the whole field: rather, it is a very specific selection of ideas that we find useful in trying to understand and work with psychosis. First, however, we shall briefly describe some of our assumptions about what psychosis might be.

The concept of psychosis and the presentation of clients

The work reported in this book is an approach to therapy with clients who have received some form of diagnosis of psychosis. 'Psychosis' refers to a range of conditions, in particular types of schizophrenia, schizo-affective disorder, delusional disorder, depression with psychotic features, and bi-polar disorder with psychotic features (see Sims, 1995, for discussion of these types).

There is a long-standing debate about whether schizophrenia is one syndrome, several syndromes, or a loose collection of symptoms such as hallucinations, delusions, and thought disorder (Bentall, Jackson, and Pilgram, 1988; Boyle, 1990; Bentall, 2003). The controversy in this area is usually about schizophrenia, but whether other 'syndromes' of psychosis, for example bi-polar condition, form distinct syndromes, is also debatable. We have tended to adopt the position that it is most useful in clinical work to focus on specific symptoms, and assume that they are 'dimensional'. Even if the categories of psychiatry do prove eventually to have valid uses they are usually unhelpful as a way of thinking about, or talking to, clients in psychological treatment.

From a social constructionist perceptive, Georgaca (2000) and Harper (2004) have criticised what they describe as the 'conventional' psychiatric view of the symptom of delusions, in particular that these are meaningless isolated beliefs and beliefs that are utterly different in form and content from non-delusional beliefs. For example, based on case studies, Georgaca suggests that two clients with delusions were able to justify their beliefs in ways similar to non-patients. Harper points out how many of our assumptions concerning normal beliefs are not supported by evidence. These writers question basic assumptions about the concept of delusion. They also raise questions about the very foundational assumptions of conventional psychiatry, for example its claims to objectivity or neutrality with regard to values, and the tendency to describe phenomena out of context. A comprehensive outlook on psychosis needs, we believe, to take these issues into consideration.

Another way of describing psychotic features is to talk of 'negative' and 'positive' symptoms (Stahl and Buckley, 2007). It has been argued that one cluster of symptoms ('positive') is composed of delusions, hallucinations and thought disorder (positive) while, in contrast, another cluster of symptoms ('negative') involves the absence of emotional expression, and absence of action or talk in general. There is also debate on whether there may be other clusters, for example 'disorganisation'. This distinction is controversial, particularly whether negative symptoms really are different from depression. Whatever the truth of the matter, the distinction helps one to look out for a range of features and to consider that it is possible to have negative symptoms without depression.

In contrast to writers such as Bentall, the phenomenologists Parnas and Sass (2002) argue that, at least for schizophrenia, there is some sort of core or essence of this condition, and that this is not a matter of any specific collection of symptoms, but rather certain hard-to-define transformations of the self, for example becoming over-aware of the details of how an habitual action is carried out or a change in the relationship between feelings and thoughts, or the unity of the self. We very much agree with Parnas and Sass that there are transformations of the self (see later section), as others do (Hemsley, 1998), but will remain neutral on the issue of a unified essential change in psychosis.

Whatever patterns etc. of symptoms may or may not exist, what is found in routine clinical practice tends to be the following:

• There is usually some reported alteration of how the self or others are experienced. This can be subtle, a way of just no longer feeling oneself to be as before a breakdown. The client often struggles to put this into words: sometimes the alterations are explained by a delusional account. Alternatively the transformation can be quite dramatic; for example, a client can believe that thoughts have been inserted into their mind or report that parts of the self are missing.
• There are alterations in the way a person behaves; for example, the person has stopped interacting with others, or is afraid of the public, and has withdrawn from public life. These changes are often the same as those found in anxiety problems.

- There are almost always problems of anxiety, depression, hopelessness or anger, or an emotional detachment from their experiences and other people.
- A client can have one or many features from the full range of psychotic symptoms, that is, hallucinations, delusions, delusions of reference, etc. Furthermore, these greatly fluctuate over time.

SOME KEY FINDINGS CONCERNING PSYCHOSIS

As stated, we will not here present a review of the vast literature on psychosis (see Bentall (2003) for an excellent comprehensive review). Rather, we will present just a few key findings from quite diverse areas of research that we have found illuminating and helpful, and which we tend to draw on when doing our work.

The transformation of the self and the everyday world

A major and long-term influence upon our thinking about psychosis has been those approaches termed phenomenological (Laing, 1960; Chadwick, 1993). Phenomenology has many definitions and types; for example, some versions are described as existential and others as transcendental (Moran, 2000) while some might be thought of as 'empirical' or falling within the tradition of analytic philosophy (Nagel, 1979; Johnson, 1987). For simplicity we will take phenomenological approaches to be at least ones that attempt to describe and analyse the reported experiences of clients, that is, what it is like for the client, how things are experienced, how things appear. In phenomenology there is also an attempt to capture these experiences in their naturally occurring complexity and wholeness. There are two topics in the tradition of phenomenology we have found particularly informative: the first concerns descriptions and understanding of the self, and the second, an analysis of our attitudes to, or experience of, the everyday world.

Laing describes 'ontological insecurity'; that is, whereas most people have a secure, taken-for-granted sense of actually being a person, of having an identity over time, of being such and such a person with a specific history, in contrast, many psychotic clients lose this secure sense of self. The loss may be temporary during severe and acute phases, or may last years. For Laing (during his phenomenological phase) this was a developmental failure and he believed that they had never developed a secure sense of self.

There are, as stated earlier, a multitude of specific manifest features of psychosis, for example hallucinations, delusions, thought insertion, ideas of reference: these are well described by Sims (1995). However important or vivid these descriptions are, we find ourselves in agreement with the phenomenological tradition that over and above all these details of specific experiences, there is in psychosis a reported alteration of the experience of self, self-with-others, and self in the world, that is persistent and often profoundly troubling for the person.

The alteration in the experience of self is suggested by many comments patients make. For example, long after the acute phase of psychosis some patients make comments such as that they do not feel themselves anymore and that they sense that something is missing, that they cannot talk or act with others as they used to do, they are just not the same person. What exactly this change might be is often not expressed clearly, and it may be that there are no everyday words to describe it. Some patients appear to use metaphors in the attempt to capture these new experiences. Some changes in the experience of self are very disruptive and disturbing, for example the experience of having one's thoughts withdrawn, that is, actually taken out of one's mind.

Laing is well known for his descriptions of the altered self, of 'ontological insecurity', but ideas about the altered self both predate Laing in writers such as Minkowski and Conrad (see Bovet and Parnas, 1993, for a review), and in recent years are very clearly expressed and developed in the writings of Parnas and associates (Parnas and Sass, 2002). The article by Bovet and Parnas (1993) is an excellent summary of phenomenological findings particularly about the person's altered experience of the self. These changes were also documented in German phenomenological psychiatry (for example, the philosopher and psychiatrist Karl Jaspers (1959) was probably the first to draw attention to these changes).

The second topic of importance is a person's normal experience of the everyday world and how this is transformed in psychosis. Matussek (1987/1952) pointed out that over and above all the well known features of psychosis, such as hallucination, patients with psychosis report a wide range of alterations in perception of things, time, space: often these changes seem subtle and difficult for people to put into words. Some excellent descriptions of changes are found in Hurlburt (1990).

Although not a 'phenomenologist' working in the tradition of continental phenomenology, the philosopher Searle has developed concepts of consciousness, everyday experience, and meaning that may help, we believe, clarify these alterations of everyday experience described by the phenomenologists. Searle (1992) points out that when a person uses an everyday question such as 'Can you make me a cup of tea?', the statement has implications (for example, the person may want tea with milk and sugar as usual). However, the simple request of asking for tea also seems to imply 'assumptions' about the world and how things should be done: for example, the person making the request would be surprised if the other person brought a cup of cold tea, or brought it next week or made up a cup of leaves with no water. Note, however, that the person explicitly specifies none of these excluded possibilities. Even more surprising would be to be informed that the kitchen is invisible or has turned into ice. The point Searle is making is that any ordinary perception or action, claim about a state of affairs, etc., seems to involve not only implications we could in principle articulate (Searle has sometimes called this a Network), but also a 'Background' of dispositions that cause or influence a person to perceive and act in specific ways. The Background for a person is not conscious, or unconscious, knowledge in the form of claims or statements about the world. Rather, it is a set of dispositions that structure our actions in the world, our ways of doing things.

We act in the everyday world *as if* taking a great number of things for granted. Phenomenologists have used many diverse terms to try to capture this: the 'natural attitude', 'common sense', 'vital contact with reality' (Minkowski, quoted in Bovet and Parnas, 1993). In psychosis, however, what was taken for granted, what for a person had been 'common sense', seems to be lost.

Rhodes and Gipps (in press) have argued that that which Searle called the 'Background' is altered during psychosis. For example, in extreme psychosis a client might claim others can walk through walls, or that other people's thoughts are in his or her head. Most people will 'know' this cannot be so and yet know this without any scientific knowledge, nor without consciously drawing upon common-sense generalisations. It is suggested that Background dispositions for a person automatically discount a claim such that people can walk through brick walls: the person has an 'intuition', a 'sense' that it cannot be. Background dispositions will also play an essential role in a person's normal perception of space and time, that is, the subtle features of experience described as altered in psychosis by Matussek.

The Background for a person is said to be formed by a person's history of experience in the world of things and culture: the Background maintains a way doing things in the world; it allows or facilitates a person's thinking, concepts, actions, but itself is not composed of concepts or any form of verbal statement. A person in psychosis loses, however, the constraints of their unique Background, their specific common-sense everyday knowledge. These alterations of Background in psychosis, it is suggested, might be specific or global, temporary or permanent. Searle assumes that the Background is structured in the pattern of a person's neural activity.

We suggest that grasping these alterations in being a 'self', and alterations of everyday consciousness (with suggested changes in Background), are essential for beginning to accept, understand, or even interact with a person with psychosis. If we do not appreciate the extremity of certain phenomenological changes, that is, that the very 'world' and self of the person is transformed, then we are, alternatively, inclined to viewing the person with psychosis as just making a simple 'error', and that attitude to the other soon leads to frustration, accusations of stubbornness, and even anger.

Social and emotional difficulties

It is clear from clinical work and a great deal of research (Davidson, 2003) that those with psychosis suffer a wide range of interpersonal and emotional difficulties. In general we can say that patients with psychosis are often isolated, have fewer friends, relationships, and so on, and when they do interact with others, this can involve an unending range of difficulties. Some of these problems are common to all people, such as shyness, self-consciousness, arguments, etc., while some problems might be the specific consequence of suffering psychotic symptoms. For example, it is difficult to go to dinner with friends if an invisible voice is whispering insults; it is difficult to relate to others if a banal comment can take on strange and overpowering symbolic meaning.

Research clearly suggests that clients suffer from a range of difficulties – depression in various forms (Birchwood, Iqbal, Chadwick, and Trower, 2000), hopelessness (White, McCleery, Gumley, and Mulholland, 2007), anxieties of many types (Cosoff and Hafner, 1998), low self-esteem (Barrowclough et al., 2003) – and have a very high rate of suicide and attempted suicide (Johnson, Godding, and Tarrier, 2008).

Many clients have long-standing social and emotional difficulties which predate their psychosis by several years. It seems possible that this contributes to the content of their psychotic experience (Harrow, Rattenbury, and Stoll, 1988; Rhodes and Jakes, 2000) and perhaps sometimes even the occurrence (see later sections). However, it is also likely that symptoms of psychosis exacerbate long-standing social problems and may also create new difficulties, for example loss of opportunities for meaningful work and activities of various sorts, loss of opportunities for relationships. Furthermore, any client with psychosis is open to the dangers of being 'stigmatised' by society, being seen as completely 'non-rational' and inferior.

A common problem of long-term residual psychosis is altered social perception: that is, an altered actual perception of others rather than just altered interpretations or ideas about others (Rhodes and Jakes, 2004b). Perception of others, we suggest, is a complex phenomenon: it is not only sensory (vision, sound, etc.) but involves meaning, and a sense of what is 'going on'. Given difficulties with social perception, it is not surprising that many clients try to avoid other people even if they do not have persecutory fears.

Perhaps the most striking evidence that clients with psychosis continue to suffer long-term social difficulties comes from the tradition of research on 'expressed emotion' (Bebbington and Kuipers, 1994). The evidence suggests that if patients are exposed to negative emotional encounters, for example family arguments, negative criticism, or overprotection, then they have a greater chance of 'relapsing'; that is, there is an emergence of acute symptoms followed by possible hospitalisation. These findings suggest some form of deep connection between emotions, symptoms, the person's 'grip' on their external context, and the ability to reason.

Some writers have made an explicit link between social difficulties and the formation of psychosis, in particular delusions. Cameron (1959) suggested that the person who is prone to develop persecutory paranoia responds to stress by feeling threatened and then, understandably, looks for sources of danger. He suggests that the paranoid-prone person has a developmental difficulty that makes him or her unable to understand the mental states of others. Under stress this leads to the following vicious circle: the more anxious such people become, the more threatened by others they feel. However, they are unable to understand the motivations of others in a more realistic way so they take what they fear and imagine for reality. Some people might feel threatened but would be more able to also see the situation in a realistic way. Feeling under threat, patients are also less able to check out their fears with others. This leads to them feeling increasingly anxious, increasingly threatened, and they take this for being increasingly in danger. The more in danger they feel, the more they withdraw from others, and the less chance there is to check out their fears. The paranoid delusion emerges as a response to this set of feelings and is associated with an increasing isolation that serves to protect the delusion from being disconfirmed.

One strength of this account is the link it makes between social isolation and delusion formation. Delusions form as a result of psychological and social isolation. Because the person is unable to distinguish the realistic motives of others, they are driven to more and more elaborate explanations of their increasing fear. Cameron further argues that once a delusion has formed it reduces the level of anxiety that the person feels, and this serves to maintain the delusion. Now the person at least knows where the threat is coming from. This theory stands in need of full empirical confirmation but as a working model it usefully links delusions with failures in social understanding and social interaction. That people with psychosis have difficulty understanding others is a point that has also been made by Frith (1992).

Some recent research has emphasised the role of social and emotional difficulties and therefore might give some support to at least parts of Cameron's theory or similar theories. MacBeth, Schwannauer, and Gumley (2008) have noted an association between difficulties with attachment relationships, social distancing, a sense of threat, and ideas of persecution. Freeman et al. (2008) in an experiment with non-patients using a computer generated simulation of travelling on a train were able to show that 'paranoia' (defined here as an unfounded sense of threat from others) was found in a substantial minority and was associated with anxiety, depression, worry, negative ideas of self and other, interpersonal sensitivity, unusual perceptions, and inflexible thinking. Most of these variables point to the importance of emotion and social relations.

Birchwood, Meaden, Trower, and Gilbert (2002) have investigated the similarities between a person's relationship to 'voices' and his or her social relationships. In one study they assessed how powerful patients felt in relation to other people and whether patients felt equal to others. They carried out the same assessments between the patients and their reported relationship to 'voices'. They found that participants reported the same troubled relationships with their voices as they had with real people. It is of particular relevance here to note that participants often felt bullied, inferior, and less powerful than others. Such findings underline the importance of investigating voices within the context of a person's sense of self and other.

From research we have carried out (Rhodes and Jakes, 2000) we believe that for most clients with delusions there are a wide range of difficulties concerning global motivations of different kinds such as achieving stability, achieving competence in daily activities, having a sense of direction or purpose, and being free from physical and mental pain; but the most conspicuous and common difficulties, however, concerned various types of social motivation, ranging from basic socialising and intimacy to issues of respect from others. The overwhelming impression was that many clients were profoundly isolated, withdrawn, cut off or alternatively had suffered intensely in terms of experiencing negative events, conflict, difficulties in relating and interacting with others, and a profound sense of being devalued by society. We return to these problematic motivations and their relevance to psychotic meanings in the next section.

Approaches to the origin of meaning

That there is meaning in psychosis is an ancient claim, very well illustrated in many statements by Shakespeare. There are, in particular, fascinating comments made by Theseus (Act V, Scene I) in *A Midsummer Night's Dream*. He says of lovers and those with madness:

> . . . such seething brains, such shaping phantasies,
> that apprehend more than cool reason ever comprehends.

He goes on, however, to outline how wishes or fears can influence perceptions of these persons in such altered states:

> Such tricks hath strong imagination,
>   . . .
> Or in the night, imagining some fear,
> How easy is a bush supposed a bear.

It would appear that here Shakespeare is suggesting that emotion has a powerful influence upon perception, via imagination, such that one's grasp of reality is altered.

Jung (1907) argued that delusions and hallucinations have symbolic meaning and that they symbolise emotional trauma and difficulties. Freud had speculated on delusions in *The Interpretation of Dreams* (1900), but it was Jung who made the first direct attempt with patients to explore possible links between delusional ideas and aspects of the person's life. He studied and wrote about one case in particular using 'free association', suggesting that for this woman the central issues were around wish-fulfilment, frustrated sexuality, and a sense of personal 'injury'. He examined the origin of these themes in her life. He commented that the woman made a claim of being Socrates, that is, that there was an analogy, but that she did not present her claims as analogies. The analogy, he suggested, was that she saw herself as a victim of injustice in the same way Socrates was the victim of injustice.

If delusions and other ideas found in psychotic states are to be understood, then we believe these areas need to be researched without assuming the complex and controversial theories of the psychoanalytic tradition. To do this we have carried out several pieces of mainly qualitative research relevant to the area of the origin of meanings in psychotic states.

In one article we presented details of four case studies (Rhodes and Jakes, 2000). We first analysed the interviews of 14 deluded participants using interpretative phenomenological analysis (IPA; Smith and Osborn, 2003) and then selected four cases to illustrate a range of problematic motivations. For all 14 we first examined how participants spoke about their short-term and long-term difficulties and their goals in life. On the basis of this we generated a typology of problematic motivational themes. Taking the delusional statements or narratives of participants we speculated on what type of motivational theme the delusion suggested. For example, if someone said that others hissed insulting comments at all times, we might suggest that this expressed a theme of contempt by others. For each participant we were then able to compare the theme of the delusion according to our system of classification with the themes of the person's life-difficulties and life-goals. For the majority of cases we found a thematic correspondence; for example, a patient who has a delusion that she is the target of contemptuous whistles and insults (social alienation) also reported years of feeling different to the others, not belonging and having 'strange' eyes. Her delusion seemed to mirror, though with distortions, her life-long interpersonal difficulties.

We identified the emotional significance of the delusions by 'putting aside' those aspects of the delusion that seemed impossible and asked 'What kind of social or emotional problem might this delusion suggest?' A delusion of a gang planning to murder a person might, for example, suggest a sense of feeling oneself to be an outsider, as not belonging: it also might suggest a preoccupation with violence. By further interviewing the patient, it might be found that the person was beaten as a child. Such thematic links obviously do not prove causation, but this does seem a reasonable hypothesis: that is, that the content or meaning found in various aspects of a person's psychosis is the product of earlier life events and interpersonal processes.

In one further and somewhat different analysis using qualitative and quantitative approaches (Jakes, Rhodes, and Issa, 2004) we noted how several themes from the basic list (discussed in the last section) tended to 'go together' or formed a pattern, were very common, and of great importance to clients with delusions: eventually we conceived these as five specific 'core clusters' of problematic motive themes. These clusters are as follows:

1 Intimacy/sexuality: this involves either not having an intimate relationship, or having conflict in an intimate relationship.
2 Superior achievement/leadership: for some clients their goals seemed to involve 'superior' or 'powerful' achievements, for example being a great leader or making important contributions.
3 Social alienation/inferiority: many clients regard themselves as 'outsiders' and looked down upon by others. This experience seems quite common, particularly for patients with some form of persecution.
4 Control/dominance aversion: clients with this theme referred to the perceived attempts of others to 'control' or 'dominate' them; for example, one client summed up her relationship with her punitive mother as 'not a matter of love but doing what she says'.
5 Annihilation anxiety: the person is concerned with death, injury, accidents, illness; for example, 'Something might happen', 'My mother and sister work too hard', 'I thought I had AIDS for years'.

We have argued (Jakes et al., 2004) that these clusters are similar to concepts generated by other researchers, and usually by other research methodologies. Power (similar to achievement/leadership) and intimacy were central concepts in the narrative research of McAdams (1993) while social alienation and control aversion are similar to ideas of Gilbert (1989). Annihilation anxiety furthermore seems linked to Gilbert's ideas about seeking 'safety' as a fundamental need. The latter may also, however, be linked to Heidegger's concept of 'angst' (Moran, 2000), which is meant to reveal a person's fear of death, but also indicates, as Moran explains, a sense of 'homelessness – we are not at home in the world'. The two concepts may not be identical but it is interesting to note how the clients identified as having annihilation anxiety had many fears simultaneously and did not seem ever to be at rest, or ever at peace.

Many delusional systems or narrations of clients can be related to, understood by, the sorts of motive and problem clusters we have described (though some delusional systems would require additional themes to those mentioned here). In our studies we could not link the delusions of a small number of participants to their specific life themes. It may be that for some clients delusions and hallucinations do link to underlying goals and problems while for some clients they do not (see Nelson, 2005). However, given that some clients are very unwilling to talk about their personal difficulties, not seeing a link can sometimes be the product of simply not knowing enough about a person.

While we have presented the themes of motivations as if they were ongoing fixed properties or features, these themes can also be seen as involving changes over time and therefore a sort of 'narrative': for example, the narrative of eventually finding love; the narrative of struggling to find success and being at last recognised; the narrative of travelling, building, coming 'home' to a safe place.

The attempt at tracing the origin of meaning might be thought of as one version of 'hermeneutics', that is, an approach to interpretation of meanings. It is only with some clients (this is further discussed in the chapter on presenting alternatives to delusions) that we might present any sort of interpretation of a symbol as described above; however, in attempting to understand most clients, to build a complex picture or formulation, we consider the possible motivational/interpersonal meanings of psychotic content and let that guide our work.

Another approach to the origin of meaning focuses specifically on the role of explicit metaphors and other figures of speech in the person's thought and experience. In Shakespeare's comment above that a 'bush' might well be perceived as a 'bear', there is, we suggest, an implication that a 'bush', given its shape and colour, is similar in some way or analogous to a bear. However, with great fear, the bush can be taken to be a real bear. In reading many transcripts of interviews with deluded participants (Rhodes and Jakes, 2004b) we began to notice that in a wide range of ways participants used various 'figures of speech' (metaphors and metonymies). After analysis, we suggested that the use of metaphors and metonymy might be present in the thinking of participants at many different stages of psychosis (that is, well before psychosis, at onset, and during chronic conditions). We speculated on various possible pathways for the transformation of metaphoric meanings. For example, a person might criticise himself or herself as 'rotten to the core'. At a later stage, as psychotic processes manifest themselves, such a person might begin to have hallucinations of a rotten smell. The metaphoric model of 'rottenness' might become so entrenched in a person's thinking and experience that eventually perceptions are automatically infused with this conceptualisation, this meaning. We argued that such experience is metaphorical, while a verbal claim such as 'I smell of rotting flesh' is intended to be literal, that is, to be a statement about the way things are.

We do not suggest to a client that his or her experience is a metaphor or derived from a metaphor (though one might, for example, in later stages of therapy where clients no longer believe their delusions). We have, however, found it useful for the therapist to think about the client's experiences as the product of processes involving metaphors. Furthermore, it can be useful to ask patients 'What other experiences in your life have been *like* that?' (We return to this in the chapter on narrative.)

Another perspective we have found useful in thinking about the origin of meaning is research concerning the role of narrative in psychosis. This tradition of research is separate to that of specific narrative therapies. The narrative approach attempts to capture a person's complex narration of events, experience, and self. France and Uhlin (2006) present an excellent review.

One idea of narrative research is the suggestion that clients with psychosis often seem to be 'stuck', and stuck in what appears to be an impoverished narration. For example, a client described in Rhodes and Jakes (2002) at the height of his psychosis would only talk of the imminent attack of two demons. He said this again and again: nothing else from his life seemed to enter his conversation. Only after many sessions, when he appeared to feel more secure, did he even begin to mention other issues. This feature of being 'stuck' was described by Keen (1986), and likewise by Holma and Aaltonen (1998).

Thornhill, Clare, and May (2004) carried out work looking at the narratives of clients who were considered to have in some way recovered from psychosis. They found three major types of narrative, namely 'escape' from illness and from the psychiatric system, 'enlightenment' involving understanding their own life history, and 'endurance' of the condition.

From the way delusions are described in psychiatric literature one might be led to think that delusions for a person exist as single isolated statements or beliefs. In reality, as narrative research suggests, most delusions are at least elementary narrations. These narratives change over time, usually becoming more complex, even if the basic outline remains the same (Lysaker, Lancaster, and Lysaker, 2003).

The three approaches described in this section, namely motivational thematic links between events and psychotic meanings, links between metaphors and psychotic meaning, and the role of narrative, all form part of a constructivist approach to meaning.

Cognitive processes

As stated earlier, this chapter is not a systematic review and we will only discuss some current ideas that we have drawn upon in our clinical work. In contrast to the previous three sections, the findings in this section tend to be based on experiments, surveys using structured questions, and the development of causal theories.

The focus of cognitive psychology for psychosis has tended to be on specific symptoms, in particular delusions and hallucinations. The work of Garety and Hemsley (1994) and Freeman and Garety (2004) have been important in this field. Their work suggests the following useful conclusions:

- Delusions are variable: they are not fixed and completely static as seemed to be assumed in much traditional psychiatric writing. Delusions vary in intensity of conviction, distress, preoccupation, and the degree to which they interfere or influence a person's everyday life.
- Hemsley (1998, 2005), in particular, has emphasised how a person's knowledge of the world, of regularities, seems affected deeply by psychosis.
- Freeman and Garety have looked at the influence of emotions on delusions. They review evidence that suggests extreme states of emotionality are relevant at onset and as part of the maintenance processes for delusions.

Freeman and Garety (2004) present a model of delusion formation and maintenance. Essentially it suggests that various negative life-events interact with a person's emotions and beliefs about (1) the self and (2) other people. In predisposed people such life-events induce 'anomalous' experiences: furthermore, the interpretation of these experiences is influenced by a person's tendency to 'jump to conclusions', that is, a style of reasoning where little evidence is used before a decision is made. Once an unusual belief is formed various maintenance factors operate such as a possible bias towards evidence that appears to confirm the specific negative beliefs and avoidance of potentially disconfirmatory situations by withdrawal. Continuous depression and anxiety might also play a role in maintenance. The model Freeman and Garety present is a fusion of diverse ideas; in particular, it takes Maher's (1988) idea that delusions are a person's attempts to describe and explain strange experiences they undergo, and couples this concept to their findings on reasoning and emotion.

Although the Freeman and Garety model leaves much unexplained it seems likely that many delusions are, at least partially, the consequence of struggling to find meaning for unusual experiences. Jaspers (1959) had also thought that some delusions were based on experiences: he called these 'secondary delusions' as opposed to 'primary', the latter being delusions which were claimed not to be based on experiences, but to arise spontaneously in a completed form. Whether in fact all delusions arise as explanations of unusual 'perceptions' has been questioned by Bell, Halligan, and Ellis (2008): on a test of anomalous perceptions they found no significant difference between non-hallucinating patients with delusions, and non-patients. The usefulness of Freeman and Garety's model, however, is that it provides a framework pointing to a range of diverse areas we should explore when working with delusions. It is helpful to have a model that places the person's experience of negative emotions as central to the experience of psychotic symptoms. Their model also considers maintenance factors, and again points to a wide range of areas one could consider in planning therapy, for example the role of anxiety and 'safety' behaviours.

Moritz and Woodward have presented experiments which suggest that a JTC (jump to conclusions) style only tends to operate in situations where a person has to make a choice between options that are simple, distinct, and obviously different (Moritz, Woodward, and Lambert, 2007). In another fascinating experiment (Moritz and Woodward, 2004) they presented pictures from the Thematic Apperception Test (TAT) (these are very ambiguous and sometimes unusual pictures of social situations) to patients and offered a range of interpretations of what was occurring in the pictures. Patients with delusions tended to accept a greater number of different interpretations and more unusual ones. They suggest patients display a 'liberal acceptance' of interpretations. We think this idea compatible with Hemsley's notion of not using previous 'regularities' about the world and the idea we presented earlier of alterations of the Background to a person's normal consciousness. Put simply, without an automatic grasp of how the world has been we will not have reactions, 'intuitions' that allow a person to experience unusual ideas or perceptions as unlikely.

The early work of Slade and Bentall (1988) has had a strong influence upon CBT for voices. They noted how voices might be induced by stressors in the environment, but also how they might be influenced by a range of factors such as a person's belief system and the quality of sensory input. In this tradition, Morrison, Renton, Dunn, Williams, and Bentall (2004) emphasised a person's reactions to inner thoughts suggesting that if someone has a self-belief that he or she is 'bad', then the extreme emotional reaction might increase the voices. Morrison et al. emphasise that a person can have a whole range of beliefs, sometimes inconsistent, about the nature of mental phenomena, and these too will mediate a person's reactions.

Frith and associates have made an important contribution with their 'theory of mind' (TOM) approach (Frith, 1992). Their research suggests that some patients lack the ability to understand how others are thinking, for example to predict what others believe. It is clearly crucial for social interaction that we are able to understand the other: for example, that a dentist does not want to hurt a person when carrying out dental work. One patient we knew complained that a new barber had been nasty on purpose by giving him a short hair cut. It turned out that the cut he was given did fit the exact request he had made, but the barber he normally had would have done it differently. The status of the TOM evidence is not yet settled and might only apply to a subset of clients with psychosis, perhaps mainly to those with very severe and chronic symptoms (Garety and Freeman, 1999).

A further influential contribution relevant to much therapy for psychosis has been the work of Bentall (2003) and associates on 'attributions', that is, how a person explains good and negative events. Bentall originally suggested that blaming others, seeing others as the cause of difficulties in one's life, prevents the person from blaming himself or herself, and hence, helps a person maintain high self-esteem. Subsequent findings cast doubt on this claim (Garety and Freeman, 1999) but the finding remains that some patients, particularly those with persecution ideas, tend to blame others. We have certainly noticed this feature with some patients with persecutory belief systems; for example, one patient claimed the Ministry of Defence had made sure he lost all his jobs throughout his life and that he was not responsible. Bentall's work points to the importance of investigating how a person explains major events in life and how this might relate to delusions.

In a development of the above ideas on cognition, Fowler et al. (2006) have suggested that there might be a 'catastrophic interaction' of cognitive abnormalities (their term for the cognitive differences found in psychotic patients) and trauma. Trauma or everyday difficulties have a disproportionately negative effect upon reasoning and emotional processes, each process accelerating the other, resulting in delusions. Steel, Fowler, and Holmes (2005) noted how in post-traumatic stress disorder (PTSD) it is reported that patients experience past trauma as 'happening now'. They argue that in these patients the original memories do not seem to be marked for context. The experiments of Hemsley had already suggested that patients with schizophrenia demonstrated problems of processing information relevant to context. Steel et al. found similar problems of contextual processing in patients with schizotypy.

Biology, events, and the environment

There has been a great deal of debate as to whether psychosis is caused by social events, or by biological changes. Most studies in these areas are not experimental but are surveys demonstrating associations between variables. This limits the ability of researchers to make causal inferences but these findings do point to potentially important areas.

There now seems a very large body of evidence that the environment is linked to rates of psychosis. In one study there was a demonstrated increase of psychosis with urbanisation, that is, people moving from the countryside to live in towns (Sundquist et al., 2004). This study carefully controlled for the effects of other relevant variables and showed these not to be sufficient to account for the changes. Why living in a town may lead to difficulties is open to speculation. One recent study suggested that the perception of potential danger, particularly being the victim of crime, might play a role (Schomerus et al., 2008).

Several studies have demonstrated a higher rate of psychosis in people in lower socio-economic classes (Mirowsky and Ross, 1983; Cromby and Harper, 2005). Mirowsky and Ross suggest that a central aspect of being poor is an experience of not having control over one's life in addition to a range of aspects such as stress and lack of opportunity.

Research suggests that there is a greater incidence of some types of psychotic conditions amongst British of African and Caribbean origin (Sharpley, Hutchinson, McKenzie, and Murray, 2001). Specific research suggests that this effect cannot be explained by genes since there is not a greater incidence of psychosis in families living in the countries of origin, nor does a 'drift' hypothesis seem adequate (that is, that people with psychological difficulties are more likely to move countries) especially since the incidence of difficulties seems to vary from high to low in different ethnic populations. Furthermore, the effect is more pronounced in second and third generation Afro-Caribbeans than it is in first generation immigrants. What might explain these effects is still not clear, but some suggestions are the effects of racism, living in poor parts of cities, low socio-economic class, family organisation, and isolation. Whatever the exact mechanism, it seems that it involves social and environmental pathways.

Several pieces of research have investigated how the social environment of the family might influence the incidence of psychosis. Tienari et al. (2004) have published research following up children born to mothers with schizophrenia. The children were in fact brought up in adopted families and therefore not brought up in the social environment of the biological mother. The fascinating aspect of Tienari's research was that he investigated the social functioning of these adoptive families and examined the distribution of the incidence of psychosis. The general finding was that there was a greater incidence of psychosis in dysfunctional adopted families and a protective influence of being adopted by well-functioning families. Dysfunction was defined as showing evidence (collected from direct interviews) suggesting 'critical/conflictual', 'constricted', or 'boundary' problems. According to this research, there is a clear genetic or biological influence, but one greatly modified by the social environment.

From such systematic and large-scale research, it seems reasonable to suggest that there is, in fact, some kind of interaction between biological factors such as genes and psychosocial influences of the family and society in general.

While some families might be negative in their style of interaction, considerable evidence suggests that some families engage in physical, emotional, and sexual abuse, and that this might make a very important contribution to psychosis (Read, Mosher, and Bentall, 2004). Many studies have investigated reported abuse and 40% to 70% of psychotic patients report having been abused as children. Several years ago when we started working with psychosis we had no expectations of high rates of abuse, but quickly noticed that many of our clients had severe and traumatic childhoods. We must emphasise that when we say 'abuse' we do not mean sexual abuse alone: we are referring to the full range of possible mistreatments, including sexual abuse, but also excessive violence to children, not being fed or protected, exposure to rejection, humiliation, and neglect. Some clients have also experienced cruel and persistent bullying at school. We underline these points since, we believe, in recent years there seems to be less attention given to these diverse forms of abuse.

If abuse is an influence, again the difficult questions remain of how this pathway works. Read, Perry, Moskowitz, and Connolly (2001) speculate on whether early abuse might in fact change the function and structure of the developing brain. This seems quite feasible given the growing evidence that, for example, prolonged stress does alter areas such as the hippocampus (Bentall, 2003). However, it is also clear that such mistreatment will have a profound effect upon various aspects of a person's psychology, for example beliefs about the self and other, expectations, confidence, and so forth. In addition to childhood abuse, there is also evidence that adults with psychosis suffer an increase of negative events before the onset of psychosis (Bebbington, Wilkins, Sham, and Jones, 1996) and suffer very elevated levels of trauma related to problems such as domestic violence and other forms of assault (Mueser et al., 2004). Tragically, it would seem that a large number of clients have suffered both childhood and adult trauma.

Many have argued that brain functions must be altered in psychosis, but what these exact changes are is still far from being settled. We believe, however, that brain science and theory has entered a new phase in recent years. There has been a move away from looking at localised changes, such as lesions, and a move towards patterns of functioning of the whole brain. As brain research has become more subtle, we can also now begin to glimpse the complex interactions between the brain and the environment.

Edelman and Tononi (2000; Tononi and Edelman, 2000) argue that a distinct feature of the brain is that it functions with multiple, high-speed 'interactions' between multiple areas: there are 'reentrant' interactions such that biochemical signals move to and fro between diverse areas at great speed. The pattern of these reentrant interactions is complex and continuously changing: furthermore, these patterns occupy large and different parts of the brain. The suggestion is that if these patterns begin to change, to function in a non-typical way, albeit in subtle ways, then the consequences for consciousness will be profound. Friston and Frith (1995) also explore the theory that there are difficulties of interaction between areas of the brain.

A fascinating area of neurological research is how the brain functions differently when undergoing self-generated experiences, such as imagining a 'voice' as compared to, for example, hearing a voice. Szechtman, Woody, Bowers, and Nahmias (1998) investigated brain patterns for subjects who could be hypnotised to hallucinate voices. Three conditions were examined, namely, hearing a real voice, imagining a voice, and hallucinating a voice due to hypnosis. The pattern for the real and hallucinated condition turned out to be somewhat different from that found for imagining voices (in particular one area called the anterior cingulate). This suggests the brain has mechanisms that allow the conscious mind to experience some things as 'external', as 'real', in opposition to experiencing something as self-generated (for example what we dream or imagine). If such is in fact the case for 'voices', then it seems highly likely that there will be similar mechanisms for differentiating input which is visual, tactile, and so forth.

The above findings relate to hallucinations; however, it might also be the case that such mechanisms for differentiating 'outside' as opposed to 'inside' are relevant to situations in psychosis where, for example, two real people are seen at a distance but given a psychotic interpretation such as the two are plotting murder. That is, the two strangers are automatically, without deliberate thought by the perceiver, perceived *as attackers*. The meaning of 'what they are' is experienced as real, outside oneself, automatic, and not inferred.

Other research investigating inside/outside differentiation is work on touch (Blakemore, Smith, Steel, Johnstone, and Frith, 2000) and work on psychomotor actions (Georgieff and Jeannerod, 1998). Blakemore worked with Frith, who looked at how 'self-monitoring' appeared to be altered in those with negative symptoms. Frith and colleagues demonstrated how some patients had great difficulty in initiating or stopping certain types of actions.

In sum, there is a great deal of evidence pointing to a multitude of potential influences upon the possible causation of psychosis, ranging from the purely biological to sociological factors, and of course a range of more psychosocial aspects as discussed earlier. We believe all these should be at least considered and discuss this in the next section.

PSYCHOSIS AND THE NEED FOR DUAL-ASPECT EXPLANATIONS

There seems an endless debate about whether psychosis is *really* to be explained by social and emotional processes or by biological processes: the assumption seems to be that one is ultimately more important than the other. We believe, however, that both brain and interpersonal/cognitive influences will be relevant to a full understanding and explanation of psychosis. We agree strongly with Bentall (2003) when, after considering many findings concerning psychosis, including biological ones, he stated that no one set of findings 'trump' another, that is, that one sort of cause somehow is superior to the other. We wish to take up this point, expand it, and in doing so advocate what might be thought of as a 'dual-aspect' explanatory system.

It might be useful first to take an example from outside psychosis such as feeling miserable. One might ask, 'Why is Fred so unhappy this week? He's not his usual self.' An adequate explanation for that question might be: he received very bad news of a coming redundancy and he has just taken out a mortgage. One might even ask a more specific question: why did he make an appointment with Human Resources? Answer: because he wants to argue that the situation is not acceptable.

Now there is good evidence that simultaneously with all the above events will be biochemical, neurological changes in Fred's brain. Before the 'bad news' his brain is in one type of state but after the news it is in another state. Some theorists might therefore be tempted to claim that the biological explanation is somehow more powerful: we disagree with such a position.

Both styles of explanation are useful, but, we emphasise, both are incomplete. If, for example, Fred cries, then it might be interesting to know that his brain flooded with chemical X, but however detailed the brain explanation becomes (for example, one might include the sensory input, the brain of the other, etc.), we suggest these neurological explanations seem incomplete if we cannot add 'he cried when he read the letter sacking him'.

In contrast to the above, to only give psychosocial explanations might be sufficient for everyday thinking and action, but ultimately these explanations are also incomplete, that is, our specific question is answered, but we still do not understand many aspects or features of what is happening. For example, Fred might report feeling no energy, or a low mood even when not thinking about the news, or that he wakes up 'miserable'. We know the bad news started the sequence but not, for example, the mechanisms that keep the content returning into his thought or why he is so tired. To understand these sorts of effects we may need to examine brain and body functioning.

A specific answer might well be a full and proper explanation to a specific question, but it seems to be the case that for any event or phenomenon there will be important aspects not covered by the specific question and answer. Our main point here is that these different types of question, from biological to everyday psychology, are equally valid, and in the end we cannot really do without the full range, the different perspectives.

The position we are arguing for here is, we suggest, a consequence of the theory, outlined in the introductory chapter, that the 'subjective' cannot be reduced to just the 'physical' as several philosophers have argued, for example Nagel (1979), Davidson (1980), Searle (1992), and McGinn (1999). These philosophers are not arguing that the mind is a separate type of substance, that the mind can live without a body, as did Descartes: rather, that there are irreducible 'aspects' of the physical and the mental, and one aspect cannot be 'reduced' by explanations of the other aspect. Would a page of biochemical formula, for example, really be a satisfactory explanation of crying, of why someone cried, or of what it feels like to cry?

Given a dual-aspect explanatory perspective, we suggest that the many findings and possible explanations for psychosis put forward earlier will all need to be used to begin to fully describe, understand, and explain psychosis. Probably there are neurological changes, but to fixate on these and ignore the fact that many of these are in fact possibly caused by, for example, prolonged stress or abuse, seems to us conceptually dubious. In fact, one might well raise the question of why the psychosocial histories of patients are so rarely investigated or mentioned in so many 'discharge' reports written after hospitalisation.

Given the importance of life-events and the very strong likelihood that much psychotic meaning (by that we mean delusions, voice content, ideas about voices, meaning elaborated about any unusual experience) relates, in diverse ways, to current and past events, motivations, core beliefs about self and others, then all these aspects must be part of understanding, explaining, and working with a person's reactions and behaviours. However, these psychosocial aspects are not sufficient in themselves and we believe a fuller explanatory system needs to involve 'dual-aspects', that is, at least biological and psychological perspectives.

OVERVIEW OF THE ONSET AND MAINTENANCE OF PSYCHOSIS

We will now attempt an integrated overview of the previously discussed findings and concepts, particularly those we find useful in our work and attempts to understand clients. If we consider the many difficulties and alterations discussed in earlier sections, it can be argued that psychotic people suffer from a range of difficulties: emotional, interpersonal, reasoning difficulties, hallucinations, and delusions. However, from another perspective one can argue that there are transformations in a wide range of different types of capacity, some of which might be thought of as basic capacities of being a person, a self. Searle (2001), for example, suggests that two basic capacities might be described as agency and acting with reasons over time. There are no doubt other capacities and other ways of describing these; for example, people have a basic capacity to feel that they are the same person over time, from day to day.

It seems reasonable to suggest that as a person moves into psychosis there exists either a sort of continuum of changes, or perhaps, a series of stages. A serious but limited movement to psychosis may occur if a person only has one specific symptom such as becoming delusional or having a hallucination. As a person enters into deeper stages, however, perhaps here the major changes, to various degrees, are the changes in the capacities of the self, and at some very advanced stage, the very capacities which create and maintain the very existence of the former self.

To enter psychosis, we suggest, some things must push the person along this possible continuum of transformation of self into a state such that the capacity for a person's normal consciousness and sense of self alter. For some clients the 'push' might come from long-term biological changes alone; however, as many research findings indicate, it seems likely that the initiating 'push' for many is due to long-term emotional and social suffering. That is, some emotional states are so severe that they begin to influence the deep structures of self-capacity. The whole mind–brain system changes: for some these changes are temporary, for others changes seem fluctuating, and yet for others quite permanent.

What causes psychotic states, these transformations of the self, to become chronic? How are these states maintained? Again, there may be a wide range of causes or factors. For some there may be permanent biological changes such that those structures of the brain that realise consciousness are continuously affected. For other clients, the maintenance might be due to the mutual interactions of several features and include: continuous, unresolved emotional and social suffering; the influence of a wide range of negative ideas and beliefs, for example that the 'self is bad'; the continuing impact of hallucinations, strange feelings, odd perceptions, and which might all in turn increase negative beliefs and emotions. The person might also be stuck in increasingly hostile and unsupportive life contexts: for example, isolation, no relationships or work.

All these factors might not only influence each other but also amplify each other: for example, losing one's job amplifies feelings and ideas of being 'useless', which in turn increases negative voices, which in turn leads to fear, which leads to avoidance, and so on. The person reaches, after many crises, a sort of steady state of suffering, yet also sometimes plunges into new acute phases, when, perhaps, the many mutual areas of negative influence interact and amplify each other.

The person with psychosis has all the 'normal' ways of suffering, of emotional difficulties and so on, but also has the additional catastrophic alterations of consciousness and in extreme cases, changes in the capacity to be one's original pre-psychotic self. Psychosis is not 'just biology' nor just 'unusual ideas', an error of judgement and so on, but a multi-faceted multi-level profound transformation of the self.

IMPLICATIONS FOR THERAPY

The key findings and overview of psychosis presented here have implications, we believe, for how therapy should be designed for clients with psychosis. In this section we will outline what these may be.

Working with psychosis the therapist needs to make more effort than usual to understand the client, in particular to attempt a sort of basic phenomenological grasp of the 'lived-world' of the client, how the client experiences the daily world of people, actions, relations, and so forth. All clients, whether psychotic or not, present difficulties to our understanding: the range of factors in any therapeutic work seems almost endless and most therapists will not have experienced the type of suffering in question. There are also potential differences of social class, culture, age, gender, sexuality. All these might be relevant for clients with psychosis, but these clients also experience phenomena that often seem almost unique to psychosis and unique to each person. Recently a client said her problem was putting up with any noise, that it 'jumbled her thoughts' and was ruining her life. From these opening comments, one might just suggest some sort of anxiety. Perhaps in essence it was, but we suggest to obtain a deeper understanding one would need to further explore the lived experience of being 'jumbled', what exactly does that feel like? What exactly is involved? The therapist's intuition was that this was not 'just' anxiety, but rather that something was unusual about the client's presentation and that it had not been understood.

In seeking to understand clients the therapist needs to understand how a whole range of 'symptoms' and experiences interconnect, how they fuse into a whole, and how these are embedded in the daily 'world' of the client. For example, delusions are not usually just a set of explicit beliefs: rather, there is a complex, changing 'account' or 'narrative' of 'what is going on', and these expressed beliefs link to perceptions of self and other. The meaning imbues the full range of experience of the client.

Given the depth and persistence of these lived experiences, then seeing delusions or ideas about hallucinations and other unusual experiences as 'errors' is very unlikely to be helpful. The concept of an 'error of judgement', as Bentall (2003) writes, may be helpful in thinking about possible cognitive mechanisms, but is not, we believe, a useful attitude in approaching a person with psychosis for therapy. In everyday life, if we think a friend is in 'error', for example thinks your birthday is in January, not February, then we assume that by giving contradictory evidence that person will see it as we do: this is absolutely not the case with psychosis. Telling a person who has ideas of persecution that people cannot just transform their bodies can have the same effect as being told that one's surname is false or that one did not come from the town one remembers growing up in.

Sometimes a client is open to new evidence, to reconsidering beliefs, but in our experience this tends to occur only after there have been great improvements in coping, mood, self-narration, interpersonal relationships, and emotional state. Even then, we will later argue, we believe that it is better to gently construct an alternative account of what is happening as opposed to a concentrated dismantling of the negative belief system.

As indicated above, after assessment, the most useful things to try are therapeutic activities that help the person cope with the present situation, and, if possible, help the person to feel calmer, less overwhelmed by negative emotions. Research points to a central role of emotion, not just as a form of suffering in itself, but because negative emotional states may be one of the key forces which sustain psychotic processes.

The research quoted earlier pointed to the possibility that many clients have undergone chronic stresses and various types of trauma. Furthermore, there appear to be 'gaps' in the narrations of clients concerning these areas. Quite often, unless directly asked, clients do not seem to mention very serious difficulties in their lives. Their narrations appear to be focused on a specific area, for example what a voice says, the attack about to happen. Clients with psychosis, in our experience, just do not place these experiences in a wider context, even, for example, when events as clear-cut as multiple bereavements have occurred. Such observations and findings point to the need, with some clients, to build narratives of their lives, to place sequences of events within a wider context. However, such work should only be attempted if a client is willing, interested, and understands the purpose in doing such work.

Many findings point to the fact that the majority of clients have extremely low 'self-esteem' and negative ideas about themselves. In the cognitive therapy tradition these are called 'core beliefs' and sometimes 'schemas'. These findings suggest the need to help clients build a more realistic and benign set of ideas about themselves.

Research suggests that clients with psychosis are very sensitive to negative events in their social environments: for example, clients who live in atmospheres of 'expressed emotion', that is, negative emotional interaction, tend to have a much greater relapse rate. Further, several clinicians have noted that clients develop a limited, withdrawn lifestyle, what White (1989) called an 'in-the-corner' lifestyle. Many clients tend to not be in work, they live alone, and if they live with family or others, tend to have minimal interaction. A great number avoid all social situations and very often have a fear of being on the street and believe others know they are 'patients'.

Being afraid of the other, of the public, is not always without basis: research has suggested that there is stigmatisation of clients. One client said she felt tense and ashamed when, in conversation with a stranger, the latter had said derogatory comments about someone being 'mental'. Exposure to such comments, and to representations of psychosis in many films and media, must be highly distressing: it is very important with some clients to underline the fact that clients with psychosis are no more prone to violence than are the public at large, perhaps less so.

The findings concerning interaction and the environment point to the need for creating calm, supportive, and constructive living environments for clients. If there is such stress in a person's home, this may need to be a primary focus. For some clients in contrast who, perhaps, are too enclosed in a narrow world, then the focus may need to be to encourage them to take risks to explore the world, take up work and social activities. To enable this sort of exploration, clients may need help with methods of dealing with the stress that attempting the new may engender.

Whatever the causal pathways are to psychosis, considerable evidence points to how a person's states vary and often vary according to emotional and social difficulties. We hope and intend that the therapy we present in this book addresses these central issues.

Chapter 3

Assessment, engagement, and case conceptualisation

In this chapter we will consider the sorts of issues that need to be addressed at the beginning of therapy. In particular, engagement, general and specific areas of assessment, case conceptualisation (that is, how one understands the presentation of difficulties in the context of the person's life), and how one might plan the course of therapy.

ASSESSMENT AND ENGAGEMENT

Who is assessing whom?

CBT traditionally suggests that the therapist carries out a detailed scientific analysis of the problem behaviour prior to the commencement of the intervention or 'treatment'. We will suggest that although assessment is useful there is a tension between assessment and engagement, and that engagement should take precedence. It is often necessary, before beginning most forms of intervention, to allow a much longer period of time to establish a working relationship with a psychotic client than for a client with other problems. In our work we will usually not attempt to begin any intervention, other than listening, for three to six weeks. Sometimes the period is much longer.

Assessment is a mutual process. As well as the therapist assessing the client, the client is also assessing the therapist. In the case of clients with psychosis initially their assessment of us is much more important than our assessment of them. This is because psychotic clients often have few reasons of their own for being in therapy and are likely to decide that therapy will not be helpful (for reasons explained below). In the client's assessment of the therapist there will be several things that they are likely to consider. The overriding question will be 'Will it be helpful or unhelpful to attend these sessions?' They will also want to know if the therapist is a competent and trustworthy person, if the therapist will be honest with them, and if the therapist will be reliable. Will the therapist be able to understand what the client is getting at? Does the client like the therapist? Does the therapist like the client? Some clients will also want the therapist to take their side, that is, to agree that what they say is true and that other people are wrong. There may also be certain unmet needs which the client has, and which they may wish to have fulfilled in the therapy sessions (such as being cared for). We discuss this aspect of assessment and therapy below. In cognitive behaviour therapy (with a client who is not psychotic or personality disordered) one can usually ignore these issues and just set about the business of addressing the presenting problem. The situation is usually different with psychotic clients. This is due to factors external to the client as well as factors associated with psychosis. First, clients with psychosis may see the mental health service as monitoring, controlling, and supervising their behaviour rather than treating them. In some cases they may be correct about this. The client may have experience of coercive forms of 'treatment'. Furthermore, they may have a tendency to be suspicious about people in general or strangers in particular. This suspicion may be based on previous negative experiences with people. In addition, they may be wary of other people because of delusions, particularly if they believe that they are being conspired against or persecuted. Finally, they may have general difficulties in relating to other people due to difficulties in understanding other people's motives and intentions (Frith, 1992).

Developing a working relationship

Several strategies are important during this process of the client's assessment of the therapist. Focusing on listening and trying to understand clients' problems from their perspective, and conveying this understanding to them when possible is helpful. During the first sessions it is helpful to ask clients what their main concerns are and to get some idea of their personal histories. It is important to allow clients to go at their own pace and we generally indicate to clients that there may be things that they will not want to discuss with us at the present time. To be helpful the therapist needs to be able to join with clients while retaining their own perspective on a client's story. Establishing this space is the first task in narrative CBT with psychosis. Many CBT-trained therapists, new to this work, will want to be more active in therapy. It is useful to remember that several studies (for example Sensky and colleagues, 2000) have found that 'befriending' or supportive counselling seems to be quite helpful with clients with psychosis, so it is worth curbing the desire to rush in and do something. Non-verbal cues are important here. Not having a hidden agenda of 'fixing' the client for someone else (for example the referring psychiatrist), or indeed 'fixing' the client at all, is important. Being clear who the client is (that is, the psychotic person and not their family or the referrer or the case manager) makes it easier to engage with what the client says. Setting up a regular time and place and a secure, pleasant place to talk are all helpful.

It can be informative to visit the person in their own home or on the ward, particularly if their motivation for therapy is low. This can, however, produce certain difficulties. Helpful relatives or flatmates cannot be relied upon to respect the confidentiality of the room that one is conducting the therapy in. One of us interviewed a client over a number of months in a shared rehabilitation flat. Two clients shared the flat but there was only one common room. Arranging a confidential space was difficult as it depended upon the other client not walking into the shared space. Another client was living at home in a house with an open plan space. That the client's parents could walk by severely limited the type of conversation that we could have, even if the client's parents did not actually walk by.

Above all, there can be a lot of pressure either from others, or from oneself, to work at changing the client's delusional beliefs, voices, or ways of living. This is an unhelpful position to take. Rather, one should try to understand the client's problems and not feel it necessary to alter anything for a considerable time. Actually one should not really feel the need to attempt to alter anything until one is convinced that the client wants this and that they would be better off if a change occurred. And this is often not very obvious.

Working in teams

It is important to be clear about what information you will share with the rest of the treating team. Some therapists have now taken to giving their client a list of the circumstances under which they will divulge information about the client to social services, the police, etc. This is obviously not helpful in engaging a suspicious and paranoid client in therapy. We give an idea of what information we do not share, and mention that in certain circumstances we have to communicate with other members of the team. Usually we mention suicidal intentions or self-harm as particular circumstances in which we would be obliged to communicate with third parties.

What you can say to clients will depend upon what you are able to negotiate with your team. Some community teams have an unexpressed philosophy that 'we are all the same' and 'we all do the same'. Having a discussion with the team or the team leader about the boundaries of the role, note taking etc., is important in establishing a space to be able to talk to the client. Here a useful distinction can be made between record keeping, which is an objective account of your treatment of the client, and notes of a more subjective and impressionistic type that are kept for the purpose of clinical thinking and planning. It can be helpful for such clinical records to not be identifiable as relating to a particular client. What is possible will depend partly on the organisation's procedures but above all it is important to be clear with the client about the situation. Successfully developing a therapeutic relationship will also depend on what other roles you have to take on within a team. It is preferable not to be the case manager of a client with whom you are carrying out therapy for psychosis. This is partly because you will be obliged to be far more active in the life of your client if you are a case manager. Sometimes clients will assume that you are offering complete confidentiality. It is important to address this when it comes up to avoid having the client feel that you have misled them later in the therapy.

Commenting on the client's assessment of the therapist

Some clients will openly express suspicion about the therapist, or will convey this by non-verbal means. In these cases it can be useful to talk with the client about whether they are engaged in a process of assessment of the therapist and to encourage this process. This approach can also be useful if the client begins to incorporate the therapist into their delusion.

A client told one of us that he believed that the therapist had passed on confidential information from the previous session to his teacher, who had made reference to this during a lesson. Fortunately this type of response is not common. In such cases we feel that it is important to be clear that we do not agree with the claim but that we cannot prove this to be the case. We believe this because if we reply in an evasive way this might encourage the client to believe that the statement is true. Such a belief about the therapist is very unlikely to be long-standing, and is likely to be relatively responsive to alternative ideas over time (Nelson, 2005).

One approach is simply to ask how the client understands the therapeutic situation and what the client believes the therapist might be trying to do. This can be stated in very tentative ways, for example 'Do you have any fears about therapy?' 'Are you worried about what I as a psychologist might be doing?' Simply having an open discussion around these issues can help to neutralise their influence and give time for the building of trust.

Suspension of disbelief, collaboration, and collusion

There is a general agreement in the literature (Nelson, 2005; Kingdon and Turkington, 2004; Chadwick, Birchwood, and Trower, 1995) that it is important to avoid confronting clients about their delusional beliefs yet at the same time it is also important not to give active consent for or agreement with delusions. In our experience it is in fact very rare that a client will ask directly at the beginning of therapy if the therapist agrees with the client about the truth of a delusion or the reality of voices or other psychotic features. One reason for this might be that there are so many other social and emotional issues to discuss, for example overwhelming feelings of anxiety, isolation, or interpersonal conflicts.

If pressed by the client on the reality of a claim, it can be helpful to take the position that we are not well placed to make a judgement on this issue, or that we do not see our role as telling clients what to think. That is, we are not in a position to authoritatively decide if clients are right or wrong about what they believe and that clients have to make up their own mind on this issue. Conspiracies do happen and many aspects of a delusional system might contain some truth; for example, a partner might have had an affair, or others may have been aggressive towards the client. A client might make a claim based on telepathy or communication with spirits: we might well say here that such topics are highly controversial and that among psychologists themselves a full spectrum of opinions is also found. We would also add that what the particular therapist's opinions are is not really relevant to doing good therapy and helping the client.

Although there is general consensus that explicit agreement with clients about delusions is a bad thing, there is less agreement about where this might begin or end and there are different opinions about the correct approach in this situation. In general we do not think it useful to tell clients that one believes that they are deluded and that their beliefs are impossible. To not express oneself on such issues is, of course, only the same approach we adopt in everyday conversation or therapy for emotional problems, that is, we do not automatically point out to others when we think they have mistaken beliefs, particularly if such beliefs are very important to the person involved. Being candid about other people's religious beliefs, for example, is not generally regarded as socially appropriate behaviour.

Generally it is possible to simply avoid expressing an opinion on the truth of delusions and other claims. If one sees one's role as helping the client articulate his or her understanding of what has been happening (with a view to changing things in a helpful way for the client) then the view of the therapist often does not arise and is not the most important thing (Chadwick, 2006; Nelson, 2005). This position is easier to maintain, as indicated earlier, if one has divested oneself of other roles that are incompatible with this neutral position such as case manager.

Most clients are content with being listened to and not being immediately contradicted, as usually has occurred. One important aspect of the psychotherapist's role can be to be able to eventually enter into a conversation with clients about whether their views on these matters are correct or helpful. It is difficult to set up such a conversation if one insists on beginning it by assuming the conclusion. In this, people with delusions react just like everyone else. It is important to find a way to 'join' with any client and this is doubly important in the case of psychosis (Rhodes and Jakes, 2002). One important quality in the therapist is to be able to tolerate listening to a client talking about paranoid delusions without feeling the need to contradict those beliefs. And in many cases it may be unhelpful to attempt to modify the delusion at all, as we discuss later.

SOME CONCEPTUAL ISSUES CONCERNING ASSESSMENT AND MEANING

When we carry out assessment in NCBT we do, of course, examine diverse areas of a person's experience, for example thoughts, actions, voices, and so forth. We will touch upon some of these where appropriate throughout this book. Another question, however, is, what sort of psychological phenomena are we actually assessing? A standard and straightforward answer might be as follows: we examine thoughts, beliefs, emotions, behaviours, etc., and sometimes we talk of assessing 'schemas'. In this section we will discuss the concept of schemas and consider two other issues concerning meaning.

What is a 'schema'?

The word 'schema' seems to have at least three meanings. First, the term often means 'core belief', that is, where a person holds a long-standing belief about self or others, expressed in many ways, for example that he or she is 'inferior', or that 'nothing works out for me'. On the whole, Padesky (1994) appears to use the term schema in this way.

The second more technical concept of schemas is that a schema is a structure that somehow lies behind or beyond particular expressions of a thought, that is, that the schema is like a template that can generate lots of specific copies (Bartlett, 1932). In this sort of conception we cannot know the schema directly, but can only collect and examine the examples it creates, and on the basis of these examples, hypothesise what the schema content or structure might be. So, from the writing of a patient we might take 20 statements about the self, and conclude that the person has a schema with the meaning or theme of 'I am not likeable'.

The third concept of schema is the one given by Young and colleagues (Young, Klosko, and Weishaar, 2003). Here schema is defined as 'a broad, pervasive theme or pattern' that is 'comprised of memories, emotions, cognitions, and bodily sensations'. This definition is broader and more inclusive than the first two. It was designed in the context of working with severe difficulties of personality.

In our practice and thinking, and in this book, we will tend to use the first definition and sometimes the second definition of schema: for example, discussing with a client how many comments might indicate one theme and that some deep structure generates this theme can help some clients see how they are doing the same sort of thing in many different contexts.

In this book we are concerned with therapy and do not wish to go into an extended analysis of the concept of schemas as may be needed in cognitive science, but we do wish to register our unease with the clarity of the concept, particularly the second definition. In various CBT textbooks, as stated, the schema is defined as an abstract structure, a sort of meaning template that warps incoming new information. We are not sure, however, what an abstract 'representation', somehow in the mind or brain, really is or could be. Following Searle's philosophical analysis (1992), we are not convinced the mind works like a computer where 'software' might involve some type of abstract representation and that somehow this software generates specific experiences. We are more convinced by the actual occurrences of what can be either observed directly or reported by introspection, that is, we are more convinced of the existence of subjective mental life on the one hand, and on the other, of public actions and discourse (that is, actual talk involving metaphors, narratives, reported experiences, etc.). We accept, of course, that psychological features, for example memories, are somehow structured, perhaps as dispositions, in the living brain. The concept of the schema is a hypothesis to make sense of certain observed facts: it may be that a better theory than that of schemas as such could also make sense of these observed phenomena.

Construction verses discovery

Assessing a problem and the person is not just about finding out what is 'already there'. It is correct that clients do arrive with many things they want to say, and things they could readily say if we ask. However, as Greenberg and Pascual-Leone (1997) argue, a great deal of therapeutic work is helping clients express in words, symbols, and narratives, things they have not been able to articulate before. In therapy there is an important process of meaning construction.

These new constructions can be about problematic feelings, ideas, behaviours, but these constructions can also be about the 'positive', about 'strengths', 'exceptions', 'initiatives', and so forth which for a whole variety of reasons have not been put into words by the person. Helping to construct new meaning with clients is a key contribution, as will be described later, of solution focused and narrative therapies.

The real nature of thinking, concepts, and experience

There is perhaps a prejudice that may go like this: metaphors are just 'decoration', vivid ways of talking, while the real thought or content is literal. Following Lakoff, we accept that if, for example, a person reportedly has negative thoughts about himself or herself, then it is possible these thoughts are always in a metaphoric form and that there is no separate pre-existing literal content as such. The person thinks, and feels, 'I'm a waste of space', and rarely if ever thinks whatever is the equivalent, for example 'I have failed recent work projects'.

A further and more subtle point Lakoff is making suggests that even ordinary words such as 'mother' or 'man' come loaded with metaphoric or metonymic meaning; in fact, a word like 'mother' comes with a complex model, often involving stereotypes, of what a 'good' or 'typical' mother might be. A simple statement such as 'I'm not a good mother', though 'literal', does in fact hook up to complex cultural notions of appropriate ways of being, in a particular society, for a woman who has children. These cultural expectations often add to the burden of clients.

It is for these reasons that constructivist therapies in general pay very careful attention to the actual words, phrases, and discursive practices of clients, and like to consider where these practices have their origin and how they affect clients. Of course, for most words, most of the time, we must assume a shared meaning, otherwise communication would be near impossible. It is, however, very useful in the course of assessment and therapy to consider carefully certain key words and phrases a client might use and to check out the associations of meaning the client can give.

BEGINNING ASSESSMENT

In this section we present areas of assessment carried out with almost all clients whether they have specific symptoms such as delusions and voices or whether they are presenting emotional and interpersonal difficulties as the main area of concern. A detailed assessment with clients is the norm but there can be situations of crisis when this is not possible and also situations where the client will simply not accept any type of extended discussion. For such cases it can be useful to use classic problem solving (Hawton and Kirk, 1989) or solution focused approaches (Rhodes and Jakes, 2002): the crucial difference here is that one might end the session with practical suggestions and not carry out extended investigation at that stage of work. The following assessment ideas and practices are aimed at clients who are stable enough to engage in extended therapy (see Appendix A for a summary of key questions and some areas covered).

Current main problems

A good place to start is with the client's current concerns and complaints. We do not try to turn these into symptoms, and we try not to listen out for symptoms. Clients are often referred for work on delusions, voices, or anxiety, but this may not be the most important problem from the client's point of view; for example, the client may report that his or her main problem is being depressed or as having a financial problem or not having a job or a relationship. A simple question can be: how do you see your problems at present? Most clients tend to describe several problems, these being a mixture of symptoms, emotional and social problems; like many non-psychotic clients, they may not give the most important problems first, and may only give the most upsetting difficulties on further inquiry. All these presenting problems should be explored with the client and over time agreements with the client can be made about which are of most concern and in what sort of order they could be addressed. Some clients do know and state that they are suffering from specific symptoms and will start by saying that they wish to be helped, for example, to cope with unpleasant voices: some clients know that they are prone to becoming delusional and in a straightforward way want help with this.

In many cases, particularly where there are delusions, clients will not be likely to agree with other people about the nature of their problems: this can be an area of conflict if not approached with care. Our general stance, as suggested earlier, is to work with the presentation given by the client and in the solution focused phase one can seek solutions completely within the frame of the client: for example, for a client who thought demons were about to arrive (Rhodes and Jakes, 2002), we repeatedly asked what he could do, how he could cope. We did not state that we believed there were no demons: to do so would have simply stopped all communication.

One crucial characteristic of cognitive therapy is that the relationship between therapist and client needs to be collaborative. This has been helpfully developed in the CBT of psychosis as a way of promoting engagement with the client. It is important for the therapist to identify the client's understanding of his or her problems and goals: and it is important to really be interested in these goals rather than seeing them as a way of working on the client's delusions or hallucinations. This process is also helped by adopting the attitude of 'joining' or seeing the world from the client's viewpoint emphasised in narrative solution focused therapy and other systemic therapies.

Usually, over a number of sessions, problems with positive psychotic symptoms will emerge if they are relevant. If they do not it is worth checking with the client if these issues are still a problem. One way of approaching this is to indicate that someone else in the team has suggested that voices or some particular experiences are a problem and that you wonder if that is right? This leaves it open for the client to deny that these are problems without contradicting the therapist. If the client indicates that these are not problems then obviously one will not want to address them in the sessions. It is easy to have a hidden agenda of changing symptoms, if we believe that these are dysfunctional. Fortunately, most clients can identify problems that can be worked on independently of whether there are delusional aspects or not. So, for example, if the client reports depressed mood, and the details of this are not too closely linked to the delusion, then the depression can be worked on using solution focused work, activity scheduling, and other approaches in this book. We return to the issues of how and whether to work with delusions in the chapter on alternative perspectives.

Current social situation

The very useful work that has been done in addressing positive symptoms of psychosis in the CBT literature has had perhaps the unfortunate effect of de-emphasising the social dilemmas of the psychotic person. Psychosis is almost always accompanied by difficulties in interpersonal relationships, but these are not always presented as problems to the therapist. It is useful to know how many social contacts the client has, how often the client is in contact with these people and, most importantly, the quality and depth of these relationships. Does the client have any meaningful close relationships with others? This is best assessed by asking clients for examples of their interactions with key people in their life. Does the client have any friends? Here it is also useful to have an idea of the client's understanding of why they are socially isolated. Sometimes clients will relate these problems to their delusional narration, or to non-delusional beliefs about themselves or others; sometimes the client will simply accept that this is how it is and have no particular explanation of this situation. This varies depending upon, among other things, the psychological-mindedness of the client. Sometimes clients will relate the problems they have to a non-delusional belief about themselves or other people; for example, the client may believe that people are not to be trusted and are dangerous or faithless. Such an interpersonal belief sometimes seems to be part of the set of attitudes which gives rise to the delusional belief (for example delusional persecutory beliefs) or it may be a consequence of their experiences since becoming psychotic. The quality of people's interpersonal relationships can give relevant information to help with understanding their interpersonal core beliefs but is also important because the inability to form relationships is part of the maintenance cycle for delusions.

Suicide and self-harm

Suicide is a high risk for patients with psychosis (Johnson, Godding, and Tarrier, 2008) so in the assessment and at subsequent stages, one needs to be aware of potential suicidal thoughts, plans, and intentions and therapists need to know what steps to take if there is a sudden acceleration of risk. With very suicidal patients it is useful to meet the psychiatric team involved and set up arrangements so that it is clear what everyone will do in an emergency.

In discussing suicide it is interesting to note that Johnson et al. suggest that a key feature of work should be the development with clients of positive future plans. This is a central feature of our work in developing solution focused ideas, considering a preferred self, emphasising long-term community involvements, and thinking with clients about personal values and purpose. The 'Tidal Mode' described by Barker and Buchanan-Barker (2005) is an excellent resource for working with suicide, particularly for staff on wards. It too draws on solution focused and narrative approaches.

Social situation immediately prior to the development of psychosis

Understanding the social situation prior to the onset of the first psychotic episode (and also subsequent episodes) is important in a number of ways. First, it gives us an idea of what may have been the precipitating events, that is, what problems have led to the person becoming psychotic. This gives an indication of the meaning of these events to the person. Often this meaning is not articulated by the person but suggests strong clues to the observer. These meanings are usually indicative of important problematic interpersonal beliefs or schemas. This is important information in understanding and working with clients' narrative of their life or for work at a schema level. The same information can also be obtained, to a lesser extent, from subsequent exacerbations of the person's psychosis. With these latter events, however, it is not always very easy to separate cause and effect. If someone is admitted to hospital is it because their symptoms have changed so that the social system cannot tolerate them or because the social situation has changed so that the environment cannot tolerate their symptoms? Understanding the person's core beliefs is central to the development of a narrative CBT case conceptualisation.

Developmental history

The developmental history of the client's interpersonal relationships is also of critical importance. In taking the developmental history one should be trying to discover what the person's interpersonal beliefs are with regard to (1) themselves, (2) other people, and (3) the world. Thus, the developmental history can give important information about the development of ideas about the self and others that can help to place the client's symptoms in context. It can give information about the development of the client's delusions or voices. An idea of the best level of interpersonal functioning the client has had also helps the therapist to understand the client. If the person has functioned socially at a reasonable level at any time in the past, this indicates that more benign schemas are available to the client, even if they are currently dormant. The relationship with the client's primary caregiver and family of origin, any history of child abuse or mistreatment, the relationship of the client to their brothers and sisters and to peers at school, are all potentially important.

The quality of relationships is best assessed by asking clients for examples of typical interactions with their mother, father, siblings, and peers at school. We find that often delusions can be understood as expressions of problems that began in early development. The degree to which the person has withdrawn emotionally from other people and the world in general needs to be assessed. A key question is whether clients have any current relationships and if so what the quality of these relationships is. Furthermore, do they express a desire for better relationships with others? In therapy the therapist is often the only person with whom the client has a significant link. This relationship when developed can be used to enable clients to reality test some of their psychotic and other beliefs about people in general. It can also be the place where the client can begin to try to develop a human relationship again after years of isolation. If there are other important people in the client's life this is helpful as improving the quality of these relationships may often be a key goal. The quality of relationships with others will sometimes reflect the relationship clients have with themselves. This can be directly assessed by asking clients for beliefs about themselves and their beliefs about others. Information about this often also comes from the client's delusions or voices. For example, if the client reports a bullying voice, is bullying experienced in other relationships from or to others? Do clients bully themselves?

Contextual analysis

The original behavioural technique of functional or contextual analysis (Martell, Addis, and Jacobson, 2001) and its variations are particularly useful in assessing all types of emotional and behavioural difficulties; voices and delusions are no exception. We are not behaviourists as such and therefore include, as appropriate, a wide range of areas to focus on when doing such an analysis; for example, we might also ask about various types of meaning, actions, motivations. Essentially this type of analysis involves taking a recent situation in which a problem occurred and examining a wide range of events, processes, and so on, that preceded and followed the specific problem in question. This provides an account of how the symptoms are related to social, psychological, and other aspects, and what the consequences of the problems are. This can be very useful for identifying potential areas for treatment.

Often, for example, voices will be noticed and are distressing when the client is alone and in contrast less troublesome when in company. Other common triggers include thinking about past experiences or lying awake at night. Another common precipitant is some type of difficult emotional experience. Something happens that the client feels depressed or angry about and this leads to voices condemning the client.

Delusions can be explored in the same way. The variation in strength of conviction can be examined, but it is often the degree of preoccupation with the belief, or the distress about the belief, that is most important. A client had believed he was being conspired against by society in general and by his ex-wife in particular. This belief had been held with absolute certainty for the two years during which the client was in therapy, but the degree of intrusiveness of the belief varied in relation to various ups and downs in the client's life. With many of the clients we have seen over a number of years this same pattern can be noted. Again if the client reports depression or anxiety or interpersonal problems, one can carry out functional analysis on these problems, looking at context and variation. Contextual analysis, which focuses on current situations, can be added to by exploring associated meanings and the narrative of events that are linked to the voices or delusion.

SPECIFIC AREAS AND APPROACHES

Delusions

When in the initial assessment it seems to be the case that the client has a delusion, that the delusion is having an adverse effect upon the client, and that the client does wish to work to change at least aspects of the delusion, then we usually set about a systematic assessment of the delusion and how this connects to aspects of the client's life. We will discuss here an interview schedule (see Appendix B) we have both developed in research and modified in practice with many clients over years. The schedule is a 'guide' in that we might ask these exact questions but endlessly modify these as appropriate for the person and occasion.

Our first aim in the schedule is to really understand the delusional account or narrative in its complexity. On the whole, delusions are not simple statements: rather, the person is in a complex altered state that has often persisted for years and as part of that state makes many attempts to express 'what is happening'. For the convenience of therapy we do eventually summarise the person's delusions into a small number of clear statements, for example 'A gang is following me all the time', but of course this is only a small part of the global situation and its history. As stated earlier, we think it very useful to fully explore the time at onset and the time before onset. Some clients have often not thought about this for years and so it can be quite difficult to access details. It can, however, sometimes reveal crucial aspects not otherwise mentioned. To understand what might be maintaining a delusion it is very useful to explore how it fluctuates in different situations over time and also to see how the person often has made some extreme changes to lifestyle, for example never going out during the day.

The final questions focus on the person's life history and present concerns: these questions might be asked at any stage and might be asked very near the beginning of the assessment or instead after the above areas have been covered. Some of these areas will be covered again in much more detail during therapy, for example how a person would like their life to be. The idea here is to just get a first impression so a decision can be made as to whether to return to an area or instead that it might be better not to focus on an area.

The schedule, if followed all the way through, on average will take about three sessions to complete. Ideally the therapist should take very detailed notes using quotes where possible. When finished it is useful to reread the whole interview to grasp what the client is saying as a whole and to think about interconnections. We usually return to the information in this interview several times while working with a client: repeated attempts at understanding it forms part of generating a narrative case conceptualisation about the client. It is also interesting how details given in the original assessment often only make sense after much more work has been done with the client.

Voices and visions

When assessing voices it is very important to remember that, for an individual, voices can be experienced as negative, as positive, or as both. Some clients do state that they wish to keep aspects of the voices they hear. We explore voices keeping these possible ambivalences in mind. Once it is decided to explore voices then we explore areas similar to the ones discussed concerning delusions, that is, a full exploration of what the voices are, how they began, how they vary at the present time, and look at a person's life history.

In exploring what the voices are, several aspects can be explored; for example, where do the voices occur, inside the person or outside? If outside, then how are they transmitted to the person? Sometimes we might here give the person a range of choices; for example, some people say voices are spirits or due to telepathy, and some say they come from within, which of these, or other possibilities, might it be for you? Another crucial aspect is the person's relationship to the voices; that is, are the voices perceived as powerful, are they malign or benign? Can examples of this be given?

For many clients voices start at some point and then develop over time (Nayani and David, 1996). It can therefore be interesting to explore how the voices manifested themselves at first and then how they developed. Quite typically the voice develops a 'character' over time and sometimes the number and nature of voices change. Often the client has not thought about this for many years and if these memories return, interesting aspects can be revealed for the client.

It is, we believe, very difficult to find quantitative assessments which can be reliably used for voices, though the one designed by Hustig and Hafner (1990), presented in Chadwick et al. (1996), can be employed with many clients; the main reason for this difficulty with measurement is that for many clients the voices vary enormously from a few minutes per week to all the time. It is also the case that there is extreme variation between different clients, making the use of one instrument for all difficult. Some clients state that they cannot clearly remember how the voices have varied over the previous week.

For many clients we have, therefore, found it useful to construct with the client a set of subjective and person-specific criteria; for example, one client might after discussion suggest the following: (1) most days most of the time; (2) just some days, a few hours; (3) two days; (4) just one day. A different person, however, might give quite different criteria, for example does not have persistent voices but rather has short intense outbursts. For some clients, it is sometimes only feasible to ask about the day before or in fact the few hours before the session since they say that they just cannot remember the rest of the week. For visual hallucinations we always construct with the client a subjective scale since these types of experience seem particularly person-specific and unique to specific contexts.

Expressive arts based assessment

In line with other constructivist therapists such as Mahoney, we find it useful to incorporate into our assessments, at different stages, forms of assessment that draw upon various types of artistic expression, for example the use of writing or visual art. For many clients we ask them to keep a simple diary: sometimes we give the client a sheet with the question: 'Please write out what thoughts or emotions have been on your mind today'. At later stages of therapy, in some cases, we might in fact ask the client to write about specific episodes or times in their lives.

We have found it very informative to ask clients to provide metaphors for how they are feeling and to express their ideas on certain topics: how this is done and the questions used are given in Chapter 5.

With some clients it can be very useful to explore expression in different mediums, for example photographs, drawings, music. Some clients find that they have strong memories of certain characters or episodes in films or television programmes. Assessment using such material might occur at any point in therapy but we sometimes, near the beginning, give a sheet to the client with the following questions:

1   Does any story, or character, express your thoughts and feelings about your self or life?
2   Can you either draw a picture, or find a picture or photograph, that expresses your thoughts and feelings?
3   Does any piece of music or song express your feelings and thoughts?

When the client returns this work we might simply ask why such and such a picture was chosen and what it might mean. The therapist should not jump to interpretations nor make assumptions about the content but rather ask for personal associations.

Quantitative assessments

Shapiro (1961) argued that for measuring change in the individual case, one should develop an individualised questionnaire for each client based on their own descriptions of their problems and their own descriptions of the intensity of their problems. This can be a useful strategy. A simplified version of this technique involves asking clients to define their problems in their own words and then to define steps towards improvement again in their own words. This then constitutes the scale of improvement. For example, a person might give: (1) I feel low; (2) I feel miserable; and (3) I feel depressed.

We rate degree of conviction in the delusion by asking clients to make an estimation of how certain they are that the belief is true on a percentage scale. We also ask them to make the same rating using the verbal descriptions: from 'Absolutely certain it is true' to 'Absolutely certain it is false', with a middle position of 'No idea if true or false' (see Appendix C). These descriptions are presented as points on a line which is given to the client, so it is possible for the client, by pointing to the given descriptions, to indicate increasing degrees of certainty or doubt. We use similar descriptions to indicate degrees of emotional distress or preoccupation. We ask clients to indicate which of five statements best corresponds to how the previous week has been (see Appendix C).

We use several measures for depression and anxiety such as the Hospital Anxiety and Depression Scale (Snaith and Zigmond, 1994) or sometimes the scales designed by Beck and colleagues. For a simple but very useful indication of self-image and self-esteem we use the Evaluative Beliefs Scale as designed by Chadwick and colleagues (1996). For clinical purposes, drawing up a simple analogue scale can be useful. An analogue scale can be constructed by using a 10-centimetre line the end points of which are given opposite relevant labels. The client makes a mark on the line to indicate his or her response.

CASE CONCEPTUALISATION AND THERAPY PLANNING

Given the client begins to engage with therapy, then several decisions have to be made with regard to therapeutic focus, length of therapy, areas to be covered, and therapeutic approaches to be used.

Most textbooks written from a pure CBT perspective tend to emphasise a formulation of the symptom(s), that is, a sort of explanation of what caused the problem and what factors maintain the problem. In contrast to this, various systemic therapies have suggested that a therapist first needs to think carefully about how any problems occur in the complex context of the person and the person's social system, but also within the context of the 'referral' system, in some cases psychiatric, and the context of the therapy service system (Burnham, 1986). If one considers the context of the problem/person, the client's attitude to change, and so forth, then the following sorts of question need to be answered:

- What is the client's attitude to change? Is it seen as something desired or otherwise? Is the client ambivalent?
- Are other people in the system more eager than the client?
- What are the goals, motivations, needs, of the network around the client, for example family, GP, community mental health worker?
- Does the client believe change is possible?
- Does the client have well-worked-out theories of the cause and any possible treatments? Are these ideas helpful or otherwise?
- What are all the relevant problems and what is the most practical order of focusing on these? In particular, are any delusions or preoccupations such that these will prevent work on any other areas?
- Has the client a specific clear-cut problem, or, many problems? Are they constant or always changing? Does the client have long-term problems of self-esteem, self-image, and interpersonal functioning?

Answers to the above need to be collected, assembled, and thought through, and a dialogue opened with the client.

Given tentative answers to these questions, the next most important set of decisions is to consider offering therapy or not, and if offering therapy, to decide whether it should be short term (less than 20 sessions), or long term (up to about 50 sessions) or in some cases supportive intermittent therapy, that is, a sort of therapy or counselling that might be extended over many years if not permanently, though with a low frequency.

We will not cover in detail the latter type of extended ongoing supportive work. Meaden and Van Marle (2008) outline a useful version, one aimed particularly at providing approaches to coping, but also emphasise the importance of understanding the client. Barker and Buchanan-Barker

(2005) likewise articulate an approach designed for long-term support and help for periodic crises. Barker and Buchanan-Barker draw greatly upon solution focused and narrative therapies; their approach to care is highly compatible with one in this book.

What sorts of problem and person are suitable for short-term therapy? Essentially, short-term work is indicated where there is at least one clear specific problem of concern to the person and the 'personality', or rather the 'functioning' of the person is such that it does not produce major 'therapy inferring' (Linehan, 1993) behaviours.

Longer-term work is suggested if there are many problems, or if there are serious long-standing problems; for example, where clients think they are utterly worthless and have little motivation or are so afraid of being seen or judged by others that they will not leave the house. Longer-term work is usually needed for someone with distressing delusions, particularly since these delusions often prevent clients from taking any sort of action or making changes. However, in some cases one can conclude that longer-term therapy would be helpful for the client, but the client may not be a 'customer' for longer-term work, and an alternative can be to consider short-term work. For example, one client we assessed had a long-standing delusion: he was sure that he was being persecuted by a former employer, and that this had been going on for over 10 years. He lived a restrictive life and we thought he could have benefited from a longer-term psychological therapy, but he was not interested in this, as he saw no reason for it. He did, however, agree to come for a very brief therapy of some four sessions to work on coping with his worries.

The NCBT approach is suitable for many types of trauma and interpersonal difficulty. We do not know if it is sufficient for those with extreme and multiple physical, emotional, and/or sexual abuse, and where these may have influenced the capacity to function in fundamental ways. For such clients, we believe, new therapies or modifications of present long-term therapies may be needed, for example schema therapy (Young et al., 2003) or DBT (Linehan, 1993).

Short-term therapy

We often do short-term therapy for clients with voices, mood disorders, and clients with specific behavioural difficulties. It is rarely done for clients with very disruptive delusions or severe depression: as suggested, these two conditions in particular seem global in their interference.

The most typical pattern for short-term work is: first, assessment and engagement, then solution focused work, and if needed to proceed to specific CBT techniques as appropriate, for example exposure therapy (Wolpe, 1990) for anxiety conditions. For voices we tend to follow an SFT phase by a sustained focus on problem patterns, for example situations where voices increase. We move in general from solution generating to a focus on problems but often there are several phases of moving back and forth between solutions and problems. If in short-term work one does use cognitive techniques such as looking for alternative explanations, then the voice content or delusion can be treated as a sort of negative thought, and the issue of the actual reality of these phenomena is not brought into question.

Longer-term therapy

The most typical pattern of therapy we use is as follows:

- the initial assessment, an outline of the person's narrative, and establishment of alliance
- solution focused work and/or any work aimed at coping in the present
- work exploring core beliefs about self and other, usually with the aim of constructing a conception of a preferred self within a compassionate and self-accepting framework
- where appropriate, a narrative exploration of past difficulties and trauma but also helping to construct a narrative of past strengths and resources
- symptom-specific work if needed and considered useful, for example investigating alternatives to delusions and beliefs about voices, locating triggers for symptoms, CBT work for mood disorders or interpersonal problems
- a phase exploring increased involvement in the community and finally issues of ending therapy.

We might not do all of these phases of work with everyone and other types of focus might be used if indicated. We might, for example, use specific procedures as developed in some versions of compassion therapy (see Chapter 8) for clients who engage in persistent very critical 'attacks' upon the self. For some clients, there might be extended work with staff in residential settings.

Suitably adjusted, these phases are useful for delusions, voices, emotional difficulties, social difficulties, and various combinations of these difficulties. Specific therapeutic ideas for delusions are described in Chapter 7 and work for hallucinations in Chapter 8.

There is a distinct focus on involvement in community activities during the end phase. By 'community', we here mean social relations, work and education, interests, self-care, and some philosophical and existential issues concerning purpose and value. We might in fact be working on any of these throughout therapy, but tend to return to these with added emphasis at the end.

We see the overall pattern of therapy as focused on a sequence beginning with the present, moving to the past, and then returning to the present and future. A similar pattern, we believe, is found in other therapies for clients with long-term difficulties.

Evolving formulations

We make a careful distinction between conceptualisations we share with a client and ones we think about and develop over the time of working with a client. We maintain this distinction since we wish to be very cautious, that is, we do not want to give to the client inaccurate or incomplete conceptualisations. Furthermore, however accurate a conceptualisation might be, we do not wish to give ones which could be distressing to the client or misunderstood, particularly in the early phases of work. We are also cautious given our critical realist perspective and hope to reflect on how our own cultural and interpersonal expectations might influence how we construe a client.

Case conceptualisations can tend to focus on the unfolding of meaning in the life of the client over time or can focus on the causation of processes and events, for example what might have caused the onset of symptoms or their fluctuations. Most of our conceptualisations are about the former. We might, for example, be working with voices and need to understand the origin of very specific insults repeatedly hallucinated by the client. We might eventually see that such insults fit or are consistent with a person's self-image, and that the latter was formed by extensive peer bullying at school. Meaning is then placed in its developmental context.

Conceptualisation aimed at explaining the causal occurrence of symptoms might typically use a simple stress vulnerability model (Zubin and Spring, 1977); for example, it might be the case that the person hears a great increase of voices after arguing with others. Such causal explanations are, as argued earlier, incomplete since a complete explanation might at least involve both biological and psychosocial perspectives. With some clients both the continuity of meaning and causes of onset might be combined into one very broad conceptualisation: for example, that a certain person had a breakdown might be said to have occurred due to a set of overwhelming stresses and the meaning content is illuminated by placing it in a life narrative context and persistence of certain meanings about the self.

We will now consider conceptualisation as it may be used in different stages of therapy.

Conceptualisation and assessment

By the end of the initial assessment phase we might or might not share a conceptualisation with the client. In contrast to conventional CBT we are not convinced that a conceptualisation is always useful at this point. We are cautious for several reasons: first and foremost, any attempt at conceptualisation which appears to explain a symptom can be seen as a rejection or doubting of the client's narrative and ability to know 'what really happened'. Second, we believe a full understanding can only be attained over long periods of working with a client and with repeated attempts at understanding the presented information.

The conceptualisation can, however, guide what areas to focus on as therapy proceeds. For example, should one work with a delusion or not? Are voices relevant? Does the person have a positive self-image, or the very opposite? Are there indicators of serious childhood trauma which might be relevant and has the client indicated interest, or antipathy, to exploring the past?

Conceptualisations and solution focused work

In the original models of de Shazer and White, formulations of the problem are not employed in the thinking of the therapists and conceptualisations are not shared with clients. The client should choose areas to work on and the main aim is to find exceptions, 'what works', whatever the link, or no link, to the presenting problem. For many types of client this can be done but in our own practice we have found that for clients with psychosis some 'guidance' as provided by assessment and conceptualisation can be useful. For example, some issues can be 'embarrassing' for the client; if the conceptualisation suggests an area is relevant, though it is not something the client has mentioned explicitly, then it can be useful to broach this and then explore solutions. If this is done, however, great care must be taken to make sure the client does now agree that this area should be looked at and that this exploration does not alienate the client from the therapy.

Formulations and case conceptualisations are usually used in CBT to explain difficulties. However, it is also possible to focus on solutions in a conceptualisation, for example what a solution in principle could be, how the client might react to such a solution being suggested, what might have stopped a client using what at least appears to be a potential solution. Questions such as these can be thought about in a session break and the generated conceptualisation can guide the suggestion of ideas and tasks to try between sessions. An example of how a conceptualisation might guide direction in the solution focused phase is given in Chapter 4.

Narrative conceptualisation in later stages of therapy

We most typically begin to share a conceptualisation with a client in the middle or even later phases of therapy. We would not attempt to give an alternative account, for example one implying the person's delusions are false, until a very strong alliance has been formed with the client, until the client has begun to improve their self-conceptions, and until we believe such a challenge would be useful. This is discussed in detail in Chapter 7 on alternative perspectives.

Some conceptualisations, of course, are not so challenging to a client's notion of what is real, rather they are straightforward attempts to describe and explain a person's usually negative emotions and meanings, drawing upon descriptions given by the clients themselves. These ideas, often connecting present ideas with past events, are relatively easy for clients to understand and to consider as possibly true. In constructing these conceptualisations we draw upon typical cognitive therapy approaches that explain phenomena in terms of negative beliefs, meaning in general, and repetition of behavioural patterns. Each conceptualisation is unique, and if appropriate we would tend to draw on any of the theories outlined in Chapters 1 and 2.

Formulation

To design a formulation we typically assemble information concerning the present, that is, meanings, motivations, emotions, ways of interacting, and then consider these in the light of the person's development. We assume that present meanings have a history and the latter throw light on the former. We speculate what aspects of a person's past context could have been crucial and how such a context might influence a person's sense of self, meanings, actions.

In terms of thinking about motivation, we do not use just one specific theory, but tend to draw on those diverse ideas used by at least some groups of CBT therapists; for example, we draw upon ideas developed by Gilbert and colleagues concerning bio-social motivations for cooperation/ belonging, need competition and rank, need for care and attachment, but would also consider the shaping role of culture (Bourdieu, 1990; D'Andrade, 1992; Kashima, 1997; Baumeister, 2005). To understand content that seems symbolic, in addition to ideas about the specific person, one might need to understand how something is viewed and valued within a culture, for example stereotypes of 'male' and 'female' and assumed prototypical attributes.

Our preference is to state a formulation in everyday English, using nontechnical language and concepts where possible. In doing so we are influenced by the model of 'intentionality' (Searle, 1983, 2004) which involves the claim that everyday common-sense concepts such as 'desire', 'belief', 'action', 'feeling', etc., are in fact fundamental and perhaps inevitable when describing and explaining human experience. Furthermore, we attempt to use the minimum amount of inference and to keep any accounts as straightforward as possible.

The following is an example of a formulation: the details of the therapy for this case are given in Chapter 5.

Example of assessment and conceptualisation: Lesley

Lesley began therapy stating that she believed she had transformed parts of her body to male body parts. She said she had done this at a time of despair when she no longer wanted to be looked at by men. However, she regretted the change and thought that now she looked like a 'freak' or a 'blob'. She agreed, however, that people did not react negatively to her or shout insults. She explained that this was because others were being polite. To cover her body she would wear large tracksuit tops and bottoms all the time and a large T-shirt whenever she went swimming.

The assessment suggested that she was mildly depressed but extremely anxious. A questionnaire indicated social difficulties, a very negative view of herself, and a benign view of others and what others thought of her. She said that she was 96% convinced that her delusion was true, that she thought about it almost all the time, and was extremely emotionally distressed about it.

Her life history suggested many difficulties. During her twenties her partner had repeatedly beaten her. This relationship ended when he openly brought other women home for sex. Life as a child had also been very difficult. She said that her mother was very critical and her father was more interested in his dogs than his children.

In an early session Lesley told me an episode, a narration which clearly had strong meaning for her. Her father had given her money to go and buy sweets. When she returned, he took them all, and gave her none. In her childhood she also suffered from asthma, which had resulted in her spending time at a school for children with moderate physical difficulties. These stories encapsulated her negative beliefs about both herself and other people.

A brief narrative case conceptualisation for Lesley is as follows. This is an example of one that we might use in our thinking and planning, and is not necessarily the type we might share:

In her childhood Lesley experienced criticism, insults, and a sense of not being wanted. She remembers clear incidents of being rejected. She was also made to feel different from others by attending a special school for those with medical difficulties. The latter concerned her body. This may be partly the source of the theme and origin of the long-term preoccupation with her body. During her teenage years she also became preoccupied with issues of dieting, weight, and the shape of her body, in particular whether it conformed to idealised images of how women were supposed to look. Because of her looks, she reported getting a lot of sexual attention but not feeling comfortable with this and not wanting it.

Her core beliefs and emotional experience centred on her being not like others and being in fact strange and defective. She experienced herself as an inferior outsider looked down upon by others. A frustrated core motivation was therefore to be like others and to be accepted.

Further negative events for her were rejection, humiliation, and violence from a male partner over many years. This perhaps led to a collapse in any remaining self-confidence and hope. She ended this relationship in great depression. At this point she decided she wanted no more sexual relations and set about changing her body by rubbing her legs. It seems possible that in her despair she lost her sense of everyday biology (we would suggest the parts of the Background that should have maintained her previous intuitions about possible biological change).

Her delusion of being a 'freak' seems a symbolic expression of the above: a contribution to this may have been a process of metaphoric comparison. That she attempted to transform her gender also suggests that she was attempting to avoid all possible sexual contact, indicating that the motivation of intimacy was also problematic.

In the above conceptualisation we have tried to capture life-long meanings, developmental contributions, social interactions, and possible difficulties in fundamental motivations, and to speculate on the possible hidden or obscured meaning of the delusional content.

CONCLUDING COMMENTS

In one piece of research it was claimed that clients with psychosis appreciated therapists who were 'friendly' and who understood their condition (Coursey, Keller, and Farrell, 1995). Our clinical experience supports this observation and we hope the ideas in this chapter and the previous ones will help therapists to achieve these elements in their alliance and work with clients.

Chapter 4

Finding solutions

INTRODUCTION

In this chapter we will outline a version of solution focused therapy (SFT) which we have developed in our work with psychotic patients. We have been particularly influenced by de Shazer's work (de Shazer 1988, 1991) and more recently the version of SFT as presented by Eve Lipchick (2002). We have also drawn more selectively on the ideas of White (White and Epston, 1990; White, 2007).

SFT can be seen either as a theory or as a description of actual clinical practice. It draws upon certain general theories; for example, de Shazer draws upon constructivism as described by Watzlawick, Weakland, and Fisch (1974), and sometimes philosophical ideas about language and meaning (Wittgenstein, 1953), yet the core of SFT was developed by doing and by conducting a form of direct practical research on what appeared to be useful in short-term therapy (de Shazer, 1985). SFT has developed a set of guiding assumptions for the exploration of specific areas, and suggested approaches to questioning and intervention.

The assumptions about therapy developed by de Shazer (1985, 1988) in outline are the following. First, most problems or 'complaints' develop in the context of social interaction, and therefore finding solutions often involves the mapping and changing of these interactions. Second, a major task of SFT is to help clients develop new or different actions and/or meanings. Third, it is assumed that clients really do want to change, and that at least some 'resistance' might well be due to therapists approaching difficulties in ways that do not 'fit' with the client's outlook or way of being. Fourth, even apparently difficult action-patterns or experiences can be re-construed, seen in a different light; for example, it can be useful sometimes to consider what is 'appropriate' or 'normal' or useful in difficult behaviours. This idea is similar to Watzlawick et al.'s (1974) notion of 'reframing'; that is, where a new interpretation or 'frame' is given for problematic behaviours. Fifth, only a small change is often needed to begin larger 'ripples' of change. We have certainly noted that when looking back over what happened when a case is successful, the first steps were very small indeed, for example in one case doing 'press-ups' or making a phone call. It needs to be emphasised that such steps are important because of their meaning for the client. Sixth, working with one part of a 'system', for example a grandmother, can influence the whole system, that is, the network of persons involved in the problem. Finally, there are occasions when interventions might help even if the complaint is neither clearly described nor understood. Most psychotherapies claim that the therapeutic interventions, and interpretations, are designed using detailed knowledge of the problem. In SFT, by contrast, it is accepted that an intervention might work even when we do not know how or why. This of course is consistent with the constructivist notion of questioning our knowledge claims about the world.

Lipchick (2002) also articulates a set of SFT assumptions, many of which are similar to the above. She also suggests, in contrast to its reputation, that SFT 'goes slowly', that is, there should be no need to believe that one should rush and do everything quickly. SFT might or might not be 'brief' in time or number of sessions, but this really depends on the person and the problem. Lipchick also emphasises that emotions must be considered as part of the problem and also of the solution. Finally, she has greatly emphasised that it is not therapists who change clients, but that clients in the end change themselves. We have incorporated these latter assumptions into our work.

Some ideas on change

SFT involves a descriptive theory of how clients might attempt to change in the present context of their lives. It is not an elaborate theory of pathology or of the nature of the self. However, a central set of ideas in de Shazer's (1988) presentation of SFT was that people tend to follow or do what 'fits' with their general outlook, world view, and beliefs. It is assumed that problem behaviours and blindness to possible solutions are often the consequence of these beliefs, habits, and attitudes. The notion that emotional problems are closely tied to beliefs is consistent with CBT, yet for de Shazer it is a much wider and open conception. For example, there is no assumption of the direction of causation; in fact, there is no assumption of what a definitive conception of social and psychological phenomena might be.

In SFT there is a focus on how clients talk about actions, emotions, meaning, and how clients might use interpretations or 'frames' for situations; again it must be emphasised that this is not just another way of referring to 'behaviour' or 'cognitions', as in CBT. de Shazer at several points explicitly draws upon those writers who in Chapter 1 we put under the rubric of constructivism; in particular, he uses ideas from Mead (1934) and Goffman (1974). These writers tend to place the concepts of action and meaning at the centre of their theories, and certainly not ideas drawn from behaviourism or information-processing cognitive science. In later works, de Shazer (1991) continued to explore notions such as how meaning is constantly defined and redefined by use. In doing this he borrowed much from Wittgenstein.

The theory of how clients might change is open and flexible. One idea is that clients might change when 'exceptions', that is, times when the difficulty does not occur, are begun to be seen as relevant and important for change, as suggesting something new, sometimes called 'news of difference' (de Shazer, 1991). If there are exceptions, and if during therapy the client begins to see these as important and suggestive of how to change, then they may deliberately choose to do these and thereby effect change. There are, however, other approaches or pathways to change: a fundamental one is to imagine the future and again it is part of SFT to assume that this building or construction of a new picture leads to changes in outlook and action.

O'Hanlon and Weiner-Davis (1989) once suggested that in essence solution orientated therapy was about new viewing, new doing, and the recruitment of resources and strengths. This simple formula is very useful to keep in mind when doing SFT.

The key areas of focus in SFT can in principle be done in any order as the occasion demands: doing SFT, the therapist needs to be very attentive to the state of the client, the interactions, emotions (Lipchick, 2002), and language. Furthermore, as Lipchick emphasised, SFT is not just a few isolated questions; rather, there tend to be long sequences or 'discussions' around just one topic, say exceptions, and even in such sequences there will not only be questions but also comments, silences, fillers, and summaries. Again as Lipchick clearly argues, SFT should not be a quick snappy approach using clever questions, and certainly should not be an attempt to persuade clients that really they are strong and all is positive.

CORE AREAS OF SOLUTION FOCUSED THERAPY

In the SFT phase of therapeutic work we concentrate on the following general areas or topics. These questions are summarised in Appendix D.

Understanding the problem

When beginning the first SFT session we usually ask clients to describe how they see their difficulties. Given that we have done this once already in the assessment phase, this phase may involve making a short summary, a simple listing of difficulties. Sometimes this second visit to problems gives the person a chance to rethink or re-describe their main difficulties, something of value in itself since it can suggest the beginning of new conceptualisations by the client. As clients describe difficulties, we note the exact words and sentences used and we write them down.

Our most typical opening questions are:

- Given all our earlier discussions, how would you summarise your concerns and difficulties now?
- Can you tell me which problems you'd like to work on with me?
- Can you tell me more about that?

A pivotal question in SFT is:

- How will you know your difficulties are being solved?

The emphasis here is on the foundation of 'knowing', that is, what the person will actually experience, see, hear, think, in what ways and in what situations and what time period. It is very rare that we would ask this immediately, but would be thinking about this from the very beginning and return to exploring the question at several points.

This emphasis on 'knowing' needs to be thought of as both phenomenological and constructionist, that is, how will things appear for this person, and what precise constructions the person uses or creates in communicating these ideas. One needs to see the future possible situation through the eyes of the client and in his or her language.

Problem pattern sequence

It is an assumption that most, if not all, problems occur in interactional contexts and if the problem is not occurring in an interpersonal context, it will at least occur in some type of repetitive context. A focus on the problem pattern is not unique to SFT, and was a central concern of strategic therapy (Watzlawick et al., 1974).

Different writers on SFT have emphasised a focus on problem patterns to varying degrees. de Shazer (1988) suggested that some description of the problem pattern is outlined initially but that it could be a topic to return to if early efforts at change have not been fruitful. To explore problem patterns one can ask questions such as:

- Where does the problem occur?
- Who is present?
- What happens initially, and next, and next?
- What is typically happening just before all this begins?

In the first phase of work, one might simply ask these questions noting the exact words used and what aspects of the problem (for example actions versus emotions) are strongly emphasised. If one later returns to the problem pattern, then it can be useful to ask for many examples and to spend considerable time thinking about the sequence of events involved. As clients return to problem sequences, new aspects can emerge which in turn allow the possibility of exploring different sorts of exceptions and ways of coping. For example, in the first phase of description a client may emphasise behaviours and the other persons involved, but when the problem is returned to, then, this time, the client might emphasise feelings of hopelessness, which in turn then provides an opportunity to explore when the client feels hope or lack of hope.

Exceptions

Central to SFT is an emphasis on fully exploring 'exceptions' to the problem, that is, those times when the problem does not occur. There might, of course, be many potential types of non-occurrence: particularly informative are times the problem does not occur yet would 'normally'. However, any straightforward non-occurrence can also be useful to know about, for example that some preoccupying worry does not penetrate a person's dreams: at least that can suggest there are some areas left 'un-colonised' by a problem.

One must first decide whether any exceptions are reported, and if they are, what this means to the client. For one client, beginning to see dreams as problem free might be surprisingly interesting, and suggestive of hope; for another person it might be plainly obvious, of no importance, and irritating to even begin to discuss (especially if the therapist seems 'positive' and enthusiastic). The essential point here is that what might look like an exception to the therapist may not appear so to the client: the therapist may need to spend considerable time 'scaffolding' (White, 2007) the client's understanding; that is, one may spend considerable time thinking about a specific episode, finding the right words, then thinking about several similar episodes and their potential meaning. One may first need to be very concrete before any generalisation makes sense to a person.

A second important distinction when understanding exceptions is to consider whether an exception is reported as the consequence of deliberate actions by a client or whether the exception is reported as 'just occurring', something that happens as if by chance, or, alternatively, where the exception is reported but no reasons can be given for what might start or stop it. Whether any exception can be useful (for example by simply suggesting to do more of what works) is again completely dependent upon the unique meanings or constructions placed upon these exceptions.

A third important 'dimension' of exceptions is to consider the 'level' at which they occur for the person. For example, if a problem is described as 'not going outside' then some exceptions might be those days the person actually goes out, that is, exceptions at the level of behaviour. However, another 'level' might be the confidence a person had while going out; and yet another 'level' could be the meaning of going out for a person's sense of identity over time. In general, it is recommended that one works with whatever level the client uses, but if progress is not made, one needs to return to the problem and then consider what other level or areas would be useful to consider.

One possible time to ask about exceptions is after a statement of the problem; however, the therapist needs to cultivate the art of noting potential exceptions whenever they occur. For example, a client with a terrible history of abuse and mistreatment told me she had not given in to a partner who had attempted to make her prostitute herself for drugs money. I expressed simple interest in how she had managed not to do this while normally she mistreated herself. She stopped talking, put her elbow on the desk, was obviously thinking deeply, and then said she'd never thought of this. Here there was no need to 'persuade' nor to become over-enthusiastic in pointing out this positive feature of her life as this, particularly with this self-damning client, could easily have misfired.

One can begin a sequence of exception questions by asking:

- Are there times when this problem doesn't occur?
- When do you go out and not feel you will be attacked?

If there are exceptions, a range of further questions can be asked:

- What's different about times when the problem doesn't occur?
- What do you do differently?
- What do others do differently?
- How do you get that to happen?

One client, to be discussed in Chapter 5, had the conviction of having become a 'freak' with a deformed body, was preoccupied by this, and had no confidence. She was asked when she was not so self-conscious. She replied that she was less self-conscious when at her sister-in-law's and when with her nephew. What was different about these times? She said they 'listened' more. Such comments suggest potential 'clues' (de Shazer, 1988) that can be used when designing a therapeutic intervention.

Again, it must be emphasised that if exceptions are discussed it is not recommended that the therapist becomes 'over-enthusiastic' and starts to persuade clients that they should just set about doing more. This can be useful but only in certain contexts of meaning for the client. Enthusiasm can have its place, but always the meaning of this for the client must be taken into consideration and, in general, caution with this is better than an over-optimistic attitude that can be taken to indicate that the therapist does not really understand.

Hypothetical solution questions

A central focus of SFT throughout treatment is to build a picture of life without the presenting problems, and further, how someone can know there is progress towards that preferred situation, preferred way of living. One well-known question designed by de Shazer (1988) is the 'Miracle Question', namely:

> Suppose that one night, while you were asleep, there was a miracle and this problem was solved. How would you know? What would be different? How will your husband know without your saying a word to him about it?
>
> (1988: 5)

Asking this question can easily take up a whole session or more, and in general it is advised to ask it in the first two or three sessions as appropriate. Given a client's initial answer, many questions aimed at enriching the picture can be asked; for example:

- Who would be the first to notice?
- What would you do differently?
- What would I see if all this was on a video?

It is very useful to follow up the above with a search for potential exceptions:

- Does any of what you describe already occur?

It is also very useful to ask a 'Scaling Question'; for example:

- Where 10 = the life you have described, and 1 = the worst things ever were, where are you now on the scale?

Given whatever answer, it is next useful to ask:

- What could happen this week to move you a little way up the scale?

There are many modifications of the hypothetical future question; for example:

- What would life be like without the problems?
- Can you describe what a good day would be like?

We are not very comfortable with using the concept of 'miracle' and in general avoid that actual word.

de Shazer (1988) comments on the importance of noting how the Miracle Question is answered; in particular, are answers vague or, alternatively, very concrete with details concerning actions and events? If vague, then it is often better that interventions are not action orientated, but rather, one can ask clients to notice and observe things or to think over certain relevant issues.

Goals and their phenomenology

A pivotal area (de Shazer, 1988) is to ask clients what their goals are and then to clarify, where possible, how they will know the goal is being realised. We suggest that the therapist needs to attempt to grasp how the situation 'will look' from the unique viewpoint of the client. This is a sort of attempt to grasp what might be thought of as a person's phenomenology with respect to a specific change. Of course, one can only imagine how things will 'appear' and this can only be done in the medium of language, of dialogue.

Quite often it seems that clients have not pictured how life would be without problems. The focus has been on the problem and that it should stop. Clients are often surprised and interested by this question and one sees the person engage in a struggle to imagine, to construct a picture to find appropriate words. If the client only suggests that something will stop or be absent, some time can be spent exploring what new things will be happening, what will be present and not just absent.

To explore goals one can ask:

- What would you like to have happen?
- How will things be when this problem is solved?
- How will you know when the problem is over? What will this look like? How will things be different?
- What will others notice?

Frames, re-description, and puzzlement

In de Shazer's 1988 book (p. 86) there is a decision-making map for working with SFT. The map suggests that there are several 'pathways' for SFT, and that one of these paths leads to the idea of 'deconstruction' of the 'global frame'. The term 'frame' here is taken from Goffman (1974): a frame may be thought of as a type of 'definition of the situation', a phrase in turn derived from symbolic interactionism (Meltzer, Petras, and Reynolds, 1975). The term 'frame' is much wider than the idea of 'negative automatic thought' as found in Beck et al. (1979). It includes explicit thoughts, but also includes general assumptions, explicit or implicit, about situations. Frames can be thought of as similar to 'axioms' or 'rules': de Shazer notes how some clients seem to hold fast to certain sweeping claims and these are such that even if 'exceptions' seem to occur, they are dismissed as meaningless. With this presentation, clients understand most events in terms of these global frames. Two examples de Shazer gives, interestingly, involve psychotic delusions, namely, a man who thought himself the devil, and another who thought the CIA would assassinate him. The idea of the devil was used to explain everything.

de Shazer suggests taking these ideas presented by clients and assuming they are true, and then working out what the implications of these ideas might be. For the CIA situation, de Shazer just wondered how so far, given the skill and ruthlessness of the CIA, they had been so incompetent and had failed to kill the man. In this case it was already 'obvious' to the man that the CIA were ruthless skilled killers, hence this point needed no proof. There was no attempt to evaluate or prove to the man any claim. If a deconstruction of a frame is to occur, then it must be almost immediately obvious to clients that if they believe X, then Y and Z do indeed follow. The first step in work with a global frame is to fully understand it, and understand the unique meanings used in it by the client. Later one can ask a question such as: does anything puzzle you about what you believe is happening? It is not advised to attempt to prove to a client the obviousness of an implication; this usually does not work. We illustrate one use of this sort of deconstruction in a case illustration later in this chapter.

Besides the explicit deconstruction of a global frame, SFT also uses the discussion about, and elaboration of, alternative frames. That is, alternative ways of looking at and interpreting events and behaviour. This is not so much a 'technique' but rather an orientation implied in many of the SF areas and questions already presented, for example, by simply focusing and asking detailed questions about an exception. David, discussed in Chapter 6, had enormous family difficulties, and had undergone divorce and separation. He mentioned his son had visited. On further questioning, this turned out to be a regular occurrence. Knowing this, we could then ask how he had managed to keep this contact going, what did it mean? It did not seem that David had 'elaborated' in his own reflection the meaning of this family connection. Indirectly asking such questions and focusing on what might be an area of strength gently challenged the frame of total failure.

Key tasks

SFT has developed a range of tasks, that is, activities and ideas to consider between sessions. These tasks need to be modified for the unique features of a client and the unique problem, and only suggested if appropriate. In the early phase of work with clients, it is suggested that one might use cautious tasks such as the 'first session formula task', namely:

> Between now and next time we meet, we would like you to observe, so that you can describe to us next time, what happens in your family that you want to continue to have happen.
>
> (de Shazer, 1988: 2)

When exceptions have been given and clients have indicated a willingness to try actions, then a standard task is to suggest: 'Do more of what works'. This is a very common task and extremely useful. Ideally, the client is asked to do more of the same, but with something 'different' about it even if what is different is only a slight change of attitude in doing this activity. For example, making difficult phone calls which can be seen as 'something I have just got to do' but noting how useful this is could become 'something that might help me change my situation'. Again, the unique meaning of the action is crucial.

Some clients struggle with habits, addictions, and other repeating action patterns. Such clients can be asked:

• Notice what you do when you overcome the urge to X.

Some patterns of actions and interpretations seem highly rigid and repetitive. In this case, and particularly where exceptions have not been useful, a client can be asked to 'do something different'; that is, one relies on the client's creativity and willingness to deliberately try out something new, the therapeutic rationale being that anything really new could set off a chain of potential change.

There are several other standard tasks used by SFT therapists and these can be modified to fit specific clients and situations (see de Shazer, 1985, 1988).

Language

It is recommended that the therapist pays careful attention to the language of clients, that is, the selection of words, metaphors, narratives, ways of speaking, and what is not said. It is useful to note down these phrases if possible. In subsequent work these phrases can be used in many ways: one possibility is simply to use them when referring to the problems in preference to using psychiatric and psychological terminology. This can be useful in 'joining' with the client; that is, letting the client know that you can see the problem through his or her eyes. If appropriate, there may be occasions when how to describe something is discussed and new phrases encouraged. For example, in the case given later, the client would often move between phrases such as 'I'm in hell' to 'it's like hell'; these different phrases will have different emotional and behavioural consequences.

Metaphors seem to be a key feature of psychosis and have great relevance to the derivation of content (Rhodes and Jakes, 2004a). In therapy there are many uses of metaphor: from the vivid expression of suffering to ways of discussing goals. We will return to this topic in Chapter 5. One client mentioned that she would like to be 'in control of the steering wheel'. Later we could ask:

- Have there been times this week when you were in control of the steering wheel?
- How can you manage to take hold of the wheel?
- How can you make sure you stay in control of the wheel?

The role of language became a focus for de Shazer (1991) and it is central to White's approach (White and Epston, 1990; White, 2007).

Externalisation, narrative, and writing

The use of externalisation is taken from White and Epston's narrative therapy (1990; White, 2007). Externalisation can be a very useful way of exploring a problem and its influence in the life of a person. When carrying out the practice of externalisation, the problem is conceived and talked about as an entity separate from the person. White and Epston described 'Sneaky Poo', a creature that made a young child mess his pants. Using this personification, White was able to explore with the child and family ways of coping, of being ready for the tricks of this creature. Interestingly, White emphasised the negative things this creature did, but also made sure to inquire about anything positive, for example could this creature ever be of use. In working, particularly with voices, it is useful to consider that while these are normally experienced as negative, some aspects of negative voices are positive and some voices are just positive. Voices are, of course, already to some extent experienced as 'external', as outside the person, but in externalising voices the aims of therapy are, rather, to map out and explore various relationships between the person and the voice, and where possible, to encourage a person's sense of agency. Externalising a 'voice', one might ask:

- What does the voice do to you?
- How does it do that?
- How does it set about making you feel powerless?
- How have you learned to cope with its effects?
- How have you managed to keep key areas of your life free from its influence?
- Is there anything you do not want to change about these voices?

Part of the process of externalisation is to map out how a problem has an influence on any area of a person's life, for example on how a couple get on, what a person thinks of himself or herself, how daily actions are carried out. Exploring a wide range of effects in turn allows a search for possible exceptions to those effects.

Externalising a problem can be most useful in the initial stages of exploring a problem, but also as a 'second look' at problems when there is reason to suspect that a focus so far adopted is not touching the issues that really matter for a person.

The general direction of therapy

In general the phases or direction of SFT tend to proceed as follows: first the problems are fully discussed, and then goals are discussed. Next the focus moves to exceptions and a picture of the hypothetical preferred future. From these discussions ideas for feedback, compliments, puzzles, and sometimes tasks, are generated. There is movement back and forth between a focus on problems and a focus on solutions. If one gets stuck, then the process, as it were, is repeated but each time around in relation to a different topic or at a different level of activity and meaning.

The above is a general outline; the reality in the room, from moment to moment, from session to session, is complex and most unpredictable. At all times one must remain responsive to the person in the room, to emergent situations and events. Sometimes wholly new directions must be initiated as a crisis occurs. Also, as Lipchick (2002) emphasises, one must attend to emotions and the emotional atmosphere of the meeting, particularly if the emotional reaction of the client seems negative in response to a direction of therapy.

Session breaks and case conceptualisations

SFT, like other systemic therapies, uses session breaks: that is, towards the end of a session the therapist states that he or she wishes to review the notes taken and to think about the situations presented and will do this outside the therapy room. Before leaving we usually ask if the client wishes to ask for or add any information. During these breaks it is useful to summarise the descriptions given and to consider a possible case conceptualisation within a solution focused framework; that is, to think about potential solutions and how they might be received by the client. There may appear to be a 'solution', but the crucial point is how this will be construed by the client: it may simply not fit the person's system of meanings and expectations.

In our solution focused work, unlike therapists using only SFT, we tend also to consider at this stage elementary formulations concerning the formation of the presenting difficulties. The concepts we draw on for these formulations will tend to be the sort outlined in Chapters 2 and 3. The conceptualisation, as stated in Chapter 3, can sometimes 'guide' the process of exploration, leading it to areas which are relevant but which could be otherwise missed. In general, however, the aim is not to present these formulations to the client, at least not in this stage of work.

Additional approaches in early-stage work

In the opening phase of work, besides SFT, we might, where appropriate, discuss other useful activities, especially ones which are relatively easy to learn and put into practice. For example, when anxiety is a problem, we might use and suggest any method of relaxation such as slow breathing, going for walks, swimming, and in general, physical methods for looking after one's well-being. Chadwick (2006) has reported the use of a modified type of mindfulness meditation with psychotic clients. Mahoney (2003) likewise in the early phase of therapy suggests a very wide range of activities with the aim of what he terms 'centering'.

For work with voices, besides SFT, we might well discuss some other well-known approaches to coping, for example the use of headphones; we will discuss these in Chapter 8.

Solution focused behavioural work

As stated earlier, in general it is our preference to begin with SFT. Sometimes after a few sessions of SFT we might use other approaches drawn from CBT and modify these to fit the general framework of NSFT. We might do this for several reasons, for example when SFT does not seem to provide a clear way forward with the client and yet there are indications that the client does want to change specific activities such as ones related to depression and withdrawal.

Our preferred option in such a situation is to use a modified version of behavioural activation (Martell, Addis, and Jacobson, 2001). In essence, one asks the client questions such as:

- What activities are important for you and which you are not doing?
- Which activities you are perhaps avoiding?
- Can you write out a series of activities from fairly easy to extremely difficult?
- Which activities could you begin this week?

Having mapped out a series of activities the client can be asked to start doing the simplest. Ideally the client keeps a record of these steps. We would tend, however, to be more cautious in making such suggestions where, for example, the client had a very active and interfering delusional system.

It is interesting to note that if one does SFT then often it is clients themselves who, as it were, design for themselves a series of steps which in essence are a sort of behavioural activation plan. For example, one client described how he could take up exercise by doing press-ups at home and that he could phone a member of his family who he saw as the easiest person to rebuild connections with (see Chapter 6). Often the work in SFT is helping clients to motivate themselves, to draw on strengths, to begin activities they know they wish to do, for example to motivate themselves to go walking when they feel afraid of the people on the streets.

The choice of meaningful activities to take up in behavioural activation is important and all the work done in SFT on the future and on goals can point to appropriate areas to work with. The narrative assessment can point to the needs of the person which might be ignored or which must in some way be addressed. In thinking with the client how to go about doing a difficult activity it is also very useful to use basic SFT questions such as how similar activities were done in the past and how in the past the client confronted things which were feared.

If a client has a very specific phobia, then after SFT we might use some versions of exposure therapy (Hawton, Salkovskis, Kirk, and Clarke 1989), that is, to ask the client to take steps to approach a feared object or situation such as being alone or being in a group of people. We have found this useful in some cases but it is important to approach exposure very carefully with psychotic clients. Experiencing fear can be very stressful for clients and can exacerbate symptoms, at least temporarily. With some clients, while doing exposure work we might use SF questions to ask how they have coped in the past and encourage the client to use these if needed; we do not always think it useful to ask clients to stop using 'safety behaviours' as is sometimes recommended for non-psychotic clients.

If clients are not sure about the irrationality of their fear or if the experience of fear has a negative effect on their mental state, it can be useful to conduct a systematic desensitisation programme (Wolpe, 1990) rather than a graded exposure programme. The key difference in that approach is that one attempts to carry out repeated exposure to anxiety provoking situations in such a way that minimal anxiety is experienced. This is achieved by using a hierarchy of situations, beginning with the easiest situation for the client.

CASE ILLUSTRATIONS

We will now present two cases in depth.

Jack: understanding his presentation

On meeting Jack he readily talked about the difficulties in his life: he stated that the medication wasn't working, he felt suicidal, he felt like he was dying. He reported that he was scared, that he was in physical pain and felt like his 'bone marrow is being lifted out'. He also reported that he heard voices. He had been diagnosed as having paranoid schizophrenia. The tests I gave him suggested high levels of depression and anxiety.

I felt somewhat overwhelmed by the range and complexity of his presenting problems, and pessimistic that I could manage to focus on any workable area given the very incoherent way he had spoken to me. In contrast, however, he was pleasant to interact with and clearly keen to at least talk about his problems. Given this mixture of signs, I decided to offer an extended period of assessment.

As the interview proceeded it became apparent that the delusions referred to in the referral letters were still present and active. He readily spoke, though in a very confused way, about his experience of dying, being in hell, of being condemned by God or under attack by the Devil, he was not sure which. At an early stage of his breakdown he had also thought certain people were following him with the intention of harm, but this was no longer active.

The dominant themes now were of dying and being in hell. On careful examination I noticed he switched from literal statements such as 'I am in hell' to statements involving analogies such that for him it was 'like hell'. At this early state I clarified whether he meant these ideas literally, and he confirmed that he did. I wrote out the statements, 'I am in hell' and 'I am dying'; he was initially 100% convinced of the former, but settled to 90% for both during the extended assessment. Some of his experiences had been quite horrifying:

I had, a few occasions where I felt I was being eaten alive.

and,

God or the Devil is lifting out my bone marrow.

He also heard insulting and attacking voices making comments such as 'don't try to be a clever boy', and other voices which gave him orders such as 'make your move'.

I decided to carry out a full narrative assessment as described in Chapter 3, that is, a focus on the delusional situation, exactly how this began and how his life was before, present continuous experiences, and an overview of problems, goals, and early social experience.

In outline, at a period where he had failed to make a living as a musician, his marriage also fell apart. Due to a certain musical fashion, he had read up on various occult 'pagan' ideas; and then as he became unwell, he also got involved in various extreme Christian churches. His breakdown occurred in the context of strange experiences; for example, at one point he felt a great shock in his head. He saw people following him. He experienced a 'burning pain'.

On a regular basis these strange experiences continued for him, for example a constant 'burning, and acidy smell', his bones felt 'brittle', and sometimes he felt 'strangled' in bed and a 'clawing' at his face. He was not working, was seeing very few people, and not regularly seeing his ex-wife or seeing his children as invited by her to do.

Discussion of his childhood suggested considerable interpersonal difficulties. His father was described as 'hot-headed' and Jack said that he would 'torture us mentally'. His father 'constantly' shouted, 'I was tense in case he snapped', and his father used physical violence. Jack had a much better relation with his mother: he described this as 'close' but 'neurotic'. He was aware of always being 'shy', 'lazy', and 'meditative'. He told me, however, that he always had had several friends in his life, and greatly enjoyed the making of music. Interestingly, he had comprehensible clear goals for change. He wanted to be 'a good parent', get his 'health back', 'get a good job', and 'have a love life'.

All the above could form part of a narrative case conceptualisation for Jack. A brief summary is as follows.

He grew up experiencing the fear of violence, and possibly at its worse, a fear of loss or death. He was also made to feel useless and inferior by his father. In his twenties he first experienced positive events, mainly his marriage, but he then failed in his marriage and chosen career. He went on to experience strong feelings of anxiety and hopelessness. He had become interested in the occult and religion: this provided a repertoire of themes that were used to interpret his strange experiences and expectations of violence and failure. There formed a toxic cycle such that ideas, for example of damnation, and bodily sensations, began to influence each other.

The therapy

I began the first session of SFT by asking again what problems he wished to work on with me now. He gave the following:

- He is 'burning up' and 'disintegrating'.
- He finds it difficult to be 'assertive if people are vindictive'.
- He could not find a job.
- His eyes were 'bad'.
- He had no relations, no 'love life'.

The list he gave was substantially similar to the problems he had already discussed, though was not exactly the same. Problems can be presented in many ways, for example in a clear or vague way, or as fixed or changing; there can be one problem or a range of problems. Furthermore, the expressions of the problems can change over time. Some of this may of course be due to the process of assessment itself.

When the list was completed, I asked him why he thought these difficulties were occurring. Obtaining a client's perspective on 'why' is emphasised by Furman and Ahola (1992). At first Jack said that he didn't know but proceeded to say perhaps it was 'self-inflicted' and that his parents thought it was 'self-generated'. I asked specifically why he thought he was being thrown in hell; again he gave a list, that it was for 'not being obedient', jealousy, harming others, involvement with the occult.

At this point I decided to move to the topic of exceptions. As Lipchick (2002) argues, it is wise to 'go slow'; however, it felt like the appropriate time to at least begin to explore these areas given our now extensive in-depth discussions of past and present concerns.

As stated, it is important to accept the wording and outlook of the client. To do this, I asked the question, 'When are you not in agony?' Jack gave a comprehensive list of exceptions:

- When engaged on the computer.
- When walking around.
- At the drop-in centre.
- It was better when he was with people, but he added that it got worse if he worried about what they were thinking.
- He tended to ignore it in the morning.
- When at church.

These encouraging statements were noted, but not commented upon. I next asked the hypothetical future question, that is, what would his life be like without his problems, how would he live, what would be different? For the bulk of the session he then proceeded to give a detailed picture:

- He would 'feel lots of love and warmth and not be cold'.
- Would see people for who they are and would be happy with friends.
- 'I'd realise I'm close to my daughter, I'd feel a love for my daughter'.
- He would go see his children and give 'lots of cuddles and love'.
- He wouldn't feel he was a danger to them.
- He would have a love life, get a job, get fitter.

I next asked: on a scale of 10 to 1 where 10 stands for this ideal picture, and 1 represents the worse situation ever, where on the scale was he now? He replied that he was at 2. I asked what small step would move him up the scale: he said to give up smoking and take up exercise. I finished this part by briefly asking what he had tried (medication, apologies, and spiritual healing) and what he had not tried (voluntary work).

I then took a session break. Given the clarity of his exceptions, it would have been tempting to simply suggest doing more. I decided not to give direct tasks, especially given the earlier hints of conflicts and possible coercion in his family. On returning to the room, I summarised what he had said, and commented on his concern and interest in the welfare of his children and I wondered whether he felt that somehow he had 'lost his way' in life. I noted, however, that he had continued to persevere in his attempts to cope throughout his suffering, and wondered on the importance of the things he had managed to do for his children.

The second session was quite difficult in that he reported feeling worse: for the Scaling Question, he reported having slipped down to 1. The only exception to have occurred seemed to be that his dreams had not been too bad. I decided to, as it were, go with the negativity. I asked again why he thought he was in hell. He replied, 'Evil, I guess,' and that God had decided that this would happen about five years ago. When asked how he knew he was in hell he replied that his face felt like it was 'burning' and his head felt 'crushed'.

At the end of this session again no tasks were suggested but I began what de Shazer (1988) speaks of as deconstructing the frame. de Shazer suggests that a 'global' frame can be thought of 'as if they are "rules" for defining life in general rather than concrete situations'. Jack was easily able to give many specific exceptions, yet it appeared at this point that all such exceptions were discounted. Jack held the sweeping conviction of being 'evil', of being in or going to hell, and hence what difference did it make if sometimes he felt happier or managed to do something?

For such situations, that is, where, even if exceptions occur, they are discounted, a possible way forward is to consider the implications of the frame. I therefore outlined the following: he stated that he thought he was in hell and therefore dead, and yet at other times was clearly experiencing the torments of dying, and therefore was not yet dead. No attempt was made to persuade Jack of the truth of these ideas; rather, it was presented as a puzzle. The puzzle posed, I then made further comments on how he had felt lost.

The third session began with Jack stating that for him it was as if he was not 'allowed' to be happy, not 'allowed to think'. He continued that when in fact he was happy a 'voice' would attack and criticise him, for example would say, 'What have you got to be happy for?'

We again returned to the puzzle that he was already dead and yet dying. I asked how he might know he was alive, and he mentioned checking his pulse. We then moved to a discussion of how he could cope in the present, what small steps could still be tried, and when were the times he felt better. This time I wrote out the steps he had suggested (for example, writing, music, cycle rides, seeing his children), and asked him to think again about the hell/dying puzzle.

The fourth session was a further discussion of what he was suffering: he began by saying that 'people say it's schizophrenia'. I decided to stay neutral and focus on what he thought it was. He said he felt like a 'zombie', but also that he felt sad and anxious. The direction of the session, though apparently negative in focus, had moved to a gentle review of what he thought might be happening. It was also encouraging that his score concerning the delusion improved.

In the fifth session he reported doing several constructive activities: cycling and walking more, visiting his sister. Jack, however, always mentioned difficulties, for example he reported that he could not engage in a 'long conversation', and often returned to negative experiences. At one point, however, he said, 'You only go to hell when dead'. This suggested a shift in his thinking.

All subsequent sessions tended now to have a similar pattern: he reported doing more, in particular making the effort to make sure he saw his children, yet would often mention not feeling well or would consider the difficulties of what he was doing. One new topic to emerge was what he saw as the purpose of his activities. At one point Jack said it was 'to make my kids happy'.

By the end of the SF phase his conviction that he was in hell had dropped to 0%, and that he was dying to 40%. His level of anxiety and depression dropped considerably.

The last few sessions involved a continuation of the SF work, but we also had a discussion looking at different or alternative explanations on what was happening (see Chapter 7 on alternative perspectives) and what experiential 'evidence' supported the different ideas of what was happening, namely, whether he was dying and condemned or rather suffering a condition which he needed to manage. It was poignant when Jack asked if he would be like this for the 'rest of his life', and if he had failed his children. These questions opened up discussions of the type one might have in work for depression or managing a long-term medical difficulty. We discussed how what would happen was unknown, and that Jack was in fact needed and appreciated by others.

As suggested elsewhere, we do not regard the concept of 'cure' as really applicable to psychosis. Jack still suffered from unpleasant and debilitating symptoms or experiences which made his life difficult, but now had moved to a situation where he could better manage his symptoms, and experience these in a context of not now feeling dammed. Furthermore, he could put his efforts in the context of purposes in his life.

Why had the therapy worked? The core aspects appeared to be: building a detailed narrative of how he had developed; the discovery or building of a picture of his future life and purposes; a re-engagement in activities but under new 'frames', in particular, that it was possible that he was still alive and hence perhaps not necessarily condemned, and that it was possible there were other perspectives on his condition which were less damning of his character. It is interesting to note the shift from 'I am in hell' to 'Will I have this condition for ever?' While receiving the diagnosis of schizophrenia might, indeed, feel like a permanent 'condemnation', we were then able to consider that over time a good life was possible and the course of the condition unknown. We hope our case has shown that SFT is not just about being 'positive' but is also a complex focus on actions, potential resources of the person, and also on 'outlook', belief systems, or complex constructions.

Grace

The immediate problem and challenge of working with Grace was that she believed it possible that she could fly. She reported seeing Sufi angels who laughed and smoked, floated in the air, and who seemed relaxed characters. But they had said she could fly and, it seemed, made some type of invitation to try this out. Before hospitalisation Grace had locked herself away in her attic at home and had come to believe that she had been made pregnant by an angel. While in the attic she had had a serious fall. At this point she was hospitalised.

She was always polite, kind to others, and usually articulate; sometimes, however, she spent many hours refusing to communicate. On one occasion I interviewed Grace when she spoke no words to me, but instead wrote down the alphabet and spelt out single words and phrases or alternatively made physical gestures to convey meaning.

The 'angels', or what I took to be misperceptions or hallucinations, were apparently on the whole benign in their attitude to Grace. They were described as friendly, yet Grace also mentioned that they introduced an element of personal danger. This was difficult to understand. Given this almost paradoxical and difficult situation, I decided to proceed slowly and carefully in spite of the pressing concerns of staff. There was a great need to understand the complexity of Grace's beliefs, perceptions, and history.

There were seven sessions just for assessment and exploration. The narrative based interview (see Chapter 3) was carried out in full, though the order of questions or rather topic areas was modified as needed. Most time was spent on attempting to grasp Grace's 'lived world'. At no point at all did I question the existence of the angels. The 'problem' was understood as presented, that is, she saw angels and wanted to fly, but found herself on a ward, her freedom curtailed, and being given medication by medical staff.

Before describing the therapy, I will present an outline of the narrative based assessment. She reported that she had first seen angels at the age of seven, and intermittently ever since. She said 'they drink a little, and dance a little', and added 'they make me strong'. On being asked how, she said with them she could walk and feel safe in the woods, and later added, they made her feel safe walking on the streets and talking to strangers. When asked about their purpose, she said 'they protect me'; ultimately their purpose was to 'save the world' from being destroyed.

Grace did not report being abused in childhood, nor being severely mistreated; there seemed, however, two major difficulties. One, that when she left her country of origin at the age of four, this involved a complete disruption of contact with extended family. Second, when in the UK, perhaps because of their difficult work situations, she reported little contact with her mother and father. With her father in particular there seemed to be difficulties in that Grace added, 'He never spoke to me'.

In her teens she ran away with a man seven years older than her. They lived together for several years but when Grace gave birth to her son, her partner became violent. After extended violence, Grace managed to escape this man, but it was in this period that she had a breakdown involving psychiatric services.

The recent emergence of angels appeared to arise in a context of some extended conflict with a neighbour over noise levels, and perhaps continuing concern about her son who was now at college, but not living with Grace. A narrative case conceptualisation for Grace may be summarised as follows.

Her early years produced feelings of loneliness and insecurity. In this emotional void she, like many children, imagined a consoling caring entity. The concept and imagination of angel-like figures became a conceptual and motivational resource for her. The origin of the very idea of angels might have been common in her essentially Christian culture. The angels provided comfort, attention, and security.

She subsequently suffered severe trauma from the very person who should have cared for her. This may have had many effects: feelings of fear and insecurity, ideas that others could be dangerous, that those she trusted could let her down. These traumas in her adult years could have stirred early memories of feeling alone and perhaps not being safe. This produced a psychotic crisis with full hallucinations of angels who made her feel safe. They also blotted out the ugliness of her situation and life.

The most recent crisis occurred in the context of social stress and danger, but also a context where the bond between her and her son was undergoing transformation, that is, he was moving away from home as a young adult. This too might have touched upon early experiences of disconnection and isolation.

From the above case formulation it was clear that any attempt at just criticising or doubting the angels would not be accepted, and also would be experienced as a loss of safety. The challenge of the therapeutic work was to think of how she could live safely without the angels. It was clear I needed to 'accept' or rather not directly challenge the angels, yet meanings and ideas concerning the angels needed to be altered to ensure Grace did not attempt to fly.

Therapy with Grace

In de Shazer's original presentation of SFT he suggests that one should not approach a person with a theory, nor with an explanation; furthermore, he stated that he did not use, for example, any sort of hypothesis of what might be occurring for the person as is often done in other therapies, and is done in some systemic therapies (Hedges, 2005). We have always found this insistence on the unique features of a case refreshing and inspiring. So many textbooks advocate, with confidence, their favourite explanations yet years later such explanations are abandoned. We have come to believe, however, that one cannot be truly 'empty handed' in any type of therapy and, for that matter, in any type of extended interaction. As stated earlier, we strongly believe in *critical* realism, that is, we believe in the possibility of attempting to describe a mind-independent external reality, yet any description we have must be taken to be tentative, rarely sure, and influenced by our own culture, education, personality, and so forth. In the casework to be described the narrative formulation guided the therapist in doing SFT, in suggesting possible areas to explore, for example, to wonder how Grace would describe life without angels, that is, without those things which made her simultaneously feel 'safe' yet which had led her to a dangerous accident. That said, her frame of reference was respected, and all the goals she offered were explored; the narrative understanding of the therapist helped point to areas in addition to those Grace would have suggested by herself.

I began the first SFT sessions with the hypothetical future question. Her first answer was that only being on the ward would be a problem, and so she would no longer be here.

Given this answer, I said, 'Accepting that you are here, how would you wake up and feel different?'

To this she suggested various positive states; for example, she would 'feel happy', 'would feel free', and would be able to work. I then asked who would notice this and she thought the nurses would notice she was happier. I asked what they would actually see; for example, see of her on a video. She replied that she'd look more relaxed, would not pace up and down so much, would be happier to do things, and wouldn't sleep so much. I asked how the nurses would be different. She said they wouldn't think she was 'crazy'.

She went on to say she wasn't actually seeing the angels at the moment, but would after 25 years or after her death. I then asked: could she be happy without the angels? She answered that she was feeling them guide her just as when she was a child.

The fascination, yet difficulty of therapy, is that at each turn of the conversation there are so many actions and choices that can be made. The real talk of therapy when examined in detail shows the complexity of interactions and how a client can take unpredictable turns. The opening response of Grace did not seem to me a 'rich' vein to explore. We had already discussed in the narrative assessment a good future with an assumption of angels. From the assessment the sort of 'guiding' thoughts for myself as a therapist were:

- If angels provide security, can it be obtained in other ways?
- Can she establish a sense of direction, of taking control of her life, without openly rejecting the angels?

Of course there is a danger in the therapist having such thoughts; for example, a therapist could become rigid in thinking, welded to the theory or hypothesis, and therefore blind to new and useful emergent ideas. As a precaution against that I kept reminding myself to explore diverse details and meanings (as shown later).

After her comment on the future of seeing angels I asked if she could imagine her life with no angels but a life where she was happy.

This led to an extended discussion. She didn't know; she didn't think she would like it; she would be like everyone else; she was afraid she might kill herself. I asked in what way would she be different in such a future. She would not just talk to anyone, as she did now, nor would she go out alone at night. I asked her how she might adapt, how she would cope. She answered that she would be more careful about who she talked to and would keep a limited circle of friends. I asked how she might judge people: she would watch their actions and listen more. I moved on to the other areas of her life: she would be working, living alone but free. She said she loved her son but wouldn't be living with him.

The conversation then turned to how she thought everything was in her power when she had direct 'contact' with angels, but she then spontaneously made reference to the moment in our assessment when I had explored with her what she thought would happen if she fell: would she break her leg, what was breaking a leg like?

I sensed that a certain confusion had begun in Grace concerning 'flying'; however, it seemed wise to proceed cautiously. I asked why they might have suggested that she could fly. She didn't know. At this point I said I wondered whether the idea of flying might be intended as a metaphor by the angels, that in some way they were saying that a 'spirit could fly'. She liked this idea very much, and said that I was probably right. To this quick enthusiasm, I thought it was better to respond with caution: I emphasised the idea was just a possibility.

I moved on to goals again: she wanted to go home. I was not sure how to proceed at this point and was a little concerned that I might be moving too fast in one direction, and so I went right back to asking how things could be different now with the angels. She said she wasn't sure and that all the nurses thought she was 'mad'. I asked if there was anything she could do to change their opinion. She thought she could try listening more to what was being said and pay attention to what was happening.

I took a short break and on return asked her to think about how she could be happy and safe with and without the angels, given that their presence was not something she could decide herself and that the future was unknown. Added to this was a brief discussion about how the medical staff were not interested in changing her philosophy but that it was a medical duty to save lives. She agreed with this moral idea of trying to save a life if someone is seen as in danger, and she understood that the staff could only act on what they saw. In elaborating this, I had had a hunch that she would find a moral argument appealing.

At the beginning of the second SFT session I asked about her thoughts concerning the above issues. She said, 'I feel safe with and without them', but added, 'I still feel them'.

I asked again in what ways she would be different without them: she answered she would be more cautious, go out and take her time, use her 'eyes and senses'. I asked how much she did that at the present time: 'Not at all', but immediately added, 'I'm in control of the steering wheel'.

I said, 'Have others noticed this?' She replied, 'I look at cars, look and see if it is safe or not'. Apparently she had not been doing this before.

The metaphor of being at the steering wheel, of perhaps making decisions for herself, was one returned to in all the subsequent sessions. I asked, 'Are there times now when you are at the steering wheel, when you are directing your own life?' She replied, 'Yes, I eat what I want to', whereas before she told me the nurses had had to tell her when and what to eat. She was now also choosing to have a bath when she wanted.

We then came to a potential setback. She said she was doing in general what the angels were telling her to do, and to not follow their advice was dangerous, since otherwise she would end up like her aunty who was frequently hospitalised. When asked if there had been a time when she had not listened to the angels, but that things had been ok, she said no.

This was a difficult, but potentially fruitful, juncture.

I opened up the topic that sometimes a person might be told to do something negative. She mentioned how she had thought of pushing anyone who came into her attic into a water tank. I next wondered with her if any force was higher than the angels. This led to a discussion of whether angels always knew best, and would it not be the case that her God knew better. This is an example of what de Shazer (1988) called finding an 'indeterminate' point to deconstruct a global frame, that is, something implied by her wider frame of reference but not highlighted in her present concerns.

After some further discussion about how in life one receives much advice, yet one is still responsible, how listening to several people can be helpful, for example how she herself had listened to a Buddhist priest, I made the request that she watch out for times when she was 'at the wheel'.

There were two further SFT sessions and a follow-up. In these sessions we continued to focus on times when she was 'at the wheel', how she would like her life to be even if she never saw the angels. She continued to take more and more steps and soon was staying at home by herself for trial periods, then was at home permanently. The return to normal life was clearly not easy for Grace. I gave her tests for depression and anxiety several times: as she got more control of her life, her levels of depression and anxiety began to rise. It seems fairly clear that the presence of angels had a very soothing effect upon her.

This case illustrates how one needs to move flexibly between the core areas of SFT, that is, goals, exceptions, the future, coping, yet also how a rich description of the person's world view and personal history can guide questioning, can suggest areas to explore or can suggest caution in moving too fast in certain difficult areas. It is also an illustration of using language and metaphors that emerge in a client's discourse.

This case also shows how it is useful to sometimes not be too explicit too early: it was tempting to explore at the beginning how the angels could protect her and yet she mentioned danger. The theme of danger emerged at the very beginning, but seemed to disappear in our conversations. It does not feature in the presented conceptualisation. The theme of danger, however, re-emerged in the later phase: the angels do protect, were inducing a sense of safety, yet, not following their directions did suggest danger to Grace (that is, that she might become unwell like her aunty). And, of course, this appears strange since these creatures, most of the time, were constructed as benign. Timing is very important: the conversation about taking responsibility and the authority of the angels would not have helped, I believe, at the beginning.

OVERVIEW

If someone wishes to try out SFT for the first time, particularly with psychosis, then it might be a good idea to do this with another experienced therapist or alternatively a peer who is also learning. SFT is simple to learn in theory, yet quite difficult, at least sometimes, to apply in real situations. Another reason for finding SFT difficult, besides the sheer complexity of what occurs in any therapy session, is an ingrained focus by therapists on pathology and problems in general. Potential exceptions often seem invisible, tentative, only implied by what is 'absent', what is not said. Jack, as discussed, never gave enthusiastic reports of taking steps; rather, these were always tinged with doubts and self-criticism. To respect negativity, yet notice positive steps or features, is a subtle art of timing and balance.

SFT does seem an excellent way of beginning a series of therapeutic explorations, and sometimes is sufficient in itself, at least for the specific problem area of concern. SFT is also very useful for situations, problems, or presentations a therapist has not worked with before. Even now after many years of working with psychosis, we still find that clients can present difficulties we have not encountered before. In these situations, SFT can be particularly useful.

In the next few chapters we outline other additional therapeutic approaches. As we carry these out with clients, however, we do not forget what was done in this 'finding solutions' phase and may periodically encourage the client to continue these activities.

Chapter 5

Working with personal meaning

INTRODUCTION

In this chapter we shall present various ways of working with meaning, in particular, meanings related to constructions of the self and other. The first approach we present is based on Padesky's ideas for working with 'schemas', or core beliefs. This approach is very much aimed at the construction and articulation of new and benign ideas of the self and other and is therefore very much in line with solution orientated therapy.

The second section looks at exploring and developing metaphor models and conceptual blends, that is, when a person uses an imaginative scenario in understanding something. Ordinary talk and experience seem permeated with metaphoric ideas and these seem very deeply linked to how we express emotion. A focus on metaphors is not necessarily a phase of work in itself and can occur at any stage of work from exploration in assessment to building goals.

The third section illustrates how one might focus on negative themes with a particular emphasis on understanding these emerging themes or negative thoughts and emotions in the context of a person's life narrative. Here we present a case where we did not think it appropriate to start with solution orientated work or work with the preferred self. To collaborate with this client required a full examination first of negative events and experiences.

WORKING TOWARDS THE PREFERRED SELF

The solution focused work we described in the last chapter is often sufficient for some people: either the solution focused work is successful in itself or the client makes some desired but small change and does not want further therapy. Some clients during the SFT phase make good progress; for example, they begin to make important social changes and a good working therapeutic alliance is established. However, the client still experiences considerable difficulties, and if the client is deluded, conviction, distress, and preoccupation might all remain high. For such clients we have found it helpful to work with the person's fundamental ideas, beliefs, and images about the self, others, and the world. This sort of approach has been reported in the literature by several therapists (Moorhead and Turkington, 2001; Chadwick, 2006; Jakes and Rhodes, 2003).

One approach we have found particularly helpful is that of Padesky (1994, 2000, 2002). Padesky is a cognitive therapist who has developed a style that she calls 'constructive CBT' (2000). Padesky suggests that not only should we note and perhaps challenge a negative theme in a person's life, but also we should spend time building an alternative positive belief about the self and others. In addition, where possible, one should draw upon the person's strengths and resources.

We will not here review to what extent Padesky's work is similar to solution focused and narrative approaches since that topic was considered in Chapter 1. As argued there, the therapeutic move towards construction as opposed to an exclusive negative focus is useful and is beginning to emerge in the field of CBT. Furthermore, there is at least one clear theoretical model (Brewin, 2006) which illuminates how such an approach might work.

Our approach differs from the general approach recommended by Padesky in that we usually move directly from a solution focused phase to a core belief phase, that is, we do not usually focus on challenging negative automatic thoughts as a first strategy as Padesky might. There are a number of reasons for this. First, often clients with psychosis find it difficult to learn to identify automatic thoughts and are very bad at completing homework assignments and filling in thought records. Second, particularly if the person is deluded, the delusion itself colours and distorts all aspects of a person's life. For example, it would be quite possible for a client to believe that the 'homework' itself was a punishment given by the 'persecutors', or is a means of surveillance. A more frequent complication is that the delusion influences what is found in the automatic thought records, for example 'he read my mind', and to begin to work on that is to begin to challenge directly the delusional account itself. As stated, one of the central ideas of our constructional approach is to delay such a challenge until major life changes are consolidated, and preferably, when clients themselves have begun the process of doubt.

Similar problems occur for many patients who do not have delusions, but who hold extreme and rigid beliefs about self and others, for example that all people are violent. A general clinical finding is that the more extreme a person's difficulties are, the more likely it is the case that the person will hold many extreme ideas about the self and others. Young et al. (2003) have argued that clients with serious and chronic psychological problems cannot easily identify and challenge negative thoughts. It seems likely that cognitive challenging in non-psychotic reactive depression is possibly due to the relatively short-term nature of the disorder and because prior to the development of the depression the client had healthier ways of thinking which can be revisited in the therapy.

James (2001) has cautioned against the over-use of 'schema' work for basic depression and anxiety. He points out how a technique such as the 'downward arrow', that is, repeated asking of a question such as 'If that is true, then what does it mean?' can lead a person to a focus on negative implications which may not have occurred to that person before. We are in agreement with James. In our work, however, we are dealing with major chronic difficulties, have a good idea of what a person's self-beliefs are from the assessment, and do not just use negative and probing questions without a full counterbalance of building optimistic constructions.

That people with psychosis have very negative views about self and others has been described in many clinical case writings (Chadwick, Birchwood, and Trower, 1996; Moorhead and Turkington, 2001). In one study we asked clients for evidence to support their delusions (Rhodes and Jakes, 2004b). One type of evidence used by some clients was to suggest that a claim was likely to be true since it tended to fit a negative view of the way things are. For example, one client thought the persecution he received was likely since 'most people are bad and vindictive'. This idea was held with a very strong conviction.

In the course of our work we often give a questionnaire to clients (Chadwick et al., 1996) that directly examines their view of self, their view of others, and their view of what they think other people think of them. We have found that most clients have extremely negative scores concerning worth, lovability, and competence.

Therapeutic process

Using Padesky's approach, we begin by asking a series of questions, in particular:

- Can you tell me how you would finish the sentence 'I am . . .'

The same is then asked for:

- Other people are . . .
- The world is . . .

In our work we have added a fourth question that seems very useful for those with persecutory ideas:

- Other people think I am . . .

How one explores these questions needs to be adapted for each client. Some clients give a clear answer straight away, for example 'I'm rotten'. For other clients, it is useful to ask the question in a number of different ways. This can be followed by a discussion about which statement seems most important for the client as a way of summarising his or her difficulties.

Padesky also recommends that a therapist notice important emotional reactions and ask a question such as: 'What does this event (internal or external) say about you?' She also recommends the use of some published schema questionnaires such as the one designed by Young and associates at the Schema Therapy Institute, New York. It is also important to reflect on the life history that the client gives and ask oneself, 'What would these sorts of experiences be likely to teach children about themselves and about the world?' As well as the direct effects of, for example, neglect or abuse, it is useful to listen to how key figures are described. Core beliefs about the self are often formed on the basis of identification with key caregivers during childhood.

For psychotic clients we believe that it is also useful for therapists, out of the sessions, to reflect on any delusional themes or themes about hallucinations or social difficulties, and ask oneself a question such as: 'What is this about?', that is, to forget the obvious 'strangeness' of a delusion and consider what type of 'everyday' problem is possibly being expressed. For example, if a client believes that MI5 are poisoning him, stripped of its 'extravagance', the client appears to be talking about a situation where others are experienced as hostile or the self is seen as bad or persecuted. Such reflection forms part of the evolving case conceptualisation. We do not recommend, at least at this stage, that the therapist suggests such ideas directly to the client; rather, consideration of such ideas can help in guiding the therapist to ask questions about certain topics, for example 'How do you experience others?'

In the end, however, we believe it is best to be guided by the client's actual statements and emotional reactions while exploring these areas.

Given that one has established a set of statements which the client agrees are important, then the essential next stage is to explore how the client would prefer life to be, that is, to answer questions such as:

• If you weren't . . . then how would you like to be?
• If people weren't . . . then how would you prefer them to be?
• If the world wasn't . . . then how would you prefer it to be?
• If others didn't think you were . . . then how would you prefer they thought of you?

As Padesky writes, the preferred core beliefs might be obvious, for example unlikeable to likeable, but often this is not the case and the preferences expressed seem quite surprising. We suggest accepting these as given by the client.

Once the client has agreed upon a set of statements with the therapist, then it is very useful to write these out and ask how much the client believes each statement out of 100%. The ratings of each statement can be very diverse and can give a clue as to which are most important.

Building alternative core beliefs

The essence of Padesky's approach to beliefs about the self is to focus on building positive beliefs rather than contradicting negative beliefs. In her 1994 article Padesky outlines a range of methods and of these we use three in particular, namely, positive data log, historic review, and examining continua. We will illustrate all of these in the following case descriptions.

Lesley

We gave the assessment and narrative conceptualisation for Lesley in Chapter 3. In brief, she thought she had transformed herself into a gender-less 'freak' or 'blob'. This had happened at the end of a violent relationship. The developmental background to this belief was that her childhood was marked by criticism and rejection.

After the initial assessment, the first phase of work was solution focused, which we will briefly summarise. Her goal was not to feel 'self-conscious all the time'. For the hypothetical future question she said she would not be 'ashamed' of herself, she would do more activities such as swimming and would not wear a T-shirt in the pool; she said that what would convince her that her difficulties were over would be if she could have sex with a man, enjoy this experience, and that the man wanted to keep having sex with her. She added that she would be more confident if he was not just doing this because he had no one else.

Exceptions occurred when she was in the company of some relatives whom she liked. I asked her what was different about these people and she said they 'listened' more. She also did not think of her body when doing artwork at the day centre.

Given that she had reported some recent improvements, and was doing at least a small number of social activities, the solution focused tasks were to notice improvements and do more of these if possible. One task was to experiment with clothes, that is, to try wearing the clothes she really liked and not just ones she wore due to fear. To help build her confidence, she was asked to discuss specific clothes with someone she trusted, that is, the relatives who made her feel good.

The solution focused work seemed to help, but was seriously interrupted by a burglary in her home. Her levels of anxiety and depression greatly increased immediately after and continued for some weeks. At the end of this phase of work, her test scores suggested considerable improvement in her view of herself, and her social difficulties were somewhat better, but the work had had little effect on the delusion itself. It is possible that a continuation of solution focused therapy would have been sufficient. We continued, however, to use the goals and exceptions we had already elicited in this phase throughout the following periods of work.

Self-belief work with Lesley

The self-belief work began by returning to the topic of what she thought of herself. She again began to list her perceived defects. She saw herself as having 'no gender', being a 'freak', 'fat', not a woman or a man, and not fitting in with others. She added that she was not 'happy inside'. I asked why and she said she did not know.

Next I asked her how she would prefer to be. She answered immediately that she would prefer to be a 'normal woman' but if not, at least she would feel better if not overweight. She added that she felt ashamed.

Several issues were then explored with Lesley both in this session and subsequently. We explored the issue of who had been negative towards Lesley. Unfortunately she listed her father, her mother, and her long-term violent partner all as having been negative towards her. The idea of being 'prejudiced' about oneself, that is, of always accepting the negative and dismissing anything positive, was introduced and Lesley said 'I get in there first'. I asked why she did not believe others when they were more positive towards her. She answered that she became 'engrossed in my thoughts' and added comments such as 'I'm horrible', 'they see I'm gross'. Out of 100%, she thought she was 100% a 'freak' and 0% a 'normal woman'.

Lesley was introduced to the idea of collecting information for a positive data log. We began the process during the session. I wrote out 'Please look for and record any evidence that you are a normal woman' and asked if she could give any examples. After some hesitation, Lesley answered that 'I've got small feet' and 'I do my nails'. She added that she wore earrings, had periods, and got on with other women. The task of looking out for further evidence was given as a task to try out at home. Next week she came back with a page and a half of observations. Many of the comments concerned the appearance of her body and how others had reacted; for example, someone had complimented her.

When Lesley presented these answers I listened with interest but made no further comments; I did not attempt to try and persuade Lesley that these were proof she had not changed gender. Furthermore, no comments were made on issues such as gender-role.

Next I began working on an historic review of her core beliefs. Padesky suggests taking the statement of a negative belief about the self, writing it at the top of a page and then making two columns. In the first column one lists evidence for the negative belief, and in the second column evidence against the negative belief. Down the far left margin of the page, different ages are written out. A variation we sometimes use is to put the negative belief in one column, and the preferred belief in the other. In each column we write down the evidence both for and against the belief heading the column. We did this for Lesley, putting 'normal' in one and 'freak' in the other. Down the left side specific age ranges relevant to Lesley were written out, that is, 0 to 2, 2 to 11, 11 to 19, 20 to 30, 30 to 40.

After detailed discussion, the column for being a 'freak' had no evidence, except for the time period when Lesley stated she had begun changing her body, that is, in her thirties. In the 'being normal' column there was considerable evidence for all stages. She had seen photographs of herself before the age of two in which she thought she did look normal. In her teens, she said, 'boys were chasing me'. She had sexual relations in her twenties. In recent times she noted that men, women, and her family all treated her in what she regarded as 'normal' ways.

The main core belief work was carried out over six sessions although all the ideas discussed were returned to repeatedly over many sessions during the phase of building an alternative account of her delusion and questioning her delusional beliefs. Her percentage scores for believing she was normal were recorded four times and were: 0%, 60%, 80%, and 70%. Her scores for being a freak were 100%, 90%, 30%, and 40%. Her conviction that she had no gender, that is, the original statement, showed a very slight change, typically she had answered at around 95%, and during core belief work it dropped, at its lowest, to 85%.

The therapeutic work with Lesley was eventually very successful and involved direct challenging of her beliefs (see Chapter 7). Though the initial shift in the core belief phase was apparently very modest, we believe this change was a crucial turning point on which the later work built. In general where therapy is successful with delusions, first there is a very small but significant shift in attitude, and this is followed by a very slow and protracted phase of small changes. There is not a sudden 'insight' followed by complete change. When successful, something alters in the 'system' of the personality and following this it is almost as if the person can move on to build a new way of living. During the therapy with Lesley she continued to make small steps towards rebuilding her life as a person and as a woman who wanted a sexual relationship.

Betty

In the opening sessions of our work, Betty cried profusely, explaining that wherever she went, others would 'tell me off'; they would also transmit information about her using a small 'device'. Everybody had one of these, or at least adults did. About seven years earlier, she had had difficulties at her job where she reported that other people had been unpleasant, stared at her, and talked about her; this had become so difficult that she left. It was at this time that the experience of persecution spread to strangers in the streets and other public places like shops and buses. She was able to give details of many episodes to show me what was happening. She explained how she had gone into a shop and overheard comments made by the assistants that contained information referring specifically to her. Typically she would quote for me fragments of conversations such as '. . . she's the one . . . no good . . . yes, she did it . . .'. She knew this referred to her. She claimed that sometimes she would overhear the exact wording she had heard an hour earlier, and the fact these strangers were using similar insults proved that they had been listening to a device.

The questionnaires given to her suggested very high levels of anxiety and some depression. She had not worked since giving up the job in question but was now attending a day centre and had just started some voluntary work for a charity shop. She had been diagnosed as having schizo-affective disorder. The case conceptualisation was as follows.

During her teenage and young years, Betty had a persistent experience of contempt and hostility by others in groups at school. Within the family she appears to have been accepted, allowing self-confidence to develop.

Under stress in adult years, and in a difficult work environment, feelings of rejection were reactivated. She again experienced herself as an object of contempt and feeling herself to be outside the main group. External and neutral information was automatically reinterpreted as 'about' her and to be contemptuous.

Her thinking became dominated by these ideas and these were used to explain all unpleasant events. This increased her feelings and perception of rejection. These feelings and ideas were given symbolic expression as being 'told off' and by the transmission of hostile information via a 'device'.

Solution focused phase

After the narrative based assessment we began solution focused therapy. To the hypothetical future question she said that people would stop saying things and that it would take her about a year before she was sure it was over. She also described the everyday things of life such as work, a partner, and going about her business without disturbance. When specifically asked how she would react to negative events when the problem is solved, she replied that she might say things to herself like 'maybe people do like me' and 'maybe it's a one off'.

We focused on exceptions in the present, that is, when was she calm, when did she feel secure, when did she feel that people liked her, and in general what worked. She was able to give examples for all these questions. The work then consisted essentially of asking her to do more of these sorts of things, but with a particular emphasis on thinking about who liked her and how people who liked her demonstrated this.

In one part of the work she was asked what her strengths were and what her good points were. In the room we began a list: she suggested 'kind hearted', 'I go out of my way to help other people', 'would share my last pound with someone'. She was given the list to continue at home.

When discussing any episodes during the week that had made her very suspicious, we returned many times to the idea suggested above, that is, was it a 'one off', a daily sort of hassle perhaps. This construct proved very useful since for Betty the opposite interpretation was that the negative event formed part of the spread of connected persecution.

Self-belief phase

Betty had made excellent progress during the solution focused phase in that her conviction that others were telling her off dropped from scores in the range of 80% to 100% to a range from 40% to just under 10%. This was the biggest change in scores she made in any one phase of therapeutic work. Her levels of anxiety also dropped. However, she still retained a great instability in conviction, and as we had anticipated, when asked about self and others a very negative pattern had persisted. Given all this we thought it would be useful not to continue with pure SFT but to look directly at her beliefs about self and others.

All the areas Padesky suggested were explored. In Betty's case, in contrast to Lesley, most of the time Betty thought in positive ways about herself, claiming sometimes to believe 100% that 'I'm nice'. However, her main concern was that others thought terrible things about her. She believed 'others think I'm horrible' with 100% conviction. She gave several descriptions of what others thought: that she was a 'rotten person', 'nasty', and 'an evil piece of work'.

The historic review of core beliefs looked at how she had been treated by others, in particular, who had been 'horrible' and who had not been 'horrible' at different ages. The most striking fact was that while at all ages she had good positive memories of her family and some friends, her experiences of others in general had been characterised by insults and bullying. Betty had been born with a speech problem, which made the sound of her speech slightly distorted. At school others had called her 'frog throat' and picked on her in various unpleasant ways.

In spite of having a normal and supportive family, the years of bullying and social humiliation seemed to produce in Betty a deep expectation of others being hostile and rejecting; the latter seemed to be the psychological foundation of her experience that wherever she went, others were 'picking on' her or 'telling her off'.

For the positive data log she was specifically asked: 'Please look out for any evidence that other people think you're ok'.

She was asked to write about this everyday. Typical evidence she gave that others 'thought her ok' were everyday social actions such as being asked for a coffee. Sometimes, the links were less obvious, for example being asked to work on a till at a voluntary job.

Again, as with Lesley, it is striking how ordinary everyday events or features took on powerful meanings and were experienced as consistent with core beliefs. It is also interesting to note how ordinary assumed social realities, things, and properties most people take for granted are experienced as uncertain or problematic in psychosis, as was discussed in Chapter 2. Most of us, for example, do not need to 'work out' intellectually exactly who does and who does not like us. For Betty the topic arose all the time and even the behaviour of, for example, a bus driver would be scrutinised and reacted to. Psychotic patients are troubled by interpersonal themes like everyone else (for example, am I likeable?) but also are caused to be 'troubled' by the very nature of the 'real'. Lesley in the previous case example had made her list of evidence for being a woman and we just accepted it; of course, we did not suggest that surface features such as polishing one's nails were not really 'proof' of gender.

Constructing an alternative account

Betty made good progress in the core belief phase; however, the scores still suggested instability in her delusional conviction, distress, and preoccupation. If she had any type of sudden social problem, for example someone not being pleasant at her voluntary job, her delusional conviction tended to greatly escalate. The scores had begun to change in the positive direction, but could easily revert. Again, as with Lesley, the initial phase of core belief work was not sufficient, and several things had to be returned to in the alternative perspectives phase.

Three specific techniques were used in this phase. The first approach was to elaborate her ideas about the device. She only spoke of it in a vague way. After some discussion she thought it would be like a mobile phone in size but was definitely not one. I then began to wonder with her what each device cost and how many would be needed for the whole adult population. We worked this out to cost about 30 million pounds at the least. I then asked if she thought her old company would have such money. The emphasis was always on open questions and in addition questions that were floated without waiting for an answer.

The second approach was to ask Betty what she found unconvincing about her own ideas: was there something that seemed unlikely or not obvious. She was then able to list the following: she said she had no 'proof'; she mentioned that in all she overheard she had not heard her actual name; that perhaps what people had said could mean something else, that is, it might not be about her; she thought that it was possible that she had let her imagination 'run away'.

At this point a third approach was used: I suggested to Betty that perhaps what she was experiencing was 'like' what she had experienced as a young school girl in that the feelings she had now seemed very much like those she experienced when being bullied and teased as a child. I then linked the feelings she had as a girl to her experiences in the workplace and then feelings she now experienced in public. She liked this idea straight away and nodded in agreement. This work was helped by Betty having been given several metaphor sheets and getting used to generating metaphors to express her feelings, as will be explained in the next section.

The phase of building an alternative account proved to be successful, that is, her conviction reduced and she was at this point neither preoccupied nor distressed by her thoughts. She took up many social activities. She was seen for follow-up appointments for over a year and a half and continued to do well.

CONCEPTUAL METAPHORS AND BLENDS

Lakoff and colleagues (Lakoff and Johnson, 1980; Lakoff, 1987, Kövecses, 1990) have suggested that metaphors and other figures of speech are central to the way we think, that mental processes have metaphors embedded in them. Someone might say, for example, that he was 'crushed' by an emotion, 'blew his top', felt 'weighed down' by a feeling of guilt. Lakoff suggests that if we analyse such concepts we find metaphoric models which give structure to the way these concepts are elaborated and used, for example that 'anger is pressure in a container'. A radical claim is that for some topics it is either difficult, or perhaps impossible, to think of these topics without using some type of metaphor. For example, it seems very difficult indeed to think about 'time' without explicitly or implicitly comparing time to distance or space: 'the days ahead of us', 'the time passed quickly'.

When we talk about mental phenomena such as the mind, self, or emotions, we also often seem to be using metaphors; for example, 'deep inside me' suggests the self has spatial dimensions, that it is, perhaps, a container with depth. One could note expressions such as:

- He filled with emotion.
- I carry this memory with me.
- She looked within herself.
- Different parts of him were in conflict.

Lakoff (1987) suggests that a person's concepts or categories of thought could in principle have the following sorts of features:

1   Basic propositions in literal form.
2   Metaphors concerning the topic, that is, where the topic of interest is compared or described in terms of some other topic (for example, 'I'm feeling on top of the world').
3   Metonymy, that is, where we might refer to a whole object by a part (or sometimes vice versa). For example, one could say: 'During fashion week, London and Paris watch each other with suspicion'. Lakoff also suggests that certain concepts such as 'man' or 'woman' have metonymic features in that we often represent a whole class by 'typical', if not stereotypic, examples. For instance, if we ask people to describe 'a man' they would not usually give the example of someone who is 90. But why not?
4   Schematic images: Lakoff suggests that for some concepts or categories, an image, usually visual, is key for our conceptualisation.

If we wish to grasp those specific ideas that concern clients, then it can be useful to consider that a specific concept could have aspects of any or all of these features, and that the literal neutral reference of a word might only be the 'tip of the iceberg'. Some concepts which one often finds are troublesome to clients include: being a man, being a woman, masculine, feminine, success, failure, worthwhile, lovable, clever, useless, bad, good, power, and weakness. All these concepts tend to have multiple meanings, have meaning that goes beyond the literal, and often contain aspects of social evaluation.

In recent developments concerning the theory of metaphor, Fauconnier and Turner (2002) point out that if we try to understand how people talk and make sense of things, then we see not only clear-cut metaphors, but that sometimes people in their discourse construct what might be thought of as complex imaginative scenarios. For example, if two philosophers were engaged in a discussion, it would be not at all unusual to make a comment such as, 'So, how would Descartes reply to those, such as Ryle, who say he made a category mistake?' Here we imagine the situation of two philosophers, separated by hundreds of years, engaged in conversation. Such scenarios are not exactly metaphors. Fauconnier and Turner also note that many products of our imagination, for example robots that feel, are likewise not exactly metaphors. To illuminate such examples they have developed a general theory of 'conceptual blends', that is, examples of thinking where there is fusion of elements from quite diverse conceptual domains. For a 'robot', we appear to have fused in one blend the idea of a human being and the idea of a machine.

A complex blend might need at least two conceptual 'inputs', and features of both remain in the final imaginative product. A metaphor, they suggest, might be also seen as one type of blend, but a simpler one, in that what we present tends to emphasise just one conceptual domain. For example, if a person states 'My brain is lead today' we underline and emphasise features of lead: heavy, inert, and so on. By emphasising 'lead' we make suggestions about the state of a person's tiredness, but we leave these to be worked out or guessed.

If we wish to understand how a person thinks and feels on a certain topic, we need to understand and describe many things: these might include, at least, literal statements, stories, explanations, but also metaphors, idioms, and conceptual blended scenarios. These are part and parcel of everyday talk and experience. To treat these as just a way of expressing an already existing set of literal ideas might be to miss the real nature of conceptualisation and other types of mental activity (for example perceiving, feeling).

Constructivist approaches to emotion, meaning, and metaphor

Greenberg and Pascual-Leone (1997) have outlined how people may struggle to put their emotions into words. They suggest the following process. First a person needs to attend to any 'felt sense' in the body. Next, the person can then 'symbolise' these feelings. This step in particular is one that often uses metaphor and other types of figuration. The third step is an attempt to then think about the symbolised emotion in the wider context of the person's life and emerging narratives.

We can perhaps just about avoid using metaphors when talking about emotions if we use a sort of neutral language, for example if someone says 'I feel unhappy about this', but it is often the case that a person feels most emotion when a metaphor or vivid conceptual blend is expressed. There is a world of difference between saying 'I feel confused' and 'I feel torn apart'.

Therapy and metaphor

Given that metaphors and blends seem central to our deepest experience of emotion, and to our ability to conceptualise, it is not surprising that the role of metaphors has been important for several therapists from diverse traditions. Of note are the ideas of Cox and Theilgaard (1987) who write from a psychodynamic position, while Sims and Whynot (1997) have written about metaphors for use in systemic therapy. There has been less conspicuous employment of metaphor within cognitive behaviour therapy, but it is certainly mentioned and used in, for example, Padesky and Greenberger (1995).

Metaphor has had an extensive use in narrative therapy (White and Epston, 1990; White, 2007). In a case illustration, White and Epston (1990) described the use of 'externalisation', that is, where a problem is described as external to the client, and sometimes is described almost as a person, with intentions, habits, quirky ways, and so on. The elaboration of the problem-as-a-character metaphor seems to open up creative possibilities, for example with children how one might try to 'out trick' or 'outwit' the entity. It is, however, also useful for work with adults in that it seems to help clients gain a sense of distance or differentiation between themselves and their problems. For example, one might say, 'How do you manage to carry on in spite of what this problem keeps doing to you?' White (2007) has also emphasised that we should be careful in our selection of metaphors for capturing a person's relationship to problems; for example, 'to fight a problem', 'deal with', 'handle', all have specific implications, and some which may be more or less helpful. In the next section we will illustrate some diverse uses of metaphor from our therapeutic practice.

Exploration with metaphors

A central use of metaphor in therapy is to explore and discover aspects of a person's experience: to illuminate vividly what something feels like, is thought to be, implies. Metaphors are 'rich' in meaning, and often say or suggest, we believe, more than a person realises at the moment of utterance.

Some patients use metaphors quite spontaneously: these automatic metaphors are used, it seems, almost without reflection, and sometimes pass without notice unless a therapist is attentive to what is said. In our therapy we often take written notes, and here if possible, record examples we have heard. A client might, for example, use a phrase such as 'I feel like I am being punished'. It might be suitable at some point, not necessarily when just said, to refer back to this statement and ask questions such as: 'You said you felt you were being punished, how does that feel?'; 'What or who might be doing that to you?'

We are doubtful that general 'rules' can be given for asking for such elaborations of metaphors; however, it can be suggested that asking such a question must fit the emotional and social 'tone' of these moments, must be part of the purpose of work at that time, and still harder to specify, must cohere or be consistent with the emerging personality of the client.

There can be occasions where therapists themselves think of and use explicit metaphors or use a metaphor so subtly that it is barely noticed. Cox and Theilgaard (1987) give some interesting examples. On the whole, however, we tend to agree with Sims and Whynot (1997) that client-generated metaphors are most likely to resonate with the client.

Another way of generating metaphors is either to ask the client during the session or to ask the client to write metaphors between sessions. We use a simple one-page sheet with the following questions:

> Today, I feel things are like (a) . . .
> Today, I feel like (a) . . .
> When I was in a difficult situation today the other person (or people) seemed like (a) . . .

The sheet is fully explained and usually the client is asked to generate some examples while in the room. If the client is not sure what a metaphor is, we give examples from well-known lyrics or poems. These sheets, and variations on them, may be given to a client during the first assessment stage, but can be used at other stages as appropriate. They can be very useful during the alternative perspectives phase.

The following is one sheet of metaphors filled in at home by a client:

> Today, I feel things are like a fog.
> Today, I feel like a victim.
> When I was in a difficult situation today the other person seemed like a cloud.

By examining this sheet we were able to open up a discussion of what this felt like. The client in question was bombarded by critical voices and visions of disapproving shaking heads. He was, however, making great efforts to do activities and to socialise. There was, however, for him a constant feeling of not being like those around him: in a way, the term being in a 'fog', yet also feeling like a 'victim', perhaps conveys this better than terms such as 'depersonalisation' (which may not in fact be correct since that term was used originally for non-psychotic problems) or if he had attempted straightforward literal phrases. He is a victim in a fog: there is confusion, not feeling he knows what exactly is happening, sensing some sort of potential danger, feeling that he could be attacked.

It is often very useful to simply ask what a client means by a metaphor. One wrote that 'I feel things are like a balloon in the sky'. On first glance this did not seem informative. However, on being asked what it meant she told me that she had been 'trying to come out of my body'. She had been indoors, had thought she heard threatening voices outside, and then as it were, tried to float away. This then opened up a discussion of whether she had engaged in a similar process as a child when exposed to extreme difficulties in her family.

A variation on the above sheet has been a sort of structured diary where clients are asked to write for a limited time. Two questions are suggested:

1   What's on your mind?
2   I feel like I'm . . .

One client (Lesley in the previous case illustration) wrote the following:

> Still hate and unsafe in my flat. At day unit in good mood today. Did not feel too depressed about body today. I have made good friends at the day unit.

> I feel like I'm a yo-yo today. At unit I feel happy, at home I feel depressed and unsafe. Unsafe when I am in flat and out of it. The slightest noise I feel someone is in the flat everyday I check flat against intruder. Can't relax like this.

The client had been doing well in therapy, but was then burgled. This produced a feeling of great insecurity, particularly at home. It is interesting how the image of the 'yo-yo' is first given, and then followed by an elaboration of what this meant for her.

Building with metaphors

Several therapists, including Padesky and Greenberger (1995) as discussed earlier, have noted that it is possible with clients to ask how they might see a preferred future state or goal and that it can be very useful to express this in terms of metaphors. One client was just beginning to make attempts to travel to new parts of London by herself. She was afraid of any area with which she was not very familiar. She said that she assumed that if she asked for directions, others would be unpleasant and not give help. She was, in addition, very critical of herself and regarded all she did as not good enough. She gave two metaphors at this point of our work:

> Today I feel like a sensitive child striking out on a road.
> Today I feel like a brave leaf unfurling.

These images suggest a certain good feeling, perhaps even excitement and joy, and yet are in tune with her fears. We have no hard and fast 'rules' as to how one might respond to such metaphors. One might simply note and acknowledge them; however, with the above one could ask, according to context:

- How does a sensitive child feel?
- What can help such a brave yet delicate leaf? What can protect it as it grows?

Several other examples of goal orientated metaphors and images can be found in other case illustrations throughout this book. Of particular note is the metaphor of 'being at the wheel' in the case study of Grace (Chapter 4) and the one of 'eyes open' given by David (Chapter 6).

WORKING WITH NEGATIVE MEANINGS

Introduction

In the original model of cognitive therapy developed by Beck and colleagues (1979) there was an emphasis on how the depressed person tended to experience specific events in terms of negative thoughts, for example 'my friend hasn't phoned, he must not like me anymore'. Such a thought is meant to occur automatically to a person, and then, it is claimed, will cause a negative feeling. Beck emphasised that such thoughts were false, irrational, and distorted.

When we do think it appropriate to work with negative thoughts then we tend to use variations on the approach developed by Greenberger and Padesky (1995). For such clients we give sheets to be filled in at home and, in the opening stages of this work, might simply ask the client to sit for 5 to 10 minutes and to write any thoughts, feelings, etc., that have been on their mind during the day. On another sheet we might then ask them to (a) describe a difficult situation, (b) say what thoughts, feelings, or images occurred to them, and (c) consider whether there is another way of describing or understanding this event. This process is first practised in the room. Some clients seem to like doing this form of at-home task, yet others do not. We would not tend to persist with this method if clients reject it (it is appropriate with some clients, for example those with basic depression, to investigate the cognitions that might lie behind clients not doing the work, but in general, we do not think that useful for clients with severe psychosis).

As argued in Chapter 1, we do not believe all emotions, or other psychological reactions, are caused by specific thoughts, as suggested in the original Beckian model. Increasingly, therefore, we have tended to think of emotional states as occurring in a range of contexts in a range of ways, in particular, that emotions arise in a narrative context of unfolding events, and a wide context of beliefs and ways of living. We use one handout that aims to work with specific emotions and ideas in a narrative context (see Appendix E for this and other approaches to meaning) and contains, in addition to basic questions about emotions and thoughts, the following questions:

- What did you believe was happening or what did you believe about the situation? (Yourself, the others, the events, etc.)
- Do your feelings reveal anything you might have needed or wanted (in the short or long term)?
- Has this event or situation or reaction got a history in your life? What is it?
- Have situations like this happened before? Can you describe these?

There can be many variations of this sheet, modified for different clients. The version we have given is quite complex and only some clients might wish to use it; certainly such questions need to be used first in the room with the client. After the sheet has been used a few times, we would then work with the client to generate alternative ideas, possibilities, or to think how the client could cope with such emotions. In the following case illustration, the specific cognitions could only be understood by placing them in the wider context of the person's life history.

Ame

Assessment

When I met Ame he was 39 and had been depressed continuously for over four years. He also had had an episode of severe depression some years earlier. In addition to depression, he reported hearing voices telling him to commit suicide and he said he now felt no emotion; for example, he had not cried at his mother's funeral a couple of years previously. Also, his psychiatrist reported ideas of reference and suspicion.

I decided quickly that the work should begin with an extended period of narration focused on making sense of Ame's life since he stated that he wanted to understand himself and his voices. An approach such as activity setting in the early phase was contraindicated since an approach attempting to get Ame to socialise (interpersonal therapy, in fact) had been used before to little effect.

Life themes

Initially therapy focused on issues related to the past (see below). The idea of using automatic thought records was explained to Ame in the twelfth session. Following the ideas of Padesky, he was asked to record the situation, mood, automatic thoughts or images, evidence that supports or does not support the 'hot thought', and finally, a balanced view and what his mood was after finishing the exercise.

One striking and repeated negative thought was:

- 'It is my turn to die, and it's overdue.'

Others were:

- 'Some people discriminate against me.'
- 'There are signs meant for me.'

Ame was also asked to record his actual 'voices' on the thought record sheets and then to consider if there was evidence for and against what the voices were saying:

- 'He's late to take his life.'
- 'When you were born many things went wrong.'

As evidence for the above he wrote that his parents had got divorced 'about the same time I was born'.

The advantage of having already done an extensive phase of narrative work before we examined the above negative specific thoughts was that these thoughts could now be put into context, though 'context' perhaps should be thought of as consisting of various layers.

The first context was that Ame had belonged to two families of which many had now died. When asked why it was his 'turn', Ame would point out how over the years one person had died 'in turn' from each family, and by this calculation, he would be the next.

The deeper context, however, was the story of his interpersonal life. His parents divorced when he was very young and then he rarely saw his mother. At around the age of 12 he was sent to live with the family of his uncle. There, he was often teased and insulted. Later his father died during a war. In discussing these issues Ame said that he had always felt 'unwanted', as someone 'outside'. On a thematic level it seems reasonable to suggest that his negative thoughts and negative voice content point to a profound sense of just not being wanted, of not belonging, and that he was somehow defective. From an attachment point of view, it would seem that fundamental attachments had been seriously disrupted.

Metaphors of suffering

In addition to thought records, Ame was asked to complete the metaphor sheets described before. On one occasion Ame had written:

Today, I feel things are like a dripping tap.
Today, I feel like a mouse.

The day after, however, he had written that 'things' are 'like a toilet' and

I feel like an animal/rat.

These are, we believe, intensely vivid and emotional statements. The next day after doing these sheets, Ame explained that he had actually wet his bed, something he had not done since his teenage years. This also opened up the topic of bed-wetting as a young boy and how this had been a target of ridicule by his adopted family.

In my work with Ame I also gave him Young's schema questionnaire. As might be expected, he scored highly on schemas of 'abandonment', 'defective/shame', and 'isolation'. While these were useful summaries, it could be argued, however, that the statements of feeling like a 'mouse' and a 'rat' express with greater emotion and vividness what his experiences felt like.

Not all the work we did will be described here. Some crucial elements in the work were as follows: first we repeatedly reviewed the basic narrative of 'his turn next'; he examined the arguments for and against, and we contemplated issues of 'change' versus 'fate'. At least intellectually he agreed that there could be no causal mechanism. The theme of 'his turn to die' was also sometimes expressed as the theme of 'deserving' to die and here too we explicitly examined the evidence for and against such an idea.

Another variation of his negative themes was that he had been a 'bad influence' as if by his birth he had brought disaster into his family. Here a detailed account of his history was particularly important in that events could be put in their wider context and aspects he tended to ignore could be brought into relief.

Core self-beliefs and continua

Following the standard assessment for identifying core beliefs, as outlined earlier, the two negative core beliefs we chose to work on were represented by the statements 'I am strange' and 'Other people are more able'. After discussion, Ame suggested as preferred alternatives 'I am normal' and 'I am able like others are able'.

For the data log, Ame looked out for examples of being normal; for example, he wrote 'I eat, sleep, wash, walk, watch TV'. The historic review suggested many ways in which he had been able. The latter had produced no apparent change by itself.

A third method of working with core beliefs suggested by Padesky is the use of continua; for example, if a client states that he or she is unlovable, a line can be drawn from 0% lovable to 100% lovable, and the client asked to place people well known to them on the line. Padesky suggests that, if possible, it is better to work towards using a line, as above, which charts the presence of one feature such as 'lovable' instead of a line going from unlovable to lovable. There are several variations on these types of continua work, and the one we will illustrate here involves taking a concept or construct that seems to be used in an absolutist way, and analysing it into constituent parts as a way of modifying 'black or white' thinking and labelling.

Ame, as stated, thought he was not 'able' like others. I decided to attempt to analyse this construct into its various 'criteria', that is, on what diverse criteria was Ame judging himself and others to be 'able'. I began by asking Ame 'what can most people do?' He began by stating that most people could 'drive, do housework, DIY, gardening, work'. We discussed what 'DIY' involved: painting, putting up curtains, etc. He wrote later between sessions, 'work, look after children, study, shop, wash'.

On a separate sheet down the left column eventually 11 criteria were suggested by Ame, for example: reading, linguistic ability, DIY, learning. Across the top we wrote 'low', 'average', 'high'. He was asked to rate himself on the various criteria. He rated himself as low on seven criteria, but as average on three, namely, learning, reading, and housework.

We had begun discussing the first criterion concerning 'linguistics' in the room; this had a special significance since I knew he had obtained a higher degree in this subject. At first, even here, he was inclined, when asked, to put 'average'. After discussing specific details about what 'linguistics' might involve, and a discussion about what he knew others could do, he suggested 'high' was a fair assessment on this aspect. It must be emphasised that his acceptance was not instant or sure: he seemed reluctant, yet just about accepted this as the case. We discussed other criteria when he came back next session, and he changed his mind concerning 'reasoning' and 'arts', that is, he now placed himself as 'average'.

Over a few weeks Ame was asked to rate his percentage conviction on the initial core beliefs. His ratings for 'I am normal' were 10%, 10%, 10%, 20%, 20%. For 'I am able like others are able' the ratings were 0%, 0%, 10%, 20%, 20%. The changes in numbers may appear small, yet, as Padesky suggests, we believe such changes indicate a shift from absolute claims to at least the beginning of flexibility. We cannot extract the effect of this specific focus from the cumulative effect of the rest of the work, but our impression was that it was a subtle but important shift.

Concluding comments for Ame

The work was modestly successful: the voices became less compelling and distracting. Ame reported coping better with the voices, going out to music concerts, getting a place on a job scheme. At the end of therapy he said, 'I don't think I deserve to die', though he also said he still sometimes had an urge to not exist. In one meeting, three years after the therapy, he still maintained that life was worth living.

Thinking back now over this case it occurred to us that these first steps to recovery had been successful, yet his progress very much depends on his 'world', his personal context. That is, in a society where people are not 'forgotten', where flexible work can be provided, where there is understanding, family, friends, or acquaintances, then Ame could find a role and slowly build a sense of being 'wanted'. Our present modes of life put all connections and involvements at risk.

OVERVIEW

Our clinical impression is that almost all clients with psychosis have long-standing extreme negative beliefs about themselves and others; furthermore, often these are linked to various types of interpersonal difficulties. It is also our impression that the more traumatic and invalidating an adult's experiences have been, then the more severe and negative are these core beliefs and related emotions. Constructional approaches such as described by Padesky, and recent compassion based approaches presented by Lee and Gilbert, described later in Chapter 8, offer very fruitful ways of helping clients to at least begin to rebuild a benign or acceptable sense of self and others.

Change in the area of core beliefs in itself might not be sufficient to alter delusions, voices, and social difficulties, yet these might be necessary steps before other approaches and activities can be fruitfully used.

Chapter 6

Narrative and trauma

INTRODUCTION

Over the last few years we have become interested in trying to use various types of narrative therapy to work with early trauma in the lives of clients with psychosis. There are several reasons for the growth of this interest. In our clinical work we have been struck by how often clients with psychosis presented their difficulties as overwhelming in the present yet often made no or little reference to various events at the beginning of their difficulties and very rarely to events in childhood. However, when clients were asked about these times in their lives, then often clients would describe enormous difficulties involving the full range of conflicts, rejections, loss, trauma, and abuse. From our therapeutic perspective, we consider that many of these early traumatic events might well have contributed to the meaning and themes of present symptoms. They may also have had a role in causing the psychosis. Given the potential for exploring the connection of present meaning and past events, we began to wonder if a specific exploration of the past as a contribution to the present might help to 'contextualise' clients' difficulties, thus providing opportunities for building new perspectives and new initiatives in their lives. In this chapter we will outline an approach we have developed for working in the areas of psychosis and narration.

In Chapter 1 we presented the notion of narrative and its possible relevance in psychology. In the second chapter we gave various findings concerning narrative and psychosis. Here we wish to make some comments based on our direct clinical experience. First, we have found that some clients, particularly those with active delusions, have lives dominated by very narrow narrations, or at least narrations of an abbreviated type. A client can arrive and explain how something terrible is about to happen, for example the arrival of demons or an execution by a secret organisation. What is often noted is a sort of narrative repetition, or rather, a sort of story that never quite arrives at its resolution. The demons are about to come; the secret agents keep watching; the person is about to go to hell, and as for Jack in Chapter 4, he is continuously dying.

In contrast to the above, many clients, at least at first, do not seem to give detailed accounts of their lives. They might not mention any difficulties they had before the breakdown, though we have noted they usually can when asked (Rhodes and Jakes, in press). Clients very rarely mention the distant past of their childhoods, though again, most are usually able to give accounts when asked. Some clients, we have noted, seem to give very confused small-scale, micro-narratives of recent events; for example, specific difficult encounters that might have upset the person during the week. This type of ongoing, often confused narrative might, we suspect, contribute to the maintenance of psychological and social difficulties by, among other things, not leading to clear specific predictions. Sometimes we have noted that if we try to draw the client on these implications (for example as part of preparation for an attempt at modification) the client will simply not engage with the potential implications. For example, we once discussed with a client how there could be people who she could not see. She said she didn't know but appeared uninterested by this fact and moved on to another topic. Her belief in invisible people continued as before.

These various considerations led us to think about how we could work with narrative in psychosis. In designing an approach for exploring past difficulties, we have been influenced by two specific therapies. The first approach is that of Neuner, Schauer, Roth, and Elbert (2002), who have developed a therapeutic approach for working with refugees who have suffered multiple traumas. They argue that it would be near impossible to discuss all the diverse traumas such clients have suffered, even if such was considered appropriate. Their approach, therefore, is a modification of testimony therapy (Cienfuegos and Monelli, 1983). This approach was explicitly designed for working with victims of torture; in outline, the aim is to produce a written document summarising what the person has suffered. The document is then used for political purposes. Neuner et al. present a case study of their method. Over a small number of sessions the clients recount traumatic events. The details of these are written down, typed up, and presented to the client in the next session. Weine, Kulenovic, Pavkovic, and Gibbons (1998) have also used a version of testimony therapy and present findings suggesting benefits for clients. Grey and Young (2008) also make use of testimony therapy in their approach to working with refugees. (With the possible exception of Ame in Chapter 5, we have not described work with refugees suffering psychotic symptoms. For therapists working in this area the article by Grey and Young is an excellent resource in general.)

We thought the above version of testimony therapy suitable for our clients since they too had often undergone years of trauma and interpersonal difficulties. While we thought it might be very useful to explore painful issues from the past, we also thought it would be useful to consider the details and meaning of actions and events which had been benign developments in a person's life, that is, to use an approach in line with narrative and solution focused theorising. Exploration of both preferred and non-preferred aspects of a person's life is an integral part of narrative therapy as developed by White and colleagues (White, 2004, 2007; White and Epston, 1990).

Our approach to difficulties and traumas in the lives of persons with psychosis tends, therefore, to include the following elements:

- After a careful explanation of the purpose of the therapeutic work, the client is asked about negative events as already mentioned or alluded to in the assessment phase or elsewhere.
- Where possible, we first ask for simple descriptions, but then spend time exploring the emotions and meaning of the events for the person and, in particular, relate this to their self-characterisations.
- We ask about events for all major phases of the person's life: the teenage years, early twenties, etc.
- Towards the end of this work we note times when the client has coped or achieved goals. We might speculate on the meaning of these exceptions or initiatives. As stated elsewhere, our attitude in doing this work is not one of trying to 'prove' to the client that there is something positive in spite of all. Rather, it is better to remain cautious, interested in these events, but letting the client draw any conclusions to be made.
- Towards the end of this phase a letter is usually written and read out in the session. Any errors, for example dates, are corrected, and any new emerged ideas are added. The corrected letter is sent or given to the client.
- With some clients, and for some difficulties, we might spend some time considering alternative 'descriptions' or 'explanations' of reported events. In the narrative phase we suggest this should occur only if clients express explicit doubt about ideas they have discussed at other times. Again, no attempt should be made to prove the therapist's ideas as the only ones correct. The aim, rather, is to have a natural conversation where different points of view can be discussed and left open as possibilities.
- While there is an effort to place events in an historic sequence, as with other narrative approaches, there is also an emphasis, where useful, on other features of narrative such as character, metaphor, conceptual blends, and dialogue.

Our approach, we believe, is one variation of a range of possible narrative approaches in therapy. A summary of some typical questions is given in Appendix G. Other approaches using ideas of narrative have been employed in the area of psychosis not only by White but also by Roberts

(1999), Seikkula, Alakare, and Aaltonen (2001), and Lysaker, Lancaster, and Lysaker (2003). There is an excellent recent review by France and Uhlin (2006).

Therapeutic approaches based on challenging cognitive themes are reported in Larkin and Morrison (2006). Smith et al. (2006) present three cases of CBT for psychosis and trauma; the formulations given to patients, to varying degrees, present themes found in psychotic symptoms as linked to past themes found in trauma. Our approach differs in that we normally separate the exploration of the past from the direct questioning of any delusions, if done at all (see Chapter 7). We think both approaches have their uses and our approach, for example, may suit clients with many traumas distributed over several periods of life.

What might change with narrative therapy

First, a narrative approach may provide opportunity for the expression and alteration of negative meanings and emotions, that is, it may work in a fashion similar to that suggested for cognitive behaviour therapy for trauma as discussed by Ehlers, Clark, Hackmann, McManus, and Fennell (2005), Grey, Young, and Holmes (2002), Resick (2001), and Brewin (2003).

A second and related possibility is that narrative therapy for psychosis could help a person to express areas that have been 'repressed' or 'inhibited', that is, it may involve the mechanisms of change that Pennebaker (1990) and colleagues suggest may explain the various benefits accrued for persons following talking and writing about trauma.

A third possibility is that engaging in narration, particularly of forgotten or never articulated areas of strength, allows a person to build various types of positive ideas about self and other, or, as Brewin suggests (2006), strengthens the retrieval from memory of positive representations which then can compete with negative representations. This is of course also consistent with the ideas of Seligman and associates (2005).

A fourth possibility, linked perhaps to the first, is that there are some advantages in constructing a complex narrative of the previously inarticulated yet influential events in a person's life. Brewin (2003) suggests this sort of mechanism for PTSD: he argues that having a verbally controlled and accessible narrative of events may help the mind/brain to control those distressing out-of-context memories which tend to be triggered by perceptions of situations similar in some way to the original traumatic situation.

A fifth possibility is that narrative therapy can help a client clear some of the confusion we mentioned earlier; that is, by regular work in which there is an attempt to put events into context and sequence, a client is helped to be able to do this not only for distant memories, but also for ongoing confusing events. This may also help the person to establish possible links between parts of their history, and between parts of their history and their symptoms.

A sixth possibility is that the technique may be helpful by reducing the client's avoidance of the trauma and thus facilitating mourning or grieving losses.

To summarise the above, these changes could involve all or some of following: cognitive restructuring, the articulation and expression of emotions, the strengthening of positive ideation, and the construction of new perspectives. There is, no doubt, overlap between these possible mechanisms, and certainly we do not believe this list is exhaustive. Other 'levels' of explanation might also be simultaneously relevant; for example, building a narration might well, on one level, alter neurological states, and on another level, it is possible that narration in the social situation of therapy somehow changes the 'position' of a person vis-à-vis the other, that is, has social and sociological effects. O'Nell (1999) studied American Indians suffering from PTSD who had been in the Vietnam War. She suggests that in order for individuals to make recovery, they needed not just to talk in any way about their suffering, but needed to do this in a culturally prescribed ritual of narrating to the whole group. As argued elsewhere, we do not regard these 'levels' of explanation as ultimately exclusive of each other.

When and with whom to do such therapy

In carrying out all therapy it is important to be in regular clinical supervision. This is particularly important with the techniques that we will now describe. In addition, one should have experience of working with trauma with non-psychotic people before attempting to work with trauma in this group. A general rule is to proceed with caution, if in doubt to stop and reconsider outside of the therapy room, and to discuss the work with other senior and experienced colleagues.

It is important to discuss the intention to carry out this work with other members of the treating team, and in clinical supervision. This is because discussing traumatic events can be very stressful and it is important to have other people's informed opinion on whether this might be unhelpful at the present time. We think that these techniques are helpful for properly selected clients but it should also be stressed that these ideas have not yet been subject to extensive empirical investigation though other clinicians are working in the area of trauma (Larkin and Morrison, 2006). It is therefore important to apply these ideas with caution, gently and under proper clinical supervision.

It is also very important to consider who, and who not, to do such work with. We suggest it is useful for clients who have undergone serious traumas and where there is a suggestion that the client is clearly 'forgetting' or 'ignoring' these areas, and yet the areas of trauma do seem linked, albeit indirect and over time. However, of equal importance is that the client must want to do this work, must see that it has importance and meaning, if not, no attempt should be made. Sometimes, perhaps often, the client is afraid of doing such work; this should not be a barrier where the client has freely chosen to take up the offer of such an exploration.

Another important factor to consider is the client's response to this method. That is, the procedure should be begun very gently, and then the client should be watched to see what their response is. If the client has a negative response to the beginning of this approach it is best to back off and work on some other issue, possibly returning to this at a later date. Any increase in anxiety, or delusional ideas, or voices should suggest that this aspect of the treatment should be stopped. If in doubt, or if the client becomes particularly distressed, it is important to back off.

We are not suggesting the narrative approach discussed in this chapter would be sufficient for those patients who have suffered extensive and extreme physical or sexual abuse. The latter clients, we believe, might well profit from the methods we illustrate in this book, yet need other additional therapeutic ways of working, for example ideas taken from classic texts for work with trauma (Herman, 1992) or in some extreme cases, work may need to focus on profound difficulties of interaction and personality as found in the work of Young, Klosko, and Weishaar (2003). Such work is not the focus of this book.

Some clients, especially those who have suffered extreme physical and sexual abuse, might either (a) reject all attempts at looking at the past or (b) be in too precarious a state of 'balance' of just about managing to cope. Trauma and past-orientated therapies are contraindicated in such cases. In spite of the severity of such cases it might well be better to offer intermittent solution and coping focused work and only to look at the past when and if the client feels he or she is ready.

The approach to narrative we are presenting in this chapter is not intended as a stand-alone treatment, but is envisaged as connected to, and supported by, the other phases we employ, that is, coping, solution genera-tion, and work with core beliefs. In general, as outlined, we think it best for most clients to begin with a solution focused phase, and then to move through core belief work, and then on to past narration for some if appro-priate. There is, of course, a sort of limited review of the past in the core belief stage and often it is then that the need for further exploration is noted. We have, however, sometimes reversed this order, that is, have focused first on narration of the past; we would tend to do this where the client has expressed spontaneous interest in discussing past matters. The order and what is done must be tailor-made for each client.

When narrative and trauma type work is carried out it is possible that a person, in the short term, feels less well. In the case of David, in general, he remained stable, except for his scores on the Evaluative Beliefs Scale, which suggested an increase in some negative cognition about self and other. These scores continued to improve, however, in the subsequent phases of therapeutic work.

David

In the first session David began by telling me that he had been divorced twice: once twenty years ago, and the second time, just under ten years ago. He said that both his wives had had affairs. The referral letter suggested he had delusions of infidelity and depression with psychotic features, although a diagnosis of schizophrenia had been considered. He said he felt depressed, had no motivation, felt 'ashamed' of himself, and went on to explain that he had worked hard over the years yet had paid no attention to what was going on in his home life. There was a certain lack of clarity in the presentation of many of these facts; however, no attempt was made to be too clear at such an early stage.

David spoke clearly and gave very direct answers to questions. Given this, I was able to begin, quite naturally, with the questions in the standard interview for delusions (see Chapter 3). He was 99% sure both women had had affairs and that the three children from his first marriage, and two from the second, were not his.

The assessment took six sessions. His conviction levels were consistently 99% with very high levels of preoccupation. His distress was unstable, moving often between medium and high. As usual, much of this assessment focused on what his present situation was like for him, how he saw major events begin and develop, and an overview of problems as they occurred over his life. Besides difficulties in his marriages, he told me how his mother had died when he was 14, and how he had moved to England from abroad. We will return to these aspects later. It was decided at this point to begin with a standard approach of solution orientated work but perhaps to move on to the other areas he had mentioned if the work proceeded well. We will briefly describe the solution focused work carried out.

As usual, we began with a new list of present concerns. This time he listed them as lack of confidence, family problems, his health, the social problems of not going out, and meeting people. To the hypothetical future question he said he would be 'happier and outgoing' and he'd do the things he'd like to do, namely meeting his family and others, but also to 'not mind that I am on my own'; it proved useful to explore details with the question, 'what would I see on a video?' In general he described doing many everyday activities both with others and on his own. He would be talking more, laughing, or absorbed in activities such as cooking. He would know he was better since he would 'feel alive', be 'proud of himself', and be living 'day to day'. His brother and sister would be the first to notice.

In the first session we had not explored exceptions, but a very concrete picture of possible actions had been suggested. I decided to be cautious. I discussed with him how it was noteworthy that he had not 'slipped' further into difficulties. I asked him to list things he valued now, but to also notice if he could force himself, for example, to concentrate on the television and how he did things when he had no motivation.

In the second session he reported that his son had visited him as he quite often did. I focused on this, to me a surprising fact, several times, wondering how this contact had been maintained in spite of all the problems in the life of his family.

He also reported watching a film all the way through. I concentrated on how he had managed to do that. He reported forcing himself to not 'zap'. At the end of this session again the tasks were to try small steps, as he had already, and noticing how he did things.

In the third session he reported taking the initiative in phoning an estranged sister. Particularly important was the fact that he also reported wanting to now change his life, but this time to do things differently, with his 'eyes more open'.

The work from then on tended to involve discussions of how he could return to activities, often ones from the past, but this time differently, with 'eyes open'. This is an example of how a metaphor can be a very useful way of describing goals or a preferred direction in life as discussed in the last chapter. Though the work was focused most of the time on taking steps, David made several spontaneous comments about past difficult events. For example, at one point he said, 'I feel very hurt and ashamed of myself . . . at the back of my mind'. He thought he had contributed to the destruction of his marriages by not giving his partners attention and by over-involvement in work. When giving such an explanation, he would typically add that, nonetheless, his wives should not have done what they did. As argued elsewhere, solution focused work does not preclude a full attention to expression of problems. David wanted to express these concerns and I listened. The attempts at new activities, yet discussing the past, fitted naturally together.

By the end of this phase he had begun to do more social and practical actions, had taken up exercise, and had made a decision to change things. There was little change in any of the test scores, except a considerable improvement in his evaluations of others, and an indication of feeling less 'hostile' on one questionnaire. His delusional conviction stayed the same.

Narrative exploration

The narrative phase began with a full explanation of the therapy he was being offered. As with other work examining traumatic events, this explanation is crucial. The client needs to understand why it may be useful to explore painful events. I stated to David that reviewing these events in detail might give us a better understanding of his development, and hence how to move forward. The main events discussed were the break-up of his marriages, the death of his mother when he was young, coming to live in the UK, and what it was like being received into another family. During these discussions, he also began to discuss his long-term sexual difficulties.

In contrast to the above negative events, we also explored moments of happiness and achievement; in particular, he began to remember an early love affair which was an 'exception' in that it did not end in a negative way, and did not end due to accusations of infidelity. It was also moving to discuss how he had effectively become his younger brother's protector when the two had come to live with his older brother and wife in England. David had had almost immediately to go to work, and one reason was to help out his younger brother. An important part of our work was to note these acts of generosity. There were also considerable opportunities with David to explore good times he had had in his life such as organising parties and winning power lifting competitions. Here is an edited version of the letter I wrote to David; it was read out to him in the session.

Dear David,

In this letter I would like to summarise some of the things we have discussed in our work together.

We have looked at your life and noted that there have been several major difficulties and challenges for you. One very important thing in your life is that you were close to your mother but unfortunately after a long illness she died when you were in your early teens. This was a devastating event for you and at first you did not even really believe that it was possible. At the time your father was not available and there were few members of your family living on the island of your birth. Therefore, at a very young age, with your younger brother, you came on a plane to England. At first this proved to be a very difficult experience. You went to live with one of your older brothers who was welcoming, but his wife made many comments which made you feel unwelcome. Almost immediately you had to go out and find a job and did not manage to carry on with any education. Besides family difficulties it was also the case that England was not a very welcoming place at such times and you often heard about or saw unpleasant behaviour.

Despite these early difficulties you continued to work hard and eventually in your early twenties started a long-term and satisfactory love affair.

Your life had many good things. You remember going to good parties, you enjoyed your work, and were very dedicated and conscientious. You also had some very interesting hobbies such as playing music for parties and you were a very serious sportsman.

After this first love affair, there have been two very long-term relationships, each with children but both ending in a very distressing way for you. With both families, you have had a moment where you came to believe that the two women in question were having affairs with other men. We've discussed some of the events that led you to think that this was happening. You remembered that you spent practically all your time doing work and now realise that the actual intimate relationship with both woman had disappeared. I, as an outsider, cannot know the truth.

As stated, as an outsider, many years later, I cannot possibly know what happened. We also discussed the fact that you believe that your children are not your own. I said that I was most puzzled by this since you were actually having sex with your two partners on a very regular basis. You said, however, that you thought that fertilisation probably wouldn't occur unless there was a simultaneous orgasm. I am not a biological expert, or a doctor. I think it might be useful for us both to seek further information on this. It seems highly possible that all of the children were in fact yours even if your partners were having affairs. We discussed how you said that throughout your relationships you were convinced that if there was not full and proper sex then it must be that your partners have had to go and find sex somewhere else. You discussed this with your partners and both denied this. Again, we have two points of view on the nature of what has been happening.

We have discussed how you have gone through a long depression and withdrawal from the world and now it might be time to make small but sure steps back to rebuilding yourself and reconnecting with others. We have both noted some significant changes in you recently; for example, you have recently made a new friend. You have seen more of your family and you have started exercising again. You are also talking more to people at the day centres and may even make some friends from there. We have discussed how you know that you are something of a perfectionist and tend to ignore success unless it is complete and absolute in every detail. I did, however, put together with you a list of all the areas in which you have definitely succeeded throughout your life. We found that there are many things you have done successfully. We noted how you have always been a family man, you had looked after your family, you had always conscientiously done your work, and you have done a great deal of looking after your own house, for example with decorating.

We noted that you are also successful in many areas at present, for example keeping in touch with your family, living on your own, and looking after yourself properly. We noted how you have a very good relationship with one of your sons who you see on a weekly basis. You said that you think one mistake you have made in your life is sometimes to so much completely focus on one thing that you don't see the wider picture. In your own words you said that you would like to do things again but 'keep my eyes open'. Perhaps as you begin to do things you have done before, you now might be able to do them in a different way, using the wisdom you have received from some of your times of suffering. Perhaps it is time to fully realise the wisdom that no one is perfect and just because you are not perfect it doesn't mean that you have not done many good things and have many strong and worthwhile characteristics. Perhaps it is time to focus on some of the good things you have in your life, what you have achieved and done, and to not let the problems overwhelm everything else, and to focus on the good things in your life now and in the future.

All the best with re-building your life.

Yours sincerely . . .

The letter aims to summarise the areas of his suffering, but also areas of strength. To counter the self-narration that he was a total failure in relations with women, it was important to articulate the memory of the early brief but apparently happy relationship. It was interesting to note how in our discussions he moved, quite spontaneously, from a simple discussion of his wives having affairs, and to proving these claims, to his role in the period before the break-up, that is, he began to reflect that he had tended to take his wives for granted and had not given them much attention. This idea opened up a new 'angle' from which to think about events, that is, not just the topic of did they or did they not leave him, but rather did he keep these relations alive. This was returned to later in our work in the phase of directly considering alternatives on what had happened. While opening up new perspectives, new explanations, and so forth in the narrative phase can be very close to implying a challenge to delusions or other ideas, we think it advisable at this stage to not proceed further, but rather to consider this as a possibility at a later stage after careful negotiation with the client (see Chapter 7 on alternative perspectives).

At the end of this phase, David's conviction level stayed the same, but for the first time there was just the beginning of change in distress and preoccupation with his beliefs. There was also a lessening of feelings of depression. We will briefly summarise the rest of our work with David.

The next phase was schema focused. A core negative belief was that he was a 'failure'; his preferred belief was that he 'was a success in all areas'. The latter worried me as an aim since it is so sweeping and ambitious, yet he seemed to have a flexible construction of its meaning. (The problem with the preferred belief is that it is the other side of the coin of the 'I am a failure' schema. What the negative and positive statements here have in common is an unrealistically dichotomous view of success and failure. And this dichotomy is actually the problem. However, one has to work from where the client is. One would prefer that at some stage it will be possible to deconstruct the concepts of being a success or a failure.) After carrying out an historic review, collecting ideas for a positive data log, and analysing his ideas of success into various sub-criteria, he moved from 60% to 20% for 'I'm a failure', and 25% to 60% for 'success'. He now was much less distressed and his scores for depression and anxiety dropped out of the clinical range.

The final phase of work consisted of a form of very indirectly 'challenging', or rather, a strengthening of an alternative perspective, a consideration of relapse, and above all encouragement of re-engagement in everyday life. Particularly important was the fact that he and his second wife began to see more of each other and considered a possible reunion. During this phase his scores became increasingly positive, and his final percentage scores were zero in a follow-up meeting some months later.

THE GLASS VASE: NARRATIVE AND METAPHORS

We will illustrate here how metaphors can be used to understand a difficulty in a person's life, and how this may form part of a narrative approach using a letter to the client.

Rosa

Rosa was preoccupied with the idea that she had an undiagnosed virus that would lead to her death. This had become so serious that a few months before I met her she had been hospitalised and diagnosed with delusional disorder. She was showing great anxiety and depression. Two years previous to this breakdown her beloved grandmother had died. She was also feeling stress within her marriage.

The usual phases of therapy as described in this book were carried out, but we will not give all these details. Here we will describe our work using metaphor and the letter used in the narrative phase.

Rosa's reaction to the task of being asked to provide metaphors was that she was unsure if she could do it. She reacted in fact like this to many things, and as I realised over time, appeared, or somehow took on the role of appearing, less intelligent than she really was.

One of the first metaphors she brought back to the session was that 'today I felt like a glass vase'. This was early in our work and I had no immediate ideas on what the image might mean. When I asked Rosa she too offered no particular idea on why she had said this. In this work we are not at all suggesting that either client or therapist needs to give any form of interpretation and in this case we just left the meaning of the metaphor as unknown. It did, however, stay in the back of my mind as somehow interesting: it was not an obvious comment in the way certain well-known proverbs or idioms can be.

Rosa was a client who tended to focus on very immediate worries, the particular problems of that week. She was also very good-humoured, and tended to move away from any difficult subjects whenever possible. It was only by carrying out a detailed narrative exploration that many extremely unhappy events and situations of her early years were eventually described. The letter read to Rosa was as follows.

Dear Rosa,

This is a summary of some of the things we have discussed in our work together.

In an early part of our work we spent a long time looking at various things that happened to you as a young child. You reported that there had been, in fact, many upsetting events when you where a child. Some of the major ones were that your father was hospitalised and your mother and father later divorced. It would appear that access to your father from then on was only occasional. The divorce happened when you were only three. Your mother went to work and left you with your grandmother who you loved greatly. Your mother then had a new boyfriend who apparently did not like children. You told me that you were 'miserable as a child' and sometimes felt bullied.

It was striking that when I asked you about your earliest memories, one was your mum sitting on a window ledge eating ice cream. The other memory was your dad with a suitcase leaving home. Reading through my notes again I had the strong impression that you were very worried and made anxious by your mother. You said in fact that when she was at work you had butterflies in your stomach when you were thinking about her. On one occasion she was arrested in quite dramatic circumstances. I think this may have continued to worry you greatly. Once the police came to the house and there was in fact a threat that she might have go to prison.

It is interesting that once when you told me some of the many worrying things that had happened to you as a child you said 'I hope I have not depressed you too much', that is, you seemed to be worrying about me, even in this session. As I said at the time, you had not depressed me. You do not need to worry about telling me things that upset you in the past. I won't list all the things you said about your childhood but I will mention that sometimes you went to your mother's house and she had not let you in. It is striking that I once asked you to describe an image to express how you feel: you said you felt like a 'glass vase'. You also were saying at that time that you often felt ignored. I wondered whether the glass vase expresses this, in that it may be something others don't see.

You have a very warm friendly personality and are clearly very concerned about the welfare of others and therefore I think you would be very popular in many jobs and your care for others would be greatly appreciated.

All the best . . .

The image of the glass vase eventually got interpreted in our therapeutic work as her having the sense that as a child, and again as an adult, she had an experience of somehow not being present for others, of not being noticed, that somehow others just saw through her, ignored her. This was consistent with the core belief she expressed of: 'I am someone who lets others walk over them'.

Other meanings may be present; for example, a glass vase also seems to suggest something delicate that could easily break. It is also something that is empty of content. We did not in fact explore these ideas. In this sort of therapy we do not engage in complex interpretations, but would explore further meanings if the client leads the work in this direction. In speculating on the meanings implied, we would also be very careful to not impose ideas from psychological theories, that is, from the outside, rather, we aim to understand the metaphor in the context of the person's narrative of life. Our approach to interpretation here is very much in line with the ideas of thematic interpretation as developed in the methodology of interpretative phenomenological analysis presented by Smith (2004).

Much of our work concentrated on how she could take small steps to stand up for herself, for example with a neighbour, her husband's friends, her mother. The letter for Rosa also illustrates how narrative can have a role in bringing together aspects of a person's life that seem ignored or 'de-contextualised'. The person knows, in principle, about a range or set of events and yet does not see or consider any meaningful connections; in Rosa's case, how her mother had been preoccupied with illness and how Rosa was now.

NARRATIVE AND THE RECONTEXTUALISING OF EXPERIENCE

Mary

When I first met Mary she was suffering from a range of problems: she was depressed, anxious, and often heard two voices. One voice in particular was troublesome and this was the voice of a middle-aged man who, somehow, touched her when in bed. She thought it was occurring to 'punish' her. Besides these experiences, she stated that when she saw other people they often did not look 'real', were not 'proper people'. She reported very distressing experiences in, for example, supermarket queues where she experienced other people as having negative ideas about her such that she was 'strange', 'weird'.

I saw Mary intermittently over a period of four years. The therapy was conducted in three stages with very wide gaps in between. It was a notable feature of working with Mary that her life really was very difficult due to family issues and crises. She had two children at home and one older child living away. The first stage of work was solution focused for the initial presenting problems, but increasingly I had to adapt to an emerging medical crisis concerning her son. The second stage of work was affected by increasing difficulties with her daughter. At each stage I tried to balance work on long-standing difficulties with basic counselling for emergencies. By basic counselling I here mean that I listened carefully to her description of current difficulties, and if appropriate, sometimes helped her to think of what she might do or how she could cope. It was Mary's wish at each stage to suspend therapy until a specific crisis was over.

The work we shall focus on for this chapter will concern the use of past narration, and how one might link the present to the past when working with beliefs about the self in relation to voices. The other types of work carried out were mainly solution focused and basic cognitive behavioural approaches for coping with anxiety and panic, and in addition some Padesky-style core belief work. The solution focused work tended to be about her relationships to her children, in particular how she might deal with conflict, and about her feelings and actions in public situations, for example by exploring what worked in those threatening situations. We managed to better describe and link activities she could do when in public and to deliberately put these into action.

The decision to explore the past seemed quite natural since Mary had mentioned many difficulties in her childhood during the initial narrative assessment interview, and at all stages tended to talk of family problems which often linked to the role of her mother.

The specific exploration of the past was carried out in the following way. We returned specifically to her daily current experiences of her voices. She was asked in detail to describe the experience of the voices. She said she felt 'frustrated', 'annoyed'. She could not understand why it kept happening and was puzzled about this. She wondered what would happen when she died: were these spirits waiting for her? Were they 'playing games' with her? She wondered if she had done something to annoy them.

I then specifically asked: 'When else have you felt like this? Is this experience in any way similar to other experiences you have had in your life?' After some thought, she replied that she had felt like this as a child in the presence of her mother. In the presence of her mother she had felt 'frightened' but also 'alone'. She went on to add that as a child 'I was so vulnerable, so dim', and added that she had no 'self-confidence'. She said she didn't like herself. Until the age of 20 she reported always trying to please her mother, for example by doing housework.

The past and the present here were clearly 'linked'; however, there was no attempt to underline this connection, or to suggest that the experience of 'spirits' might somehow have had its origins in Mary's relationship to her mother.

It is fascinating to note that at the next session Mary spontaneously stated that she had been dreaming of her grandmother, someone she said she had loved and that Mary had 'tried to put myself in mother's shoes', had tried, she stated, to justify why her mother had been 'so cold'. On being asked why, she suggested many possible reasons, for example: Mary's father had not given support and had just left; her mother's next husband died in a car crash; her mother had developed serious depression and had been hospitalised.

In the next session we began a full discussion of her past and early adulthood, looking at events in their sequence. Not all details will be reported here. In sum, Mary reported an excellent relationship with her stepsister and grandmother, but a relationship so difficult with her mother that Mary was put into care on some occasions. Particularly upsetting memories for Mary were that on two occasions when Mary had been in hospital her mother had not visited. Mary reported that her mother had stated sometimes that she wished Mary had not been born.

After four months of therapeutic work (including a gap of two months), the following development occurred. She reported that the voice of the man had stopped and had been replaced by the voice of her mother. She also reported the following dream: a 'nice woman' had appeared at her door and said she had come 'to show her how to knit'. On sitting down in the house this woman had turned into her mother, saying in a nasty voice 'I've not come to show you how to knit'. Again, no attempt was made to 'interpret' this dream or to explain why the nature of the voice had changed.

The work continued for a while with a focus on building a picture of a preferred self using Padesky's ideas, and on coping with a strong sense Mary had that 'something will happen'. A crisis occurred concerning her daughter and we took a break of almost a year.

It was fascinating to note that a year later she was not distressed or preoccupied with her 'voices', and did not believe it was the voice of a man or her mother, but now construed it as an 'inner force'. The hearing of a voice did not now seem a pressing problem, and work continued on her anxiety and interpersonal relationships. Unfortunately, though some approaches to her anxiety worked a little, she continued to be bothered by very high and fluctuating levels of worry and sometimes panic.

In the later stages I was able to openly wonder with Mary if her present experiences of voices were in fact, at least in some way, linked to her early experiences. This possibility was further suggested by something that happened. For no obvious reason, Mary received a request to visit a government benefits office. She became convinced on arriving at this office that her mother had initiated this investigation, and would hide and suddenly jump out of a hiding place and attack Mary when she went into the building. She had gone with her sister, and though terrified, they had laughed together at this possibility.

Overview

From work with many cases over years, we have made the clinical observation that for patients with psychosis there appear to be disconnections, separations between areas of their experiences and lives. A common disconnection is between present symptoms and past experiences. It is a very rare patient who might begin work by suggesting that their life difficulties, or any meaning found in their symptoms, has anything to do with whatever occurred in the past.

Mary did not begin our work by seeing any connections at all. When we began to explore the past, and as she told me more and more, in fact, shocking details of at least emotional mistreatment, then at some point I said words to the effect, 'Mary, I think you had a very difficult childhood'. Mary replied by stating yes, but that she did have a 'laugh' in the children's home.

There may be many reasons for these disconnections. Some may be cognitive; however, it may well be that in some ways these blind spots are in various ways produced by motivational states. It may well be that Mary, at least in part, was still trying to cling to a hope that her mother could be 'good'. This sort of point has been made by those who have researched trauma in general (Herman, 1992). However, it would also seem to be the case that it is almost unbearable for people to see themselves as 'victims'. To be 'a victim' is perhaps to see oneself as weak, vulnerable, perhaps even to be seen as inferior and an outsider to the functioning group.

The cost for the person of not seeing 'the truth', of not seeing the past–present continuity, might, however, be great. The person needs a story that explains what is 'going on'. Mary could not access the narrative in which she had been a victim and her mother an abuser. However, she had to account somehow for a sense of danger, attack, being unwanted, and not like others, and to account for these things she had turned, somehow, to ideas about spirits and being punished. While possession by 'spirits' is a very frightening idea, to describe and understand the extremity of her childhood mistreatment was more frightening or somehow more disturbing.

The specific approach we used in the narrative phase with Mary could be seen as a form of 'recontextualising', that is, we asked for events and situations that were similar in some way to present ones. We wanted to place experiences of the present in the context of the past where such experiences may have first occurred.

In an article on metaphors and delusions (Rhodes and Jakes, 2004a) we have specifically argued that delusions as 'verbal statements' are not themselves 'metaphors'; rather, delusional statements such as 'I am possessed' are meant as literal truths by the patient, but may be based on experiences which can be thought of as metaphorical in origin. That is, either consciously, or in some non-conscious way, Mary experienced specific sensations that felt as if these were some form of invasion, some form of attack. It may be possible that, for example, if a person hears some new sound, then the mind makes an automatic non-conscious 'search' for that which it is 'like'; for example, is it like an animal, or like a human? We also do this, of course, quite consciously; once something is experienced as 'like something else', then perhaps from that time on the association is automatic. Bourdieu (1990) was thinking, perhaps, of a similar process when he spoke of 'irresistible analogies'.

Work of the type carried out with Mary might well be perceived as a sort of 'literalising' or 'de-metaphoring' of her psychotic experience of a voice as 'spirit' such that she moved to experiencing the persecuting voices as that of her mother, and finally to experience it as something from within her, an 'inner force'.

NARRATION OF SPECIFIC EPISODES

Much of the narrative work we have discussed in this chapter concerns long time periods in a person's life. There can, however, also be a narrative of a specific event, or of a few connected events in the time frame of a few hours or days. When some clients have been distressed by a recent event, or events that have occurred between sessions, it can be useful to attempt with the client to put these in a meaningful narrative sequence.

One client arrived making, in quick succession, a series of comments such as:

- He phoned his friends.
- I don't trust him.
- I just walked off.
- Why did he want to stay?
- It's horrible.

Something had happened, I was not sure what it was, but clearly the client was distressed. A simple request to 'tell me what has happened' led to similar unconnected statements, to anger and distress.

With this client, Jill, I had to carry out a sort of supported narrative, that is, to first establish a time point before events had begun, and then to persist in working through the events, listening if she jumped back or forth in time, but then to continue forward from where I had understood the sequence had been left off. Eventually the following was reported to have happened:

- A man she knew came to stay at her flat.
- They had slept together.
- The next morning he had been in bed with her but was talking to his friend on the phone.
- She had felt rejected by this and then suspicious.
- They had gone to a bus stop where he seemed to ignore her, again laughing on the phone.
- She had the feeling that he was laughing at her.
- She said she felt guilty about having slept with him.

The more useful psychological issues were that she had put herself in a vulnerable position, had felt the need for affection and yet felt rejected.

After establishment of the narrative, we were then able to discuss these issues and to consider that in fact she had been doing something simple and human, in that she had wanted intimacy.

This episode fitted the wider narration of the client. She had at other times explained how she thought that others in the neighbourhood did not want her there, and that she sometimes overheard the voices of her neighbours calling her a prostitute.

In working with delusions it can be very useful to focus on upsetting events that have just occurred: these often reveal the details of how a person narrates, explains, and experiences certain types of situation. These repetitive experiences are often, we suspect, what most convinces a client that a delusional situation is still going on and is real.

NARRATIVE, PRE-NARRATIVE, AND THE NON-CONSCIOUS

When Mary began therapeutic work it could be argued that many events, or rather memories of events and their implications, were simply 'out' of consciousness or non-conscious for her. That is, some memories could be accessed perhaps in principle, yet she did not do this, and also the implications, meanings, and connections between diverse aspects were 'unknown' to her.

To ask a person to persistently remember a period, and to think with the person about such a period, can be seen as constructing a narrative. The constructed narrative might then serve many roles in helping the person 'make sense' of their experiences and life.

The process of constructing meaning from that which is 'pre-verbal' or non-verbalised is also a central aim of Greenberg's emotion-focused therapy (Greenberg and Pascual-Leone, 1997; Greenberg, 2002). Greenberg describes a process whereby a patient can be invited to attend to feelings, a body sense, that which is occurring within, and then to attempt to verbalise these experiences. Greenberg describes the many uses such a process might have; for example, if a person can begin to notice that besides obvious anger there is also a feeling of being rejected, then knowing this allows the person a wider range of options.

In our work and conceptualisation of cases we assume there is a form of 'unconscious' or 'non-conscious'. We have been particularly influenced by Searle's writing on this topic (1992). At any point in time, a person is only aware of a limited number of things; outside this specific content, for example, will be all the person's memories. Furthermore, there will be all those 'states' and dispositions that the person has in their repertoire of possible reactions. Any person might be thought of as having a repertoire of potential self-states and dispositions to act and react in typical ways.

Besides episodic memory (for example for events and facts) and procedural memory (memories for ways of doing activities) it might also be the case that a person can be in a motivated and emotional state without full consciousness. For example, given Mary's childhood experiences, she might well have often been at some level 'expecting' she would be attacked and rejected yet could not consciously formulate that in words.

The notion of a pre-narrative non-conscious is not, we believe, identical to Freud's conception. We tend to be in agreement with Talvitie and Tiitinen (2006), who outline a range of possible 'levels' of non-consciousness. For example, we may not register something in consciousness because it is simply too quick or complex. At a more profound level we may not 'notice' issues relevant to ourselves and our personal history and therefore these aspects do not then form part of a person's self-conception or ideas of self-identity.

Several writers on trauma, from Herman to Brewin, have commented on the importance and usefulness of putting into words a person's difficult experiences. Brewin (2003) argues that verbalisation helps the mind/brain to cope with powerful memories that seem intrusive and automatically triggered by present situations, and which may be stored in the amygdala.

In this chapter David, Rosa, and Mary might not have undergone definitive sexual and physical abuse, yet in diverse ways they were traumatised by experiences, and perhaps exposed to either emotional abuse or at least emotional traumatic events. In agreement with writers such as Read, Perry, Moskowitz, and Connolly (2001) and Morrison, Frame, and Larkin (2003) we think trauma may contribute to the onset of psychosis, and perhaps, in some cases, be a primary cause of later psychotic breakdown. We hope the types of therapeutic work outlined in this chapter, that is, building narrative, finding metaphors, writing by clients, and therapeutic letters, may all be ways of constructing meaning, of putting disconnected past events into context and sequence, thus allowing clients to be less mystified and baffled by their experiences.

Some writers influenced by narrative have developed the idea of 're-authoring' lives (White, 1995, 2007). We are, of course, influenced by these ideas. However, we must emphasise, as stated in Chapter 1, that we are 'critical realists' and believe there is a mind-independent reality, an external reality of the world and of a person's life. We believe that people suffering from psychosis have been driven to a point where the real past is invisible to them, unknown, and where their present real needs and motivations are obscured. Our work with narrative is an attempt to get closer to the 'truths' of a person's life, and to do this against the many influences that obscure what may have occurred. Of course, as the person struggles to articulate what has occurred and is occurring, one can never be sure the exact truth is arrived at. Any new narrative must be very tentative.

OVERVIEW

Narrative has its deepest roots in everyday human communication; communication that is logical and literal is perhaps the hardest to achieve, and one that rarely taps into the core of feeling. Given the potential of narrative, it seems only wise that therapists attempt to incorporate its use in their interactions and work with clients. Telling stories, narrating events is an essential part of how people experience emotion, thoughts, and other aspects of consciousness. In conducting this therapy with psychotic clients, as stated earlier, it is important to get good supervision and to proceed with caution, and to stop if the client seems distressed. It is simultaneously crucial that clients feel in control as emphasised by Herman (1992), particularly since issues of control are central to those who have suffered trauma.

Chapter 7

Alternative perspectives

INTRODUCTION

In this chapter we describe our approach to helping clients develop alternatives to their delusional worlds. We have emphasised in the earlier chapters of this book that the delusional beliefs of clients can be understood as part of a more general narrative about their lives and the world. This perspective carries over into our approach to modifying delusions. That is, rather than treating delusions as stand-alone beliefs, we deal with them as part of a more general account of a person's life.

One of the most exciting advances of the early 1990s was the development of cognitive techniques to modify delusions. This approach has been refined with increasing clinical experience over the last 15 years. Our work has benefited from the original work done by Nelson (1997, 2005), Chadwick and associates (Chadwick, Birchwood, and Trower, 1996; Chadwick, 2006), Kingdon and Turkington (1994), and Fowler, Garety, and Kuipers (1995). In this period we investigated (Jakes, Rhodes, and Turner, 1999) the effectiveness of CBT for delusions in routine practice using time-series single case methodology; that is, in every session with clients we recorded any changes. The results suggested that one third of participants made substantial change, one third some change, and a third did not change their levels of delusional conviction. This early work included some solution focused work, but since that time we have increased the use of solution focused approaches and added extensive work on core self and other beliefs, metaphors, and trauma narration as described in the rest of the book.

History and development of cognitive therapy with psychosis

Cognitive interventions for symptoms of psychosis have a long history. Cognitive therapy for delusions was stimulated by reports that it is possible to modify delusions by using cognitive techniques of challenging the evidence on which the delusions are based (Shapiro and Ravenette, 1959;

Watts, Powell, and Austin, 1973; Chadwick and Lowe, 1990). Influenced by ideas of Maher (1988), Chadwick and Lowe (1990) treated delusions as normal hypotheses to explain abnormal experiences. In these experimental single-case study reports, clients with long-standing delusions were asked to explain the evidence that they had for their delusion. Clients were then presented with an alternative explanation of this evidence and asked to spend some time evaluating this with the therapist.

First the evidence for the delusion was evaluated; next the delusional belief itself was 'rationally' evaluated. Finally an experiment was designed which would distinguish between the delusion and the alternative hypothesis. The degree of belief in the delusion reduced markedly for the majority of participants in these studies. Furthermore, this change, at least in some cases, occurred within one or two sessions of either verbal challenging or carrying out an experiment to test the truth of the delusion. As one defining characteristic of a delusion was assumed to be that it was resistant to reason, this was a surprising finding, all the more so because the change occurred so rapidly. This empirical finding generated a lot of interest in using cognitive techniques to modify delusions.

GENERAL ISSUES IN THE TREATMENT APPROACH

Symptom or distress?

In the earlier phases of treatment described in this book it is clear that we have been addressing the distress of the client as our primary concern. This emphasis continues in the alternative perspectives phase. Although cognitive therapists aim to modify unhelpful thinking it is important to be clear that this is always a means rather than an end. In mood disorders it is clear that the distress of the client is the target of the treatment. That is, one treats depressed clients with cognitive therapy in order to improve their mood, not to 'straighten out' their negative thinking. In psychosis the most conspicuous symptoms are often cognitive rather than affective, and this can lead to the mistaken conclusion that the aim of a cognitive therapy should be to alter these cognitive symptoms (for example a delusional belief). However, cognitive therapists have argued that the goal of cognitive therapy for psychosis must be to reduce the distress that the client experiences. This can be argued on ethical grounds. If a client is not able to give informed consent to an attempt to change the delusion which he or she has, then it is crucial that the therapist considers whether the client will personally benefit from the attempt if it is successful. It can also be argued on technical grounds: if clients see no benefit in changing their beliefs then the procedure is not likely to get very far in any case. So, cognitive therapy for psychosis has emphasised collaborating with the client to change delusions in the service of reducing the distress of the client, rather than changing delusions because they are symptoms. This has profound implications in how one goes about working with a client. The first focus of the therapist needs to be on the distress of the client in order to increase rapport, and because it is actually the distress, not the delusion, that we will be trying to change. This is why in our approach we place this phase later in our sequential phased approach to therapy. It is only if the client remains distressed by the delusion that one would continue with this phase of treatment.

Position of the therapist

There are some complexities around the position of the therapist that largely relate to clients' lack of insight into their symptoms. These have been discussed in the chapter on assessment and engagement (Chapter 3), but are particularly pertinent when one comes to considering something as potentially confronting as altering the client's delusions. So, for example, in depression the therapist 'educates' the client about the role of negative thinking in generating sad or depressed mood and advises the client in techniques to alter these thoughts. As a *technique* in the service of this rather directive process cognitive therapy uses a collaborative relationship with the client (Beck, Rush, Shaw, and Emery, 1979). (But see Padesky's work (1994) for examples of a less directive use of socratic questioning in cognitive therapy.) The therapist and the client jointly agree on an agenda. They set joint goals. Furthermore, the therapist proceeds largely by the use of socratic questioning. Socratic questioning is the process of guiding clients to a particular conclusion by the use of a series of closed questions so that they are led to draw the intended conclusion for themselves. (This is named, unsurprisingly, after the method of debate used by Socrates, as recounted by Plato.) Of course, socratic questioning is used to get the client to a point which the therapist already has in mind. So with a depressed client who believes, for example, that she is completely responsible for the break-up of her marriage, the therapist will use socratic questioning to help the client to see that this is not the case. But it is clear to the client from the outset that this change in thinking is the aim of the therapy.

Now in the case of modifying delusions there is a danger that the therapist can put himself or herself in the position of trying to educate or lead clients to see that his or her delusions are false. There can be no understanding from the client that this is the aim of the therapy at the beginning of the process. It may be, as Chadwick has argued, that a more openly collaborative relationship is more helpful. Unlike the case of the depressed client there is usually no agreement on a common frame of reference or goal. The depressed client will usually be able to see that his or her thinking may be distorted and will agree that he or she wants to be less depressed. Psychotic clients will often not agree that they have a disorder or that their thinking may be distorted. If the therapist is listening to a client in order to work out how to change his or her delusion, the therapist can easily stop hearing the client's distress. In fact it can lead to the therapist taking a superior position to the client (sotto voce, 'can't you see that if there is no one in the room the "voice" has to be a hallucination?'). Clients may perceive this approach as invalidating their integrity. The other problem with the position of being the 'change agent' is that it ignores the forces in clients that are moving them to change their beliefs in a healthier direction. In fact, by trying to drive the change the therapist can slow it down. Furthermore, clients often have good reason to want to hang on to their delusions.

An alternative position for the therapist is to be less focused on change and more focused on providing an environment in which change can occur. This does not mean giving up the idea of modifying unhelpful ideas, of course. But providing a safe environment in which the client can explore his or her beliefs may be an important tool in modifying entrenched beliefs such as delusions (Chadwick, 2006). In general this approach is helpful as it allows clients to think through ideas by reducing their anxiety that these ideas are 'under attack'. It allows time to build up an alliance with the client as a solid base on which to develop a reconsideration of these ideas. With delusions it is essential to have a long period of engagement for these reasons. In our approach the earlier stages of treatment help to perform this function. But it is also important to continue this process in the alternative perspectives phase. There should be a focus on listening and trying to understand the client's point of view (see Chapter 3). It is clients in the end who must decide whether they wish to critically examine their beliefs or leave the beliefs as they are.

Goal of modification

A traditional goal in CBT for psychosis is, as we outlined above, to modify the delusion in order to reduce distress. However, on reflection one can wonder why so much emphasis has been placed on modifying delusions in working with deluded clients. Why has the CBT literature on working with psychotic clients focused so much on modifying the symptoms of psychosis? This in itself may be based partly on a medical model of the psychotic person. (If the person has symptoms we should aim to reduce them or the distress they cause.) This is why we begin treatment in the early stages with an emphasis on building something positive. If the question is 'how can we reduce the distress of this psychotic person?' then sometimes the answer will be to try to modify the delusion, but sometimes it will not. Clients may, quite commonly, be unconvinced that examining the truth of delusions will be of any benefit to them at all. Sometimes they may go along with the procedure to please the therapist. But this is hardly likely to be therapeutic. The goal of the therapy should be to work on whatever is the most pressing concern of the client. In our experience this may or may not involve work on any symptom at all. In summary, we suggest that therapists do not assume that they have to try to change their clients' delusions. In many ways our sequential approach is based on this idea.

Active versus receptive stance

Linehan (1993) has discussed how in the cognitive behavioural treatment of borderline personality disorder it is necessary for the therapist to move backwards and forwards between a position of facilitating change, on the one hand, and validating the client's perspective and distress, on the other. This is because borderline patients suffer from chronic invalidation by others and by themselves, so they need to be helped to affirm their perception of themselves and their experiences, as well as being helped to change. This seems to us to also apply to work with psychotic clients. Psychotic clients usually feel invalidated by other people's inability to confirm their ideas.

The degree to which the therapist is active in attempting to modify or change the client's world view, or, alternatively, receptively listening and conveying understanding, will shift within the individual session, and between sessions. An important source of information about where one should be on this dimension is the response of the client to one's attempts to modify or alter the client's perspective. The correct atmosphere when challenging the client's perspective should be one in which the client is happy to follow the therapist's line of argument. If you sense any resistance in attempting to alter the client's perspective you should stop and return to active listening and validation.

Delusion as part of a larger narrative

In approaching the modification of delusions it is important to see the delusion as part of the larger narrative about the person's life and his or her experience of the world. This involves understanding the world view the person holds and how that world view is related to the delusion. The delusion will often grow out of a world view based on fear and hostility or self-hate and depression. Sometimes the delusion will express a desire or a fear that the person has in a symbolic form, as argued in Chapter 2. Information-processing models of delusions provide a view of humankind as a computer which gives an overly intellectual model of how we come to the beliefs we hold. Although in some ways delusions can be like scientific theories, unlike scientific theories they very often involve expressions of the deep fears and hopes of the person concerned. The importance of emotions to the process is left out in this information-processing account. Recently the importance of the link between delusions and underlying fears and goals has been given renewed attention (Rhodes and Jakes, 2000; Harper, 2004; Freeman and Garety, 2004) but the implications of this for therapy have not been fully articulated. What we are pointing out here is that people often do not base their beliefs on an assessment of the evidence as an information-processing approach would suggest. There might be many routes to belief; for example, people often base their beliefs on the opinion of others via education, the media, and other means of cultural learning. Most people, for example, are unable to justify their belief in the atomic structure of matter, or that the Earth orbits the Sun, or that the Earth is round rather than flat. People often follow the religion of the community they grow up in, rather than selecting from the range of religious beliefs in the world, or making up a new religion for themselves. We are less rational in our beliefs than Maher's account suggests, particularly when our emotions are strongly aroused. This is also true for deluded clients. Consequently, for most clients, we spend considerable time exploring the pros and cons of the delusion being true or false, rather than beginning with the evidence that it is true or false.

As suggested, we see delusions as complex accounts, narratives, conceptions which are intermingled for the person with memory and present experiences. Very rarely can delusions be summarised as one simple belief, though doing that can be a convenient way of referring to the complex story when talking to clients. We have also argued, based on a qualitative analysis of delusions (Rhodes, Jakes, and Robinson, 2005) that clients do not fall into neat groups such as the 'persecuted' or the 'grandiose'. Rather, any one individual will have a delusional account made up of several strands of meaning or themes and these themes are drawn from wide and open domains of human experience albeit expressed in psychotic content. For example, some patients with persecution ideas also have grandiose ideas, but others do not. The profile of themes for each person is unique and needs to be understood in its entirety when doing therapy for delusions.

Gillian: the importance of context

Gillian was a woman in her mid-thirties living in Sydney. She told me that she was being followed by terrorists who wanted to use her to commit acts of terrorism. She believed that in the past she had possessed paranormal powers and that if the terrorists were able to destabilise her mental state these powers would return. They would then use these powers to commit terrorist acts. She interpreted many insignificant events as relating to her and confirming her delusion. This set of beliefs needs to be understood in context. She had had a difficult childhood and was sexually abused by her father in her teens. This abuse had continued into her mid-twenties. She married in her late teens. This marriage became quite emotionally and physically abusive. She had a number of affairs, and when her husband found out he became verbally abusive in front of her children. She left him and moved in with a new partner, but this relationship failed and she moved back in with her husband, and things between them became even worse. This was the social and emotional context in which she began to feel that she was being monitored and followed, at first by gangsters and later by terrorists. The more general narrative of her life then reflects, and is reflected in, the theme of her delusion, that is, of a world of predominantly abusive and threatening relationships. This narrative is, furthermore, reflected in the actual social situation of the client. This is important in understanding the delusion, but also in thinking about possible interventions. In this case, for example, instead of challenging the truth of the delusion, seen as an account of her anomalous experiences, one could choose to work on her feelings about her past or current relationships.

EXPLORING ATTITUDES TO CHANGE

A useful strategy prior to a direct attempt to change a delusional belief (and sometimes in place of the attempt) is to explore certain attitudes and beliefs that maintain the delusional belief.

Advantages and disadvantages

A good starting point is to explore the advantages and disadvantages of the delusion turning out to be false. We have been somewhat surprised at how freely most clients will talk to us about the possible gains from believing in the delusion. If a client convincingly explains that there would be no serious problems if the delusion turned out to be false, and that they would welcome this outcome, one may be able to proceed with an investigation of the truth of the delusion (see below). If clients do not list any disadvantages in the delusion turning out to be false, but convey by their attitude that they are not particularly interested in this possibility, one should suspect that they really do think that there would be disadvantages in this eventuality.

If the client provides a list of disadvantages in the delusion turning out to be false, the therapist should consider how realistic these are. Common examples of the disadvantages of discovering that a delusion is false are as follows:

- It would mean that the client is 'mad' or 'crazy' or has a mental illness.
- They would feel sad, confused, or frightened about having been so out of contact with reality for so long.
- They have wasted long periods of their life.
- They have been 'stupid' or others would see them as 'stupid'.

- There is a positive aspect of the delusion that the client would miss.
- Other people who told the client that they were wrong would turn out to be right.
- The client would lose face.

Another disadvantage which some clients mention is that there would be no hope of improvement; for example, if the voices or feelings of persecution are due to an external situation then they could, in principle, stop. If, however, they are due to internal factors the client may feel that there is nothing that can be done to make them stop. Clients can feel that if they have been wrong about their delusional beliefs then they will not know what is real and what is not real and they will be precipitated into mental chaos, not being able to distinguish imagination from reality.

If the client sees significant disadvantages in the delusion being false, the therapist can work on trying to alter the client's perception of these disadvantages. Often the disadvantage can be modified by clarifying with the client the details of what they believe. For example, a client may baulk at believing they have a 'mental illness' but be happy with an explanation based on a description of an altered state of mind related to extreme stress. This work will often involve normalisation strategies (described later). If it is possible to link the content of the client's delusion or hallucinations to the circumstances of his or her life, either in the present, at the time that the psychosis began, or in the client's childhood, so much the better. Often it is necessary to include an explanation about the effect of stress on the function of the mind or brain in order to explain markedly unusual states of mind. For example, one client who we worked with had believed, as part of a complicated delusion, that she had been cloned and that her clone had stolen her identity. She believed that her clone had gone on to have a happy life, whereas friends and family had abandoned her. When she eventually stopped believing this she was perplexed about how she could have come to believe so strange an idea. We related this to the very real disappointments in her life, but she remained distressed about the oddness of her belief and how out of touch she had been. It was necessary to include an explanation referring to the effect of stress on reducing logical thinking and increasing more unusual thinking to help her come to terms with this. Being wrong about a belief can similarly be normalised and the therapist can easily give personal examples of this from everyday life.

Exploring the advantages of the delusion turning out to be false can begin to contextualise the delusion in the emotional life of the client. Another way of describing this procedure would be as an exploration of the beliefs of the client about their delusion; that is, the beliefs that the client has about his or her delusional beliefs. Asking the client about the meaning of the disadvantages of the delusion will often lead to more general interpersonal issues. The downward arrow technique is often used to identify assumptions or schemas in cognitive therapy. This involves an iterative process of asking for the negative meaning of an event and its implications. So, for example, if someone lost their job one might ask about the meaning of that event for the person. If the person replied that this meant that they had 'failed' they could be asked what 'failing' meant to them, and so on until an implication was found that justified the client's emotional response. Asking for the advantages and the disadvantages of the delusion proving to be false or true can be similar to the process of the downward arrow technique for identifying interpersonal schemas and assumptions. Just as in that technique it is important to check out that the result makes sense to the client rather than rely on any one approach. However, the advantages and disadvantages map has another role as well as clarifying the underlying interpersonal schemas. The technique can be used to illustrate to the client as well as to the therapist the role that the delusion plays in the client's life. We will discuss how this can be used to change the client's perspective below. In Table 7.1 we present examples of advantages and disadvantages, and how one might work with these.

In the case of Gillian, for example, the main disadvantage of the delusion turning out to be false was that she would have lived her life on a false assumption for twenty years. She had spent much of that time hiding at home and avoiding social contact. Also the main evidence that she cited for believing that her delusion was true was a powerful intuition or feeling: if this turned out to have been wrong it would be hard for her to trust her feelings ever again.

Linking advantages and disadvantages of delusions to interpersonal core beliefs

The list of the advantages and disadvantages of the delusion being false, we believe, gives us an account, at least in part, of the client's motivation for holding the belief. There are two possible strategies when one has discussed with clients the advantages and disadvantages of their delusions being false. First, one can explore the validity of the identified disadvantages. Are these disadvantages likely to occur and if so, how bad might they be? One aim here is to modify the client's view of these disadvantages and thus to reduce the client's motivation to hold on to the delusion. This should not be seen as the inevitable consequence of exploring the advantages and disadvantages of the delusion. Sometimes the client has persuaded us that he or she is right about the disadvantages of the delusion turning out to be false. This is particularly the case if the consequences would involve the client feeling overwhelmed by depression or unable to relate to reality.

If the client's perceptions of the disadvantages are not modifiable or if the therapist comes to believe that the disadvantages outweigh the advantages then there are two possibilities for intervention. One can explore the

Table 7.1 Advantages and disadvantages of delusional beliefs

Disadvantages of changing the delusional belief	*Suggested interventions*
It would mean I am mad or crazy.	Decatastrophise the ideas of madness or craziness. Give information. Explore the client's understanding of these concepts. Normalise symptoms.
It would be frightening to have been so out of touch with reality.	Normalise being wrong. Use a model of continuum of error.
I would have no way of knowing what was real and could no longer trust my own senses.	Underline that most of the client's perceptions are accurate and normalise errors of perception (e.g. visual illusions).
I will have wasted long periods of my life.	Normalise making mistakes as a part of the process of life. Examine times when things went well.
This will mean I have been stupid; others will see me as stupid and be in the right.	Identify and reduce labelling.
If I am this mad my future will be hopeless.	Education and information giving. The eventual outcome for everyone is uncertain.
Advantages of continuing to hold the delusional belief	*Suggested interventions*
I will be recompensed for all my suffering.	In the case of this and other positive consequences of delusions the therapist should work to help the client get these needs met in other ways. For example, in this case the universality of suffering and the positive aspects of suffering could be emphasised.
My belief means that I am a worthwhile person.	Modify belief that being worthwhile depends on doing something else or being something else. Look for real areas of strength and value.
My belief means that I do not need to be angry about the things that I have been deprived of.	Find alternatives ways to channel anger. Modify reasons for being angry, the motives of the people who have harmed the client, the moral superiority of rising above this, etc.
I know who my enemies are.	Suggest that if this explanation is incorrect the real problem cannot be solved.
I have a have power.	Consider real achievements of the person.

possibility of a partial modification of the delusion or one can revisit the related interpersonal core beliefs or schemas (see below). If neither of these seems promising one can consider leaving the delusion alone and continue, if needed, to work in other areas such as getting involved in social activities and so on as described in the rest of the book.

APPROACHES TO THE MODIFICATION OF DELUSIONS

There are perhaps five approaches to working with delusions:

1   In some cases the best might be to leave the delusion itself completely alone, usually because in different ways the client has made it clear during assessment, or at other stages, that this is their wish. However, given that a client does wish to work on some area, for example, overcoming a fear of being outside, then of course work in this area might anyway have a benign effect upon delusional content. We have noted this in our clinical work and the fact that supportive therapy seems effective (Penn et al., 2004) also backs this claim.

2   One can work 'within' the delusion, that is, accept the delusional account and find solutions for any presented difficulties within this frame of reference. This sort of work was presented in the chapter using solution focused approaches (Chapter 4). An example of working 'within' the delusion was also given in Rhodes and Jakes (2002). Here the client refused to answer questions typically asked in assessment, but was willing to talk about the crisis. He believed two devils would visit him, usually the next weekend, to test him on his ability to read. If poor, he would be taken to hell. One very useful technique used at this initial stage was to repeatedly ask him questions such as 'what can you do this weekend that helps?' He generated a list of practical activities such as to pray, leave his door ajar, keep the radio on. In further sessions he reported that he was doing these activities and that it seemed to help.

3   Without directly addressing the validity of a delusion, we believe that a delusion can change when there is a focus on developing a formulation or narrative of the person's emotional and social difficulties, particularly those difficulties which appear, at least to the therapist, as thematically linked to the delusion. This sort of work was presented in both Chapters 5 and 6. While the foremost aim here is to explain, for example, why a person feels distress in certain situations, or feels depressed, we believe that for some clients if a new narrative emerges and is highly convincing to the client, the delusional account may spontaneously 'fade', though slowly, over time. We suggest that this is

what may have occurred to David in Chapter 6. In this work it is sometimes as if two discourses are proceeding in parallel: one is talk about the delusion, and another about the life history of the person. To the therapist, it may appear 'obvious' that the two are clearly related in terms of themes, and yet often the client makes no comment on this. We believe that quite often there is no need to point out these links or connections.

4   One can attempt a partial modification, an approach particularly developed by Nelson. Here one attempts to change very specific but distressing details of the delusion, but not the whole delusional account.
5   Finally, one can provide a narrative formulation and simultaneously directly question the validity of the delusion.

For the rest of the chapter we will discuss partial and full modification approaches.

PARTIAL MODIFICATION

Partial delusion modification is described in detail by Nelson in her book on cognitive therapy for psychosis (2005). This approach involves not attempting to prove the delusion false but attempting to change some details of the delusion.

To carry this out it is useful to think about the specific parts or implications of the delusion that are causing distress and to think, as is typical of cognitive therapy, whether there might be another way of looking at the relevant situation, but all the time not questioning central claims of the delusion. For example, one might not question that a voice is the voice of a 'spirit', but question if this spirit really has power over the person.

For any specific problem, a wide range of diverse beliefs are relevant. Some of these will be more fundamental, for example that a 'gang' actually exists, but other beliefs will be less fundamental, less clear, and not held with such tenacity, for example how many gang members there are, who they belong to, their ultimate intentions. The daily living difficulties of the client can often arise from these latter sorts of belief and are more open to negotiation.

With Gillian, who believed that she had been monitored by terrorists for the past twenty years, we were not able to help her see that this belief was false. The consequences of this realisation would clearly have been quite far reaching. She had lived her life on the basis of a false belief and this had prevented her from engaging in a great many activities. However, we were able to help her see that if the terrorists or gangsters intended to kill her they would probably not have taken twenty years to do this. The people who were planning this would have grown old in the meantime.

It is important that one does not modify the delusion in a negative way. Here it is useful to use information gathered in the earlier exploration of advantages and disadvantages of delusions turning out to be true or false, in particular to inquire hypothetically of the client what the consequences would be if it turned out, for example, that the terrorists were not seeking to kill her. For Gillian a negative alternative belief could have been that the terrorists would enjoy slowly torturing their victims prior to killing them but then would still execute them. Fortunately, this client did not believe the latter. She came to believe that although the terrorists were still monitoring her it was not true that they were trying to physically harm her. All of the examples of terrorists' executions in the media pointed to them taking swift action rather than waiting for periods of twenty years.

DIRECT CHALLENGING OF DELUSIONS AND BUILDING ALTERNATIVES

We will now describe cognitive methods that are used to directly alter delusional beliefs. We use this approach, as argued above, where there is clear indication that the client would definitely prefer not to believe the delusion and to stop being certain about the delusion would be of benefit. In most cases, as we have outlined above, we do not start with this approach.

Developing alternative perspectives

As our book has made clear, our preferred type of explanation makes sense of delusions by placing them in the context of emotional and interpersonal processes, and sometimes where useful, underlining how these processes might influence a person's cognitive processes such as perception and thinking. We also find it useful to incorporate possible metaphorical meanings of the delusion when this seems clear. However, it is most important, as we have already stressed, that the alternative account is acceptable to the client. Sometimes an account that gives this type of narrative meaning for a delusion is not acceptable to the client and in such cases we may opt for simple explanations, linking psychotic symptoms to stress and how this, for example, influences a person's perceptions and thinking.

Evidence map

In addition to developing an acceptable alternative belief, the other task prior to challenging the delusion is to understand the evidence that supports the delusion. In the interview schedule given in Appendix B we point out how it can be useful to ask about recent experiences related to the delusional content. For example, if someone is followed by a gang, one can ask when the gang was last seen, what exactly was noticed. In this way one can access some of the evidence the client is using as a basis for continuing to believe the delusion. There are many different types of evidence and in Table 7.2 we present a typology. We arrived at this by research that involved asking participants to give evidence for their delusions and then used interpretative phenomenological analysis to suggest a typology (Rhodes and Jakes, 2004b).

For each person one can put together a sort of map of supporting evidence used by the client. The map is important as it allows the therapist to plan how they might go about attempting to alter the delusion; in particular, what might be the 'sticking points', the experiences which the client finds difficult to ignore or understand.

For example, in the case of the client who believed that she was being followed by terrorists who were planning to kill her, one source of evidence was her memories of her thoughts leaving her mind (thought transfer) and harming other people. She also remembered receiving messages from the TV and seeing people following her around (person perception). Another source of evidence was her current interpretation of her experiences. She interpreted people's behaviour as following her around and loitering near her house to monitor her (assumptive accounting). A third major source of evidence was her non-delusional belief that people could not be trusted (prejudicial accounting). This was largely based on her experience of child sexual abuse and neglect. These beliefs form the background on which the persecutory delusion is formed. That she believed that others could not be trusted and that people were abusive, and in particular that she expected this to happen in relation to her, set the emotional stage for the delusion that she was being persecuted by terrorists. Her behaviour towards others generated more evidence in favour of her delusion. She would look suspiciously at others when she thought they were following her. This resulted in people actually staring at her in an odd way which she, of course, interpreted as evidence that they were monitoring her.

Normalisation

If we are to aim to lead the client to believe that his or her delusion is false, we need to ensure that the alternative belief that will replace the delusion is acceptable to the client. In order to achieve this, the alternative belief will usually involve a 'normalised' account of psychosis. Normalisation here means suggesting that it is in fact quite normal to suffer from certain symptoms after great stress and suffering, and furthermore, that some of these symptoms, such as hearing voices, having unusual perceptions etc., are more common in the community than is often assumed (Romme and Escher, 1993). Mentioning famous people who have had hallucinatory

Table 7.2 Typology of evidence for delusions

Type	Definition	Examples
1. Object perception	Perceiving entities, fully present, partial, or hidden	Seeing 'furry balls' moving Hearing a voice somewhere in the room
2. Sensation-analogy	Describing unusual sensations using analogy or metaphor and literal description, sometimes moving between the two	'It was like a haze of waves' 'Like sulphur' 'It was like hell. I was in hell'
3. Global perception	The whole 'world', space, or time seems different	'The sun was unreal'
4. Thought transfer	Thoughts go in or out of a person's mind	Someone claimed to 'transmit ideas' to others
5. Volition alteration	A person's actions are experienced as under the control of someone or something else	Some insects were 'making me do things I didn't want to'
6. Social perception	Seeing other people and thinking, knowing, their intentions, attitudes, etc.	'I felt they were trying to get me out' Ordinary comments such as 'she's the one' are about the client
7. Eruptive ideas	An idea, or knowledge, is given immediately to the client	'It must have been when I was 15 and they showed me my future'
8. Narrow focus accounting	The client reasons about experience but ignores context, prior learning, etc.	One client argued that he wasn't hallucinating otherwise he would hear the voices when at home
9. Assumptive accounting	The reasoning makes some sense, but only if one assumes the prior account or narrative. There is 'hidden meaning' in things	The fact that a man sits reading a newspaper in a van is evidence for the 'gang'
10. Prejudicial accounting	The client assumes a stereotype, generalisation, unusual belief about others	People would spy since 'most people are bad and vindictive'

experiences, for example William Blake, can be very helpful. Kingdon and Turkington (2004) have made extensive use of normalisation in their CBT for psychosis.

Most accounts of psychosis, both medical and lay, involve a high degree of stigma and have very negative connotations. This makes accepting that this applies to oneself particularly hard. In preparing a client for delusion modification the syndrome conception of 'schizophrenia' can be questioned or 'deconstructed' (Boyle, 1990). The variation in the presentations of people with this diagnosis can be pointed out to the client and that no clear explanation is universally accepted. One can point out that many investigators now prefer to investigate single psychotic symptoms rather than broad syndromes. We will often, as stated, explain the delusion as an expression of the client's experience of trauma or unfilled needs if this is possible.

Normalisation is also useful to make acceptable the idea, if needed, that the client has been so clearly wrong and mistaken in a personally important belief. Pointing out that being wrong about things is a common state of affairs can be helpful. The diversity of strongly held but contradictory religious opinions is a good example. The client's personal examples can be used; even better, the therapist can disclose his or her own examples of having been wrong.

Direct questioning

We begin the process of challenging the delusion by putting it to clients that one way of explaining what has been happening to them is that their delusional beliefs could be true, but that another possibility is the alternative explanation (which we have previously determined is acceptable to the client). We then propose that it could be in the client's interest to explore which of these explanations is correct because of the advantages for them (as previously determined in prior conversation with the client). If they agree we begin the process of direct challenging of the delusion. 'Challenging' does not quite capture the mood of this part of the work. It is more an open discussion, asking pertinent questions, putting facts together, and thinking with the client. If the client is not coming along with the therapist then the therapist should stop exploration at that time and return to it later if considered useful. The point is that if the client is showing a negative reaction to the arguments we are putting to him or her then we need to understand the experiential evidence and motives behind that reaction rather than trying to reinforce our argument in some way.

Usually it is best to start with specific evidence for the belief rather than with the belief itself. The evidence that the person is currently experiencing is often a good place to begin as the events can be observed to determine what is happening. The other major source of evidence will be the experiences that led the person to believe in the delusion in the first place. Current evidence, however, has the advantage of being open to detailed observation unlike the historical evidence.

The main strategies in challenging the evidence for the delusion, or associated beliefs about self and other, are those used in conventional cognitive therapy. Evidence against the current interpretations of events can be discussed with the client. Alternative explanations of evidence supporting the delusion can be outlined; inconsistencies between theses interpretations and other beliefs of the client can be indicated and behavioural experiments can be set up. These are sometimes called 'reality tests'. Generally, clients will not complete thought records so most of the work occurs in the session with the therapist. In the case of Gillian discussed above the current evidence was mainly her perception that she was being followed and monitored. It would have been possible to question this by looking at the evidence that she was being followed. How did she know? One could look out for evidence that was not consistent with the delusion. Why had no one taken direct action against her over a period of twenty years, for example? Looking for alternative explanations would be helpful here. This would involve explaining to the client the process of confirmatory bias.

Logical reasoning can be used to question either evidence or belief: a good guide to this is to imagine that the delusion is true and then work out the implications this would have in real life. For example, if the client had truly been pursued in such a blatant way for twenty years because of her special powers it is likely that other people including the security forces would have become aware of this and intervened, or that the terrorists would have taken a more active approach and kidnapped the client. Would it be likely that she would be kept under surveillance by people hanging around her house in such an obvious way? What would they be hanging around for? This particular client had a subsidiary belief that they were monitoring her to drive her crazy again so that they would reactivate her special powers. Why, in that case, did they not use a more direct approach to driving her crazy, and a more effective approach (twenty years later)?

One could also use a behavioural experiment to test the evidence or belief. So one can go with clients to observe exactly what happens when they believe they are being followed. Possible experiments depend on the details of what one discovered but might, for example, include the clients doubling back on themselves or stopping to look in shop windows to check if they are being followed. A client could also observe the numbers of people standing near someone else's house and see if these were different to the numbers standing in front of their own.

With Gillian, in fact, we opted for doing only partial modification. We did not succeed in totally eradicating the delusion, rather we altered it to the belief that although she was monitored this could not be because any harm was intended, since if so, this would have happened many years before. We will now describe a case where direct challenging was used. A range of possible questions for direct challenging is given in Appendix H.

Lesley (continued)

Lesley was first described in Chapter 3 and the main work presented in Chapter 5. We will here summarise work we carried out in the challenging phase.

After solution focused work on her beliefs about self, she still held on to the idea that she was a 'freak', a 'blob' with no gender.

Of crucial importance was that over the course of our work an ever clearer narrative of her life emerged. Eventually we were able together to note how she had been the victim of harsh, critical, and rejecting attitudes from both her mother and father. There was also a history of preoccupation with her body in various ways; for example, she had been to a special school because of asthma, she had engaged in excessive dieting.

As an alternative to her delusion I was able to suggest in various ways that she had developed an attitude of profound rejection of her self: that believing herself to be a 'freak' encapsulated a feeling of not being wanted, of not being like other people. In terms of the motivations described in Chapter 2, that she experienced herself as an 'inferior' person looked down upon by others, I greatly emphasised that this reflected or was a product of her mistreatment at the hands of others and did not actually say anything about her real self. This account was credible to Lesley, but not sufficient it seemed to push aside her delusional convictions.

The following methods of direct questioning were therefore used. First I checked again what was still 'evidence', that is, what experiences still made her think of herself as a 'freak'. She listed several features of her body – her legs, hands, shape of her lower body – that were masculine.

One specific line of questioning was to ask what did not 'fit' her account. She was able to give a list of things she noticed that did not fit her account:

- 'People want to be my friend.'
- She had had two boyfriends in recent times.
- She had recently had a sexual relationship.
- Her family did not call her names or react with horror or disgust.

This led to an extensive discussion of how these facts did not 'fit' her theory. She again, as before, would argue that some people were just being polite. I was able to suggest that others could not always be so polite, for example the new partners she had met.

During the work at this time, given that her conviction was obviously wavering, I introduced the idea of the difference between believing with the 'head' and believing with the 'heart'. She agreed that now she could at least imagine and consider she was not a 'freak', yet still felt it was true emotionally. It is interesting to note that at this point she again remembered episodes from her childhood where she had been teased if not bullied when others had called her names.

Another approach to challenging was to ask if she would believe the opinion of a doctor on the gender features of her body. I knew that she had been referred to me by a particularly sensitive psychiatrist and I had asked this doctor if she would be willing to give an authoritative opinion on Lesley's body. She had agreed. I was then careful to ascertain whether Lesley would believe such an assessment. She said she would and it was important to note that she had never in fact asked any doctor for an opinion. The assessment was arranged and the judgement given. This approach has, as stated, been termed a 'reality test' (Chadwick). It is often very difficult to organise such tests but was feasible in this case. During this phase of work there was a very large decrease in conviction and later conviction levels fell to zero.

CONCLUSION

Our clinical impression is that clients, when they change, do so slowly, incrementally, and often over long periods of time. We actually ended active therapy with Lesley while her conviction levels had become very low and it was only in later follow-ups that her conviction dropped to zero. There does not seem to be one moment of sudden realisation. Rather, clients become less interested in their delusions and get on with their lives. We do not recommend over-persistence in this phase of work: rather, it is better to discuss these issues and move on to other phases of work.

Chapter 8

Voices and visions

INTRODUCTION

In this chapter we describe the way we work with voices and visions. The general approach tends to use the same elements as described elsewhere in this book for delusions and social-emotional difficulties, though some details are specific to the characteristic manifestations of hallucinations. This chapter differs from the other descriptions of therapy in that working with voices and visions is not a separate 'stage'.

We will not present a review of the various possible causes of hallucinations (Bentall, 2003) nor present a detailed review of the phenomenology and description of hallucinations (Nayani and David, 1996; Knudson and Coyle, 2002). We wish, however, to make the following observations since these tend to influence our way of working.

First, while it is obvious that hallucinations cause great suffering, it is also often the case that clients can have benign voices and often have ambivalent attitudes to their existence (Romme and Escher, 1993). Our approach in consequence of this is very much 'libertarian', that is, we only work with voices if clients wish to, and even when clients at first say they wish to be rid of voices, we assume this attitude might change or fluctuate.

Second, it appears that hallucinations manifest themselves in multiple ways, for example as 'internal' versus 'external', 'real' or not so real (Nayani and David, 1996). Furthermore, and especially over time, people often develop personifications of voices and might also hold certain complex theories as to their reality, for example as 'mind' generated as opposed to being real 'angels'. We regard it as neither therapeutically useful, nor morally justified, to impose any one specific philosophical, ideological, or scientific world view on the client.

Third, whatever the ultimate causes may be of hallucinations, it seems that hallucinations fluctuate in their frequency and unpleasantness, and that this variation is due to the concrete living situation of the person, to social and emotional processes, and to events that occur in the person's life (Slade and Bentall, 1988).

Finally, research concerning voices has described how people develop methods of coping: Romme and Escher (1993) carried out a large survey of voice hearers, and categorised respondents as those who did or did not cope well. All groups used a range of ways of coping and these were classified as distraction, ignoring the voices, selective listening, and setting limits on the influence of the voices. Those who coped well tended to use distraction least and were reported to keep voices under control by 'communicating with them in a selective manner'.

The cognitive behavioural approaches

There are basically two approaches used in CBT for work with voices. The first is coping enhancement strategy (CES) developed by Tarrier (2002) and colleagues. CES is aimed at enhancing the strategies the client already uses: often patients themselves have developed methods spontaneously over time, and where this is the case the person can be encouraged to use these more often or in more systematic ways. Sometimes, however, methods based on research such as the use of headphones, ear-plugs, or vocalisation (Nelson, 1997) can also be taught, and, of course, Tarrier suggests the use of many techniques found in CBT such as activity scheduling and belief modification. He also recommends the use of positive self-statements to build self-esteem (Hall and Tarrier, 2003): this clearly is in line with a constructional approach.

The other major CBT strategy tends to be one of emphasising the use of cognitive challenging, in particular the challenging of clients' beliefs that their voices are the voices of powerful persons or powerful entities. Research has indicated that some clients have the same attitude to real people as they have to their voices and that often voice hearers regard themselves as being weak and inferior, and regard others as dominant and powerful (Birchwood, Meaden, Trower, and Gilbert, 2002). Cognitive therapy (Chadwick and Birchwood, 1994; Birchwood et al., 2002; Byrne, Trower, Birchwood, and Meaden, 2006) using this emphasis tends to focus on challenging beliefs about the voice's power and where possible to design 'experiments' for the person to try; for example, the person may be encouraged to ignore a threat and then see what happens.

The solution focused approach

From the very first writings by de Shazer (1988) and White (1989) on voices, both have advocated taking a stance of acceptance, not attempting in any way to argue with a person about the existence of voices, but rather to work with these phenomena so they are less distressing or overwhelming for the person.

de Shazer (1988: 140) presents a case of a woman who had heard voices for years, but had recently experienced a great increase in frequency. de Shazer lists the questions he asked as follows:

1   when she did not hear the voices
2   when she did not pay attention to them
3   when she did not argue with them, and
4   when she knew her husband knew that she was not paying attention to them.

His aim, he explained, was to find out what she was doing at such times and then to encourage her to do more of the same. Over a few sessions the frequency of voices went down and the woman was satisfied with the reduced level.

White (1989) describes a case where he had explored evidence of a woman's competence when dealing with the 'harassment' of her voices. He writes about how the voice on one occasion had tried to stop her attending her appointment. He describes how he introduced questions to 'enable her to retrieve the new story', that is, a story of competence and resistance. In a later work, White (1995) describes the importance of working with a person's relationship to a voice, and that often this relationship is one of the voices attempting to control the hearer.

The narrative CBT approach to hallucinations

As elsewhere in this book, our approach tends to draw on solution focused therapy, narrative ideas, and CBT.

The first stage consists of a careful assessment, an attempt to fully understand the client's experiences and ideas concerning what the voices are. Typical questions we might ask are:

- Can you tell me all about your voices (visions, or other hallucinations)?
- Why are your voices a problem for you?
- What is it you like or dislike about them?
- Are there good voices?
- Do you wish to attempt to stop them or rather, develop more control over them or be less distressed?
- What do you think they are? (If no clear ideas are given, we then typically make suggestions; for example, are they spirits, are they from real people, from telepathy, from your mind in some way?)
- How do the voices influence your daily life?
- How do they make you feel?
- When did they begin and how did they develop?

In the assessment phase we also use several measures found in CBT, namely the Beliefs About Voices Questionnaire (Chadwick, Birchwood, and Trower, 1996), and the voices rating scales designed by Hustig and Hafner (1990). We also sometimes give the client a sheet which explores thoughts, feelings, etc. before, during, and after the occurrence of voices (see Appendix I). Not all clients would be willing to fill in such a sheet about voices at the beginning of work, but it can be used at a later stage if needed.

The Hustig and Hafner assessment is a very simple set of scales asking for frequency, loudness, clarity, distress, and ability to ignore. Where voices are the main focus of work, we would tend to use this scale at each meeting with clients. Often we modify the scale to fit the client. For example, one client said that her voices were too frequent and therefore she could not remember a whole week: for this client we asked her to estimate how frequent the voices had been that morning.

In the same way we would investigate the complex formation of delusions, we spend time reviewing aspects of the person's present, aspects of the past, of the time before and during onset, and would use all the questions in the final section of the interview schedule given in Appendix B, that is, on problems in general, goals, and early years. We wish to understand the role and meaning of the voices in the life context of the person. As in other work we would also normally give short questionnaires on anxiety, depression, anger, social difficulties, and self-evaluative beliefs. This sort of complex assessment is particularly needed where there are both delusions and hallucinations entangled in the life of the person.

The initial assessment usually extends over three to four sessions, though it can be less, and ends with an agreement about what to work on. Before proceeding we usually review our notes, and other material, in order to produce a narrative summary or synopsis. We might at this stage consider some possible thematic connections, that is, wonder why this person hears a certain type of voice with certain types of content. Themes emerging at this stage can suggest areas that might be useful to explore more fully when a therapeutic alliance has been established. For example, in a case described later in the chapter, the types of insult heard in the present life of the person suggested possible early trauma. Hardy et al. (2005) looked at types of trauma, the exact content of the voices, and at the general themes of the voices: while very few voice hearers seemed to be reproducing exact memories from traumas they had experienced, a large number of participants did have consistent general themes between traumas and voice themes, in particular of threat and intrusive control.

Another issue to consider at this stage of treatment planning is again to try to work out the client's attitude to change. Is the client enthusiastic, lukewarm, ambivalent? If the client states a wish to change, we accept that and proceed, but proceed cautiously, being aware that doubts on the part of the client may only emerge later.

Another important aspect that needs consideration is how specific coping strategies one might develop with the client will fit or not fit the 'explanatory framework' of the person (Knudson and Coyle, 2002). The latter authors suggest a voice coping method might be abandoned if there is no fit for the person; for example, we have often noted in clinical practice that the voice of a perceived god is very difficult to work with. One client would try out no new methods of coping precisely since this was believed to go against what she regarded as this god's will. A set of explanations or personal philosophy will tend to render some change practices more acceptable than others, as may in fact be the case for any therapeutic intervention. Considerations of a client's attitude to change should begin at this early stage and be returned to throughout one's work as ideas and methods are negotiated.

Therapeutic pathways

For almost all clients our clear preference is to begin work for voices with a solution focused approach as outlined by de Shazer and others. That is, to locate those times and occasions where there are no or fewer voices experienced or where the person feels he or she is coping. However, we think it useful, if appropriate for the person, to mix methods if the person gives few or no ideas. For such a client we then tend to give information about the various standard interventions given in the literature (Nelson, 1997) and ones suggested by research into the nature of hallucinations (Slade and Bentall, 1988) such as the use of vocalisation by reading.

The solution focused coping phase is quite often enough for a client: the client may report being satisfied and does not request further work. Others, however, want to do more. We then try out a range of possible methods.

For some clients, particularly those who have made clear indications that they do indeed wish to review aspects of the past and see this as relevant, we use variations of testimony and past narration therapies. A full example is given later in this chapter.

For some we move from a coping phase to the use of variations of classic cognitive challenging work: that is, we explain the cognitive model, demonstrate the use of thought records and the generation of alternatives, and give writing tasks to do between sessions. (These methods are explained in Chapters 5 and 7.) A core focus of this approach is to challenge noxious and complex meanings a person might hold with regard to the presence of the voices. Included in a cognitive phase might be work with core self-belief, again using methods from Padesky (1994). The client is also asked to note the details of situations where the voices occur, that is, what was occurring before, during, and after an outburst of voice hearing. Such information can then be used for a situational or functional analysis.

Our most recent development has been to use ideas from Gilbert's conception of compassion therapy. This is particularly useful for those clients who engage in a stream of self-attacking statements, or attitudes, whether in the context of the voices or attack by their own thoughts. It is suggested that clients with this difficulty often develop a self-attacking practice from the way they have been treated by parents and others in childhood. We will return to a further explanation in a later section.

Does it work?

The simple answer, to what is in fact a most difficult question, must be: yes, sometimes, in some ways. When we first worked with delusions, voices, and other problems of psychosis in the 1990s we at first assumed voices would be easier than delusions. On the whole we believe that it has turned out to be the opposite. Changing voices can be very difficult indeed. For many, a good outcome is to be able to develop ways of coping so that difficulties do not overwhelm the person's life. For others, the voices greatly reduce, but on the whole, can be re-triggered by psychological and social problems. We have seen very few people who lost their voices altogether; yet we, and others, do not have really long-term data. In spite of these limitations, we believe, however, that work with voices is vitally important, and should be part of a large package of approaches including return to everyday activities such as work and socialising. It is also very useful for some clients to join a network of other voice hearers in order to share experiences and ways of coping.

Richard: voices in context

SFT stage

When I began working with Richard I felt pessimistic: his speech seemed a little distorted, he was reported to often get angry, and he quite quickly began to insist that the neighbours were shouting insults at him, namely, that he was 'backward' and 'bent' (that is, a rather old-fashioned homophobic insult used against gay men) and that what he claimed he knew to be true. A doctor had suggested to him a couple of weeks before our meeting that he might be hallucinating. He got into a temper about this while speaking to me and was obviously going to get angry with me if I went down that route, as he seemed to expect. I told him I wanted to help him cope with the situation whatever was happening, and that I could not know the truth about his neighbours.

For clients who present in this way, angry though perhaps also very fearful, we do not believe the assessment phase should be too extended. I spent just two sessions, very much focusing on the here and now. To ask

Richard for details of his past at this stage might have appeared as 'psychologising' his problems. I decided to start with SFT straight away. As argued elsewhere, SFT allows assessment and intervention to proceed in tandem. If the work went well I would be able to carry out further exploration.

Richard, aged 58, had been diagnosed many years earlier with paranoid schizophrenia and in recent years lived in a series of residential homes: these placements had usually broken down because of the voices he heard and the arguments he had with other clients or staff. He liked his present home very much and wanted to stay. It was a crucial part of my work with Richard that a staff member from the home brought him to the department, attended all sessions, and acted as a liaison.

The SFT proceeded in a standard way. For the hypothetical future question he described a picture of himself doing normal everyday things, getting on with others, being calm. He spontaneously had said that he knew his bad mood contributed to his difficulties. After the break, I suggested he was brave to say this. I asked him and the care-worker to begin recording when voices were not present. It emerged that voices were not heard while at a workshop during the day, and when watching TV, but tended to emerge at the end of the afternoon between 5 pm and 8 pm; if he did not hear them at such times, he tended to go and check by listening to the wall adjoining the house of his neighbours. The work at this stage consisted in suggesting that he engage in activities that he enjoyed, such as TV or music, and in the session spending much time wondering how he coped when he did cope. We also discussed how abandoning this home would not be a solution, and how it would be unjust if he had to move.

Some improvements were reported; I suspect, looking back, that this was not due to any specific technique or intervention, but to the cumulative effect of being listened to, encouraged, of having opportunities to reflect on possible actions, and that it was recognised that he had some strength to cope. There certainly were improvements, but these were at this stage very unstable. This pattern of instability would in fact continue throughout all our work. Given he seemed very well engaged I then decided to offer extended sessions over several weeks.

Core belief stage

The next phase of work, over several sessions, was based on Padesky's approach though considerably modified in that no record of belief percentages was kept and the focus was on what he thought other people to be, or rather, how he had been treated by others. He tended to give different answers to the question 'I prefer to be . . .' and likewise, many to the question 'I prefer others to be . . .'. I decided to condense the themes he mentioned and suggested (but borrowing his own phrases):

- I am someone who takes his time in what he says and thinks.
- I prefer others to have a warm and friendly attitude to me.

One piece of work was to consider his strengths, and for this to be continued and discussed with his residential staff.

The following was brought by Richard to our next session.

Strengths: Able to self-motivate with regard to work, can get up and leave the residence without prompting.

Awareness of what is happening within his surroundings. Example, the home: ability to solve problems as and when they arise within the home, for example changing electric bulbs, fixing faulty door locks, simple woodwork problems.

The understanding of his support needs; for example, Richard understands that he needs to help in drawing up a menu which should consist of a balanced diet, as well as drawing up a shopping list to match the menu. This makes it possible for staff to support him in this area.

We used the 'take your time' idea to discuss various incidents where he might have got angry. In the therapy sessions we would ask and discuss issues such as: Was doing such an action an example of you taking your time? What could you have done instead?

The main focus in this phase, however, was to review who now or in the past had shown 'warmth'. Richard was asked to discuss this with someone he trusted at his home and to get help in writing down his thoughts. At the next session a page of writing was returned; it mentioned three people in his present life with examples. Below is a short extract.

People who have been friendly and warm to me:

Mr N

I have known Mr N for three years. I moved into his home in 1998. He's been very understanding, caring, and very supportive. He knows my problem and he works hard to help me get over it. He always makes an effort to take me to the psychologist whenever there is need.

Mr N takes me to places I want to go. He takes me for a ride in his car and to . . . to have a meal. He also takes me to the head office. I do appreciate what he does for me.

Mr D

I have known D for nearly a year now. He's one of the few people who understands me very well. He's caring and kind. He comes to . . . House to see me often and we have a chat. He helps me to sort out problems over certain issues whenever I complain to him, for instance about how other people treat me and think about me. He does treat me well generally.

Mr P

I was beginning to build up a relationship with P. He was very kind, warm, and very understanding. He used to take me out in the car and do the things that I wanted him to do for me. I wish that he could come back here.

We next began an historic review of who had been warm to Richard throughout his life. It is important to emphasise that from at least session six, Richard had started to describe or mention details of his childhood, and in particular that it had been very difficult. He had outlined that he had been to a boarding school for children with difficulties, and that his mother had hit him often. To such comments I had emphasised that if he wished to talk about past difficulties, then we should make this part of our work together. I was careful to be both accepting and to listen, yet not assume it was the moment to proceed, and if we did, thought that this should be done carefully.

In looking for those who had been warm in the past he gave the following:

- His brother in childhood. He had also recently bought Richard a TV.
- His sister: he remembered her taking him to the railway station when returning to the school.
- He remembered a 'house mother' who had been kind. He had bought her chocolates and she had thanked him.
- A teacher who had patted him on the back and said 'you've done well'.

I found these anecdotal details moving. It points so clearly to the fact that carers and teachers can make a difference to unhappy children: that a simple gesture can last over 50 years.

For the next couple of sessions we again focused on coping. We also started a record of what worked. Richard was asked to record, with the help of a member of staff, if and when he heard voices, what 'method' was used to cope, and a column for 'did it work?' A list of possible methods from all phases of our work was drawn up. Some examples are:

- Not to continue paying attention.
- Watch TV or talk to someone.
- Try counting backward from 100, or reading.
- Remember who has shown warmth and respect.
- Remember insults are not the truth, but a way someone tries to make himself or herself feel better than others.
- Are you being someone who thinks and takes their time?
- Above all to find someone to talk to about any upsetting voices or comments heard.

Trauma work

At the twentieth session we discussed whether it would be a good idea to talk about all the traumas he had suffered as a boy. He was asked to think about this carefully. He decided to proceed.

As described elsewhere, this work I saw as a variation on testimony therapy in that the aim was not reliving, but a narrative overview with some focus on key events. I also wished to narrate exceptions to the story of suffering. The focus on the worse features, in particular being the object of physical attack and mistreatment, took two sessions. Other sessions were focused on schools he attended and events in these years and over his adult life. The core of those discussions was summarised in a letter read, corrected, and reread with Richard. An edited version is as follows.

Dear Richard,

Richard was born in . . . on the . . . of . . ., the year before the war ended. His mother was originally from London but his mother had fled to . . . to avoid the bombing. He and his brother were twins. At the end of the war, his mother returned to London with the twins. When she got back to London she found that her husband was having a relationship with another woman and his mother and father split up.

We tried to find memories of these early years. Richard said that his mother was very difficult. When she thought he had done something she didn't like, she would tend to punish him in a very severe way. For example, she would hit him on the head with her shoe and often this would make him bleed. Sometimes he had to go to hospital for stitches to recover from his wounds. She would shout at him that he didn't belong to her but that he belonged to her husband. She seemed to lose her temper. We can only guess looking back so many years but it seems that she must have been very angry with her husband for leaving her and took out her anger on Richard. She would tend to use very insulting words such as calling his brother a 'cripple' and would say to other people that he was 'backward': when she said that he 'felt the size of his little finger'. He realises now that he must have always felt insecure and insulted by his mother. However, in spite of all this he said that he never stopped loving his mother and made many attempts to have a good relationship with her. Sometimes she did not provide any food for him and on such occasions he and his brother would go for long walks to . . . Often the police would pick them up. This is when social services got involved.

Sometimes he would wet the bed and she would tie the sheets around him. Richard said the children knew they would be punished. Because of all these difficulties, they were placed in a boarding school. As a psychologist I believe children who wet the bed are often terrified.

I asked who had been kind to him throughout his childhood years and he mentioned several people. First, his sister. She used to go and play with him in the nearby field of . . . where he grew up, used to stick up for him when his mother was criticising him and would sometimes take him to the railway station or to the bus when he was going back to his boarding school. He also had good memories of a teacher called Mr . . . who would often pat him on the back and say 'you've done well'. He also had a good memory of his Scottish housemother, called . . . He bought her some chocolates and he remembers her saying 'Thank you very much'.

At 16 Richard went into an independent residential home. Eventually he learnt to work in the hotel trade and did that for several years. Sometimes he'd try and go back and see his mother but she usually didn't want to speak to him. During his twenties he then began to sleep rough. For many years he found it very difficult to settle anywhere and often kept moving and moving to new places. He eventually realised that sleeping rough was hell. For the last few years he has felt very secure in Mr . . .'s residential home. Sometimes Richard hears insults. We have discussed together, myself, Mr . . . and Richard, how there is no need to move just because he might hear an insult. The kind of words these people use just seem to be the kind of silly comment you would hear school boys saying.

The history above is the history of great challenges and difficulties that Richard went through. However, there is another history about Richard. This is the story of someone who always managed to be hard working and do his work carefully and properly. Richard managed never to become someone who took drugs, or resorted to major crime, and generally has led a peaceful life. He was never in prison.

Given how difficult the treatment at home was for Richard, I did wonder with him, how it could be that he still managed to feel love at some times for his mother. He didn't know and I wondered with Richard whether it could be that in the first one or two years, maybe when he was in . . ., at those times his mother was warm and gentle and good to him. Maybe she changed because she became such a disappointed and unhappy woman once she returned to London in those very difficult years after the war when everything was chaos and times were really very very difficult. We forget these days how a single woman would not have been receiving money to help her as they are now, and it must have been extraordinarily difficult to have several children in the 1940s. That said, we have also discussed together how she should never have done these things to Richard, that he never deserved the treatment he got. Richard said that he was always an ordinary boy who tried to do his best. The people around Richard now both at . . ., where he works, and at Mr . . .'s residential home, have confidence in Richard to carry out jobs and do things properly.

Through our work together we have discovered that when he hears insults, the best thing Richard can do is usually just go and talk to somebody he trusts and if nobody is around then to put all his attention on to something interesting, for example on television. Again, if Richard feels irritated by a resident in the home, the best thing is probably to take a deep breath, walk away, and talk to somebody about what is going on before deciding what to do next. In another piece of work, Richard has told me that he would like to be someone who takes their time in what they say and think. He also would like it that other people could have a warm attitude towards him. I am very sure, Richard, that you are well on the way to these things.

All the best in your future.

Over the last few weeks of our sessions (26 in total) the voices greatly reduced, often with none for several days. Furthermore, Richard seemed less bothered by them, and more confident in general. Two years later I saw Richard again. Unfortunately, his home had closed because of contractual difficulties, and he was hearing intimidating voices again in a similar way. We had four sessions in which we re-established all the things we had done before and again the voices stopped.

Reflections on what worked

We can only speculate on what aspects were useful. We were struck, however, by at least four features.

First, establishing a practice of helping Richard in his home situation, in his 'system', seemed to have the most immediate effect. A second major aspect, we believe, was the extended work on Richard's self-narrative in that we explored the meaning of his suffering but also remembered the 'counter-story', the narration of those who had been warm and helpful towards him. A third theme was the constant return to an attitude of doing something, of coping with the problems, in contrast to 'running away' as he had always done. A final major aspect was the establishment of a good alliance in the room with the carer, and myself, and then the establishment of better relations in his home. In point one above we indicated specific actions such as making a suggestion about listening to the radio; here we are emphasising that the interventions helped change his connections to others, that others, for example, would give him support or show care at moments of great insecurity.

There are, of course, many other aspects: we did not, for example, challenge the existence of the voices. It is interesting to note, however, at session 22 he mentioned, after a discussion of his 'urge to move' that 'I'm beginning to think it's part of my illness'. Perhaps he had begun to doubt the voices? This was noted, but we moved on; in retrospect, we think that the right decision, to open up a discussion of 'illness' may have been useful, but equally, it might have backfired, for example by giving a sense of shame at being mistaken.

There was also no attempt to deliver to Richard a definitive 'formulation' as explanation of his symptoms. Rather, as discussed elsewhere, there is an ongoing dialogue of putting events and features in a context. The letter does make some specific links, for example that children who wet their beds might be terrified, but does not suggest he hears voices with this content due to past abuse.

The aim of the letter is, rather, to make his suffering more comprehensible, to put it in a developmental context, but also to underline the other story of doing his best, of at least sometimes being accepted by others.

Hew and visions

Hew reported frequent upsetting voices and visions. He believed that these, on the whole, were manifestations of a 'spirit world'. He had read up on these topics and some years previously had consulted a 'medium'. She had told him that a 'door had been left open' but, very sensibly, that he needed to 'root' himself, and that he should do something like weight-training.

When I met Hew, he had suffered from visual and auditory hallucinations, depression, and social withdrawal for years. He had, however, made attempts sometime before meeting me to get involved in amateur dramatics, but had given up when offered a part. He explained that he thought the voices would 'mix' him up.

In this casework illustration I shall concentrate on the work specifically for 'visions'. The visions had appeared to him as being on objects in his flat, for example the carpet near the TV, on the TV itself, and on his bed cover. The visions were of faces and animals that moved. He thought the things he saw changed, or moved, to 'show it's living'.

The approach I developed for working with Hew's visions could be said to have proceeded mainly on two different but interconnecting levels. One was on the level of specific actions, exceptions, and goals. The other level is harder to describe, but could be thought of as 'orientational', both concerning ideas about the nature of things, but also his attitude to living, coping, commitment, and change.

As stated earlier, Knudson and Coyle (2002) suggest that for coping methods to actually be used, they must, in various ways, 'fit' the interpretative frame of the client. What may have happened for Hew throughout our work was an alteration in the 'interpretative' frame, that is, his constructions or more general ideas concerning hallucinations.

Hew's attitudinal dilemmas could be characterised as follows: one interpretation he was drawn to was that it was important to attend and listen to the voices/visions since they were from spirits. He had wondered for some time whether a dead relative had been trying to contact him. One can speculate, of course, whether this 'role' of being in contact with spirits gave him a sense of purpose; the latter was not discussed with him since I considered that to do so would be to move too fast or would be too far removed from the client's concerns. It is fascinating to note that at one point he said he had had a 'hunger for the voices'.

The new emerging interpretative frame could be described as an attitude that whatever the visions/voices were, he needed to live his own life. Furthermore, though some aspects were positive or important about the voices and visions, he was also angry that the voices could say a comment such as 'go see a prostitute', that they 'nagged him', and that he even heard sometimes the voice of 'Hitler'.

How was the shift in attitude achieved? I believe by simply giving Hew time to discuss these things without myself trying to prove any 'point' to him. The discussion took place, however, in the context of thinking about change. It could be argued that the 'assumption' of our discussions was: so why not change things in your life? The latter was perhaps started by the hypothetical future question and by returning several times to the question of goals.

The other level of work was at the level of specific actions. Exceptions to the problem were as follows:

- He had sometimes coped with visions in the bedroom by moving objects to different positions.
- He had no visions while walking around.
- They were less if he was 'busy' and if he kept up 'good humour'.
- They did not occur in direct sunlight.

The intervention at the level of actions was simply to do more of the above. He got a cotton sheet to cover a specific area around the television. He began to engage in former activities such as reading, going to the gym, learning French, and seeing his sister. The visions stopped. Some weeks later he told me he had removed the sheet and was not experiencing the visions. He also added that he 'didn't care' about them either.

The above approaches were also useful for the voices; in particular, getting involved in desired activities helped to change his relationship to them. Given his apparent ambivalence about the voices, at one point I discussed with him the idea of listening for 15 minutes, but not at other times. This is a technique discussed by Romme and Escher (1993). The effect, however, was that he reported that in the 15 minutes he was getting angry with the things they said, and I think that this anger was important in helping him to change at a more attitudinal level. At the end of the work he reported no visions, fewer voices, and most significantly that he did not feel so distracted or preoccupied with the voices.

Compassion and self-attacking voices

Gilbert and colleagues have described how there are types and possibly different functions of self-criticism (Gilbert, 2005). While some people may dwell on mistakes with the aim of improving performance, might say to themselves something to the effect of 'come on now, try a bit harder', other people engage in a form of self-attack which can involves feelings of hate, sometimes self-disgust, and in the most extreme cases might actually involve a physical attack upon themselves.

We will not here review the emerging theories that attempt to explain these diverse behaviours (Gilbert, 2005). Our clinical observation is that while some people are gentle in their self-criticisms, and only do this occasionally, some clients do engage in various forms of ferocious self-attack and seem to do this nearly all the time. Furthermore, clients seem to regard the way they treat themselves as completely normal, it is the way things are. The apparent purpose suggested by the client might be, for example, to learn or improve, but if we listen to what clients call themselves, the actual words used and the degree of harshness, of hate or disgust, then the severity of this does seem quite shocking on occasions. The attitude to self in such cases does not seem to be one of simply trying to improve competence or other features (though that can be the reason given), but seems to be an attitude that the self deserves to be punished, to be attacked, and perhaps even destroyed. Whatever the immediate declared purposes are for clients, it does seem to be the case that engaging in such self-attack has very detrimental long-term effects, for example it might keep a person depressed, and relevant to this chapter, might have a role in the maintenance of negative voices.

Evidence and observations given by Gilbert (2005) and Lee (2005) suggest that the habit of self-attack might well have its origins in childhood interactions with parents. In the case example below this seemed to be confirmed by the client's description of her childhood experiences. We have noted how a pattern of extreme self-attack does seem to go with extreme mistreatment in childhood, particularly where the child is insulted, 'put down', made to feel inferior. Sometimes this mistreatment might be thought of as one form of emotional abuse.

Research carried out by Birchwood et al. (2002) found that many voices were perceived as powerful, dominant, shaming/insulting persecutors; furthermore, where people experienced themselves as feeling inferior or powerless towards their voices, then these patients were found to experience similar relationships to others in their social worlds.

Gibert and Lee have suggested that in cases where there is powerful self-attack, then the use of basic cognitive challenging often will not be sufficient: clients might understand intellectually that they are not the terrible things they call themselves, but they still feel they are, they just feel they are 'bad' or 'worthless'. Compassion approaches to therapy hope first to develop an attitude or feeling of compassion towards oneself before asking the person to challenge specific ideas or to think of positive alternative perspectives. In the next section we will present a case to show how compassion ideas can be employed with voice hearing.

Elaine

Elaine developed severe depression with psychotic features in her late fifties. She had a range of symptoms including delusions and voice hearing. When

I began to work with Elaine she made great improvement but was still depressed and hearing very persistent negative voices. In contrast to these difficulties, it was clear that there were many sources of support in Elaine's life. She was in a committed and long-term relationship, had many friends, and a wide range of interests.

We began the work with the usual detailed assessments. Besides the tests used, Elaine did writing tasks at home. She was able to provide a page of writing recording what her three voices were saying. The content was generally insulting, giving lots of instructions about what to do. Given her great enthusiasm for music and literature, I asked what art work might express how she felt. Eventually, she suggested the following song by Orlando Gibbons.

> The Silver Swan, who living had no note,
> when death approached unlocked her silent throat.
> Leaning her breast against the reedy shore,
> thus sung her first and last and sung no more.

The metaphors she gave for herself were as follows:

- She felt like a 'yacht with a broken mast on a choppy sea'.
- In a situation the other person seemed 'like an inadequately briefed total stranger with neither the skills nor the interest to try to listen or communicate'.
- 'That things were like a giant net from under which I need to escape with inadequate tools to facilitate the process.'

The metaphors suggest feeling lost, trapped, and somehow an object of indifference to the other.

The work began with solution focused therapy. There were several exceptions to the problem of hearing voices, for example playing an instrument and doing housework, but the most useful with Elaine was the hypothetical future question. She described getting back to her former self, doing interesting activities, being social, but someone now with more confidence.

When asked: Who would first notice? She said her partner, but at this point became tearful. The idea that anyone could notice at all when she was or was not hearing voices was very disturbing to her. We were able to have a useful conversation then about whether anyone could in fact notice, or did in the recent past.

The main outcome, however, of the solution focused phase was that Elaine said she had decided she just must not delay things any longer, that she would take steps to do things, she wanted to get on with her life.

At this stage, she was also asked to record her thoughts, feelings, and activities before any outburst of voices, and record the same during the voices and after. We looked at this together. It suggested voices might be induced when she was upset, or, in particular, where she was 'unassertive', that is, where she felt she ought to have said something but had not.

At the ninth session Elaine reported she was doing well, but in the tenth reported a very distressing week. The basic problem was one of a neighbour leaving a mess due to repairs. Elaine did not express her dissatisfaction, and then found herself crying, upset, and having very attacking voices. I had not been sure about whether to proceed to other work, but realised her capacity for self-attack might need addressing. The work presented here is a version of how Lee (2005) describes her work with self-attack and compassion. The work has several stages and we shall number them for clarity.

First, the basic method of using an automatic thought record was explained and Elaine was asked to complete sheets at home. Second, how Elaine thought and spoke about herself was explored in detail. Some examples were as follows: that she was 'inefficient', 'stupid', 'unreliable', 'useless', 'lazy', 'self-indulgent', 'odd', 'inept'. She used these terms about herself a great deal.

At one point she mentioned that often she was not sure if others liked her. I asked if she thought I liked her. She answered 'probably' given that I did not keep looking at my watch in the sessions. I was struck by how she had to rely on this external behaviour in order to form an idea of how we might be relating to each other.

Third, the next stage was to ask if she had been exposed to a lot of criticism in the past, and did the present reflect the past in anyway? Her mother had, in fact, been extremely critical. She was exposed not only to comments, such as being called 'lazy', but to very threatening statements:

- 'I'll knock you into next week.'
- 'I'll give you a thrashing.'

Excessive physical punishments had also been used. Some episodes of attack or criticism were discussed in detail. On one occasion at the age of eight, Elaine played a violin on stage at school, but a string broke, affecting the performance. When, after the performance, Elaine went to sit next to her mother in the audience, her mother refused to acknowledge her, as if ashamed. Looking back at this time, Elaine said that 'objectively' there was an 'underlying cruelty' displayed by her mother. Other episodes were discussed.

Fourth, for homework, Elaine was asked to summarise episodes and attitudes of her childhood experiences and what in the end this made her 'conclude' or believe about herself. These were as follows:

Examples of criticism

Mother thought physical perfections were paramount.

Everything I did must be done to the best of my ability and even then was probably not good enough.

My opinions are not valid and in any case should not be aired. I should speak only when spoken to. There was a good chance that I'd be put into a home if I did not watch out for my behaviour and then I'd wish I'd never been born.

And to the actual statements 'the conclusions I came to about myself' and 'I was made to believe that' she wrote:

I was on this earth on sufferance only and could unwittingly put a foot wrong.

I was not just physically unattractive but generally unlikeable. I was 'too big for my boots' and my views were both unwelcome and invalid. Even when I had tried very hard at something (a science test for example) a less than perfect mark indicated that actually I had not been thorough enough.

Fifth, Elaine was asked to consider the positive and negative aspects of her mother and father, and, in addition, to consider if she wished to continue to take to herself the same attitudes as her mother. The list suggested many characteristics, but most striking was how her mother had been experienced as harsh and critical. Her father had been warm, but was perceived as not standing up to his wife.

Elaine could easily see similarities in attitudes between how she now treated herself and the attitudes of her mother to her. She was, however, very sceptical as to whether her mother could still be the source of these attitudes after so many years. We decided to leave this open, but proceeded to attempt to change her 'self-attacks'. One useful discussion here concerning connections over time was to first discuss specific ways she had felt that week, and then consider if this was similar to her childhood beliefs about herself. There were some interesting and clear similarities.

Sixth, one of the essential ideas of the compassion approach is that before a person can begin to use cognitive challenging, a shift in fundamental attitude and/or emotion towards the self is required. Some people, when they begin automatic thought records, simply transform the exercise into yet another harsh and critical self-attack. Sometimes, this is not exactly specific words, but an attitude or tone in the way evidence is reviewed. The whole issue of compassion needs to be fully explained at this point such that the client can see how a self-attacking attitude has permeated the person's inner thoughts or inner dialogues of self with self.

A key part of Lee's (2005) approach is to develop compassionate imagery. She suggests asking the person to build, in as much detail as possible, an image of a perfect nurturer. For Elaine the image she developed was of a woman in her forties/fifties, with a 'lively face' and 'smiling' eyes'. The woman would listen, comfort, and probably reach out to touch Elaine.

In addition to an image, I also asked what music Elaine considered might be of such a nature that it could induce a feeling of compassion. At the next session she gave me a tape with four pieces. She told me that before my request she had already thought it would be a good idea to choose the music she wanted for her future funeral. I was a little surprised by this but she reassured me that her choice was not at all morbid, and was music that expressed compassion. One of the pieces was the music mentioned earlier, that is, 'The Silver Swan'.

At this point in our work, Elaine made such progress that she reported hardly having to use either music or images. She told me she had in fact on one occasion used a piece of music by Bach before attempting a reframe of her negative thoughts. She was not sure the music helped since she found it difficult on that occasion to listen to it, yet she moved on to a successful compassionate reframe.

An example of a compassionate reframe is as follows.

Self-attacking thoughts:
He didn't really listen to what I was saying, nor, when it became apparent that he didn't get the message I left on his answering machine, did he even bother to ask whether I had had a particular reason for phoning. I can't imagine that he would be so bored and off-hand with his other friends. It must be something about me. I should have let . . . make the phone call. She has never complained that he seems to want to get off the phone as soon as possible. They often talk for ages. He obviously prefers to talk to her rather than to me.

Source of critical thought and identity of critic?
Me.
Compassionate reframe (music):
'Come unto me all ye that labour' from Handel's 'Messiah'

He may have been very busy but not liked to say so, choosing instead to try to have as brief a conversation as possible, which led to my feeling that he wasn't really listening. He may have been embarrassed into being dishonest in saying that he had not received my 'phone' message, i.e. he may have listened to it and intended to return the call but having not done so straight away, and a week having gone by, leading to my ringing again, preferred to pretend he hadn't got any message. In any event everyone agrees that he always was incredibly self-absorbed and that now that he has been retired for some time he has also become increasingly selfish about putting his own little routine and rituals ahead of anything else, so I need to allow for this.

Extent to which I endorse reframe: 75%
Mood rating (1–100): 70
When we have lunch together on Sunday it is my intention to be as buoyant as possible and certainly I will not raise the subject of our recent telephone conversation, but I suspect that I will need to keep this resolve in the forefront of my mind early on in order to achieve an easy, relaxed attitude in his company.

The results showed a marked improvement and in fact the voices stopped. The questionnaires suggested that Elaine's levels of anxiety and depression fell well below the clinical cut-off points, and she now had lost the negative self-beliefs on the Evaluative Beliefs Scale. It is interesting to note that all these positive improvements occurred in the context of difficult negotiations for Elaine about a forthcoming major surgical operation, and hence, her life certainly had severe pressure at this point. At a follow-up appointment some months later, that is, after her operation, she reported feeling well, was engaged in a range of activities, and most striking, she had not experienced a return of her voices. I spoke to Elaine two years later and she told me her life was going well and the voices had not returned.

OVERVIEW OF THERAPY FOR VOICES

In thinking of Richard, Elaine, Hew, and Ame (from Chapter 5) it appears that what has happened is the following. First, to help some clients what is very useful is to make real changes in their present life, in particular their social life. For Richard this involved setting up a supportive social system. Such social changes may not be possible for some clients (for example

Ame), but where possible at all our work indicates that changing relations in, for example, how a person receives help and care, could be crucial. While compassion was a prominent and explicit feature for Elaine, compassion was also a central feature of the system of help established by the carers of Richard.

A second major feature appears to be the exploration of meanings and narration. It would seem reasonable to suggest that at least three clients were dominated by negative views and narrations of self. Therapy seemed to involve an expression and exploration of these perspectives followed by a slow and tentative discovery of alternative narrations and ideas for the future. While it is conventional in textbooks to separate 'emotions' and 'meaning', this distinction is not clear when in actual work with a person: work with narration was based on meaning, but was very emotional.

A third aspect of therapy for at least two clients (Elaine and Hew) was that during the work they appeared to make a 'decision'. Both declared having made a decision that they did not accept the way things were and now was the time to change. For Elaine the decision seemed to emerge directly after the future focused descriptions. The issue of making a decision to change is, we believe, something crucial for therapy yet difficult to know how it comes about for a person. The hypothetical future question may be one way to induce this in at least some clients.

All cases were, perhaps, vulnerable to future relapse. Given that Elaine had not heard voices for most of her life, however, it seems possible she could again become free of them. For Richard, however, it seems he can be mostly free but only given a certain benign social environment. Ame made the least change and still heard them though infrequently; he was the person for whom social changes were most difficult (and, it must be emphasised, which had already been the focus of a previous therapy).

The aim of this chapter is not, of course, to explore the causation of voices, yet on the basis of our work we would like to make the following observations: for three clients (all except Hew) the voices and their content did not, on the whole, seem to represent specific content (though the words Richard heard perhaps were from insulting episodes) but seemed to represent or express how the person had been 'treated' in the past, that is, how they had experienced key relationships. Richard and Elaine heard critical, insulting, and bullying voices. Ame, in contrast, seemed to hear a sort of nihilistic prediction and content that expressed a sort of utter hopelessness; this too might reflect how he felt treated by his adopted family. In contrast to these very negative experiences, Hew appeared to be fascinated by the special meaning of his voices. Roberts (1992) suggested some delusions come to be a sort of 'purpose' in life for some patients. It appeared that meaning of the voices gave Hew a sense of purpose, that, for example, there was an important message to be heard from a spirit world. Perhaps in the end we might say that voices express in complex ways, aspects of the self that are dreaded but also, sometimes, aspects a person desires. In short, they emerge and fixate themselves within a person's complex system of motivations and social relations.

As we hope it is apparent, we do not have one set procedure for working with hallucinations. A person's needs, goals, attitudes, behaviours, relationships, meanings, etc., all need to be taken into consideration. For some clients a focus on solutions may be sufficient. For others locating the voices in what is often an unexpressed narration of suffering may be necessary. Furthermore, to change voices might involve the clients changing their relationships to other people in general and the self-to-self relationship.

Chapter 9

Movement to recovery and ending therapy

INTRODUCTION

In this chapter we will consider how one might work with clients to help them become more involved in various types of social and other activities. We will then consider some issues that occur during the actual end of therapy and how one might work intermittently over long periods of time.

RECOVERY AND INVOLVEMENT IN THE EVERYDAY WORLD

Potentially throughout our work with clients, but particularly in the last phase, there is a focus on involvement in a wide range of personal and social activities from re-involvement with old hobbies, making steps towards voluntary or paid work, and reconnecting with social networks. In this part of the chapter we will briefly consider research concerning what has come to be called a 'recovery' orientation and how our approach might help a person move towards recovery. Finally, we will consider various social and activity programmes that can be useful in pursuing recovery.

In the opening chapter we speculated on how therapy might work and suggested that we hope to increase the access of positive meaning, but also to help clients build personal and social resources. The activities discussed here, that is, social networks, work and education, interests, and self-care, are fundamental ways we hope of building resources in the lives of clients. The work of building these resources potentially involves the whole psychiatric system and network of family or friends when these exist. We believe, however, that one-to-one therapy can also play an important role in helping clients think about these resources, how they may pursue them, and to tackle problems such as fear and lack of confidence that can block involvement. Further discussion of such issues is found in Gumley and Schwannauer (2006).

Recovery

There are now different meanings and senses of client recovery. One meaning is to simply recover from a symptom, that is, symptom-remission. Another outlook and definition of recovery (Deegan, 1988; Jacobson and Curtis, 2000; Davidson, 2003; Shepherd, Boardman, and Slade, 2008), however, suggests that clients can be in recovery with or without current symptoms. In this sense, recovery involves a range of activities and attitudes aimed at the enhancement of life, self-direction or autonomy, the doing of activities aimed at ameliorating symptoms or coping with difficulties. The attitude of recovery might be thought of as: yes, I am prone to certain symptoms, but I can influence these and get on with a life I wish to have.

In reviewing several definitions, Jacobson and Curtis (2000) suggest recovery can be conceived in the following way: (1) it involves a process over time; (2) each person's recovery is unique; (3) the person is active and takes responsibility; (4) it involves the person making choices about how they wish to live; (5) it involves hope; and (6) a person gains a sense of meaning, of purpose and direction in life.

Davidson (2003) has carried out highly illuminating qualitative work in the area of recovery. Based on phenomenologically inspired interviews with clients attempting to make progress and recovery in the world, he depicts first a very vivid picture of what it is like to be 'inside' schizophrenia, and then in contrast what might occur as a client begins to live on the 'outside' of this condition. He suggests that the process of moving outside involves the following: a rediscovered sense of belonging and hope; the experience of some success and pleasure; the beginning of an enhanced sense of agency and belonging; and finally, active efforts at coping along with greater community involvement.

Therapy and recovery

While a recovery orientation must in some important and deep sense emerge from the client, and cannot be 'imposed' from other people, we hope that several features of the therapy we have described in this book might contribute to a person moving to a recovery orientation, or alternatively, that it is a therapy which a person who already is engaged in the recovery process will find useful.

The solution focused (SF) stage can help in several ways: SF approaches involve an attitude to the client of 'the best ideas come from you'; this attitude, we believe, is one that can promote autonomy and self-direction. Another crucial feature of SF approaches is the use of future focused questions. These promote the development of goals and sometimes a change in attitude such that the person 'decides' to do things. This was clearly shown in the case illustration of Elaine (in Chapter 8). Typical and useful steps begun in the SF phase often involve daily activities and social-ising, that is, involve attempts at getting back into everyday community life. While the SF phase often involves a focus on specific ideas and actions, the core beliefs and narrative phases, we believe, can contribute to recovery by their emphasis on enhancing self-characterisation, and furthermore, a review of the identity of the self over time.

These points are illustrated by the case of David given in Chapter 6. In the SF phase he made a clear and definite decision to get on with things and then carried out specific actions such as doing exercise and phoning a relative. In the narrative phase he began to think about difficult phases of his life in the context of struggles in his childhood and during his teenage years: this we suggest let him think of himself as not just a 'failure' but as someone struggling against enormous difficulties. The core belief stage helped develop a richer and more positive self-characterisation, in parti-cular one of a person who had done well in some areas, at some times, in spite of difficulties. It is interesting to note that after narrative exploration in therapy he made the decision to attempt to 'move on', to not bother about what he had thought his wife might have done. He became more concerned with the present and future.

A great deal of research and clinical observation suggests that recovery involves getting involved 'in the world', or in 'the community'. From our observations of clients over the years, we believe this to be the case. A note of caution, however, is made in the research of Corin and colleagues (Corin and Lauzon, 1992; Corin, 1998). Corin examined clients with long-term diffi-culties who lived in the community, and made a contrast between clients who had frequent hospital admissions, and those with few. She characterised the former as struggling, but failing, to achieve very conventional roles of work and family life. In contrast, some of the non-hospitalised participants, but ones with symptoms, had developed what she termed 'positive withdrawal'. These participants were not so much interested in conventional jobs and family life yet saw themselves as engaging in important projects of personal development or of a philosophical and/or religious type. Some participants put great importance on friendship, and some saw themselves as having a valued network of people seen in daily community life such as the staff in cafes. The findings of Corin apply to clients suffering chronic symptoms, and therefore not necessarily to those who make a full symptom recovery within two or three years, or who live most of the time, besides the occasional relapse, without significant symptoms.

Putting Davidson's and Corin's work together, it seems reasonable to suggest that for most clients, most of the time, recovery and well-being involve substantial involvement in work, other people, meaningful activi-ties, while for a small subset of persons there is an active choice of an alternative and distinctive lifestyle of 'positive withdrawal'. The latter, Davidson points out, also finds a parallel in the wider community, for example in the lifestyle of those who choose to live in isolated regions or in monasteries and other types of retreat and sanctuary.

AN OVERVIEW OF TYPES OF ACTIVITIES

What aspects of community living or activities do we encourage clients to get involved in? In this section we will discuss activities we regularly focus on, and mention some we have read about and that have been developed in diverse services and in different parts of the world.

Much of our work, at all stages, is directly aimed at both helping clients overcome obstacles, such as fear of involvement, and sometimes helping clients discover or rediscover motivation, potential skills, and forms of knowledge. Often we ask clients to get involved in activities which are already potentially available in their world: for example, to rebuild a friendship which may have been strained during the onset of psychosis or to improve desired family relations. Sometimes, however, some clients will need more support and help to initiate activities: this support can be something quite minimal, such as a suggested visit to a specific library, but may sometimes involve a full community based programme. We will mention some interesting examples of the latter.

The social world

All phases of therapy potentially involve a focus on changing social inter-actions and almost all clients make attempts in this area. This may not be the case for some clients, as Corin's work suggests, and one case presented in this book might be Ame in Chapter 5 who stated he really did not wish to socialise at all.

There are now several initiatives, in different countries, to develop services to help clients with social relations. The best known are those services and therapies which can help with family problems, for example services aimed at reducing 'expressed emotion' (Bebbington and Kuipers, 1994). Green (2003) makes the point that while such services may be useful, many services do not routinely give advice to families about things that they should or could do as opposed to things families should stop doing. The carers Green interviewed reported developing strategies on their own, and not receiving wanted feedback on whether these were considered appro-priate. Of course, professionals likewise might not know, but it seemed from this research that such carers would at least appreciate some coopera-tive open discussion about the everyday solutions they had developed for crises.

A considerable percentage of clients with psychosis are also parents. Research by Evenson, Rhodes, Feigenbaum, and Solly (in press) suggested that this role provided a deep sense of purpose and satisfaction for fathers, yet also involved many worries and stresses. A similar pattern for women has also been reported. Several of the clients in this book were parents, in particular Jack for whom family relations were central (Chapter 4), but also David, Mary, and Rosa. With the first three of these clients our therapeutic work focused directly on ameliorating family relationships and helping the client with self-esteem concerning their roles.

The research by Evenson et al. noted how, on the whole, official services seem quite blind to the fact that so many clients have children. Some participants stated that when hospitalised, they did not want children to visit given the unpleasant nature of some wards. Evenson et al. suggest hospitals could help by setting aside protected space for such visits.

Jack suffered from a very profound sense of failing and over time his increasing doubt had led to less and less involvement with his family. A crucial part of our work was to turn this around, to help him see that he had an essential contribution to make for his children and ex-wife, who had stated she wanted his continued involvement as a parent. We suggest that if clients have children, then this area can be one of great importance and may, as was the case for David, be something that can be explored as an area of strength, or perhaps better here, of noteworthy contribution in the person's life.

Intimate sexual relationships are central for many clients, yet such topics are rarely addressed (D'Ardenne and McCann, 1997). McCann (2000), however, investigated how clients experienced attempts at direct counselling on these issues, and found no increase in symptoms, and that such discussions were welcome. Three clients in this book had particular difficulties with their partners (Rosa, Lesley, and David). Lesley began a sexual relationship during our work: it was striking how her self-esteem led her to doubting her partner's motivation (her attitude at first was 'he only wants me for sex since he can find no one else'). There were several discussions around the evidence which suggested whether he really wanted her or not, if he was in fact 'disgusted' with her body or not. Drawing on both her positive data log concerning her preferred self and the work on seeing alternatives to her delusion was crucial in the slow building up of her confidence in exploring this new relationship. This specific relationship in fact ended during our work: it was gratifying to see that she did not collapse, stated she could be happy with or without a partner, and in fact started another relationship a few months after which has now continued for several years.

Where possible, re-establishment of old friendships and acquaintances can be very enabling for clients, and formed part of the work for Jack (Chapter 4), Lesley and Betty (Chapter 5), and David (Chapter 6). Clients may abandon friendships for many reasons, particularly following a dramatic onset of psychosis. There are certainly great barriers for clients in reconnecting or making new friendships, not least the problem of stigmat-isation. Again, however, self-esteem plays an important role.

Developing new friendships may be an area where there is a great need for community programmes. One such initiative has been developed by Larry Davidson (2003), who describes how he and colleagues have devel-oped a project for 'supported friendships', that is, where a person with long-term psychotic symptoms is paired with either recovered clients or non-patients. Data from their research suggest that these initiatives have been greatly welcomed and made important differences to the lives of clients.

Work and education

If a client shows some interest, we cautiously encourage clients to look for voluntary work, for paid work if feasible, or for involvement in educational programmes. As stated, such activities will not be suitable for all clients as Corin's research on social roles and systems of personal meanings indicates. Casper and Fishbein (2002) examined self-esteem and work: their research showed that work only helps self-esteem if the work is experienced as satisfying and successful. Not just any work will do, and they note that some clients have self-esteem without work.

Ideally clients organise such initiatives themselves. However, there are in many local areas diverse supported programmes that can be of great help in this process. Diaz, Fergusson, and Strauss (2004) describe a fascinating project in Colombia where clients first attend a rural centre involving therapy and work, and later attend an urban centre. Of particular interest was the time and care given to negotiating with potential clients their involvement, a process that could be extended over months. Attendance is voluntary, and might continue for many years. On the basis of interviews they suggested that a turning point for many clients was a change in meaning such that the clients saw that they needed to do activities that were intrinsically beneficial for themselves. The change in meaning, however, was often not one of accepting a conventional psychiatric explanation of their difficulties, but often arose as a transformation within their own meaning system. Once work was started, and if meaningful, then work provided a sense of purpose, contribution, and independence.

In our clinical work we have made considerable use of a local initiative in supported education: some clients enter any courses they like, and have access to counselling in the college as appropriate. The more intensive alternative programme, however, is a specific year-long course for clients with more extreme difficulties. The classes involve, among other things, computer skills, communication, and the use of video. An evaluation suggested positive effects (Isenwater, Lanham, and Thornhill, 2002).

Self-care

Besides clinical observation and reports from clients that exercise is experienced as pleasurable and useful in diverse ways, there is also systematic research suggesting benefits from such activities (Ellis, Crone, Davey, and Grogan, 2007). It was very striking how David (Chapter 6) began by doing sit-ups and press-ups, eventually going for an early morning walk of one and a half hours.

There are, of course, a multitude of ways of gaining the benefits of exercise. Some clients have reported the benefits of dancing: Betty and Lesley (Chapter 5) both went to local groups for traditional American line dancing and enjoyed this enormously. It occurred to us at the time that the structure and socialising involved in such types of dancing might also have contributed to its success.

We suspect that all traditional and conventional activities aimed at enhancing mental and physical well-being can be useful for clients with psychosis: for example, better diet (Hallahan and Garland, 2005), massage, yoga, tai-chi. Ideally these sorts of service would be available to clients in supported contexts but also in the non-psychiatric services of the local community. We have encouraged attending meditation classes for some clients and Chadwick (2006) suggests this may be useful for psychotic clients.

Independent interests (skills and knowledge)

In becoming ill, many clients give up interests they have enjoyed. Where possible, we suggest re-engagement in these. Some clients, when asked how they might live, express an interest in new activities. Again, we encourage these where possible.

The range of interests is, of course, completely open and where possible it is useful for clients to use normal community resources for learning and practice. There are many fascinating programmes. Bizub, Joy, and Davison (2003) report on how involvement in learning to ride and care for horses has strong psychosocial benefits.

Many clients report great interest and benefit from engaging in learning and producing various forms of artistic activity. Tolton (2004) gives a fascinating first-person account of how he uses poetry both to express himself and even to contain the beginnings of what he sees now as delusional thinking.

For some clients there are enormous benefits from attempting to write short or extended biographies. We are at present working with a woman (not reported here) who suffered multiple abuses, and who on her own initiative set about writing an account of these years during a period she was in hospital. She reported this was a breakthrough in recovery for her.

There may be a multitude of reasons why sustained interest in, and practice of, skilful activities may have benign effects, for both clients with psychosis and people in general. Csikszentmihalyi (1997) has investigated over many years how people experience activities and argues that in certain conditions a person will experience 'flow'. Flow is said to be a state in which a person experiences a challenge, yet manages to produce a skilled performance. Typically people feel content, even joyful, and fully absorbed in such activities. He suggests that the state of flow involves a certain 'order' in a person's mind, as opposed to being in a distracted and disordered state. If anxiety and psychosis involve 'disordered' mental states, often with poor skills of attention, then the deliberate practice of flow-orientated activities may produce a form of benign order. It is noteworthy that Elaine (Chapter 8) reported no voices during the practice of a musical instrument. Lesley (Chapter 5) took up visual art and reported great satisfaction and that it allowed her to express herself. Ame had had before his breakdown a great interest in classical music; in our meetings he was encouraged to attend free concerts and to listen to music again at home.

Csikszentmihalyi gives an anecdote of a psychiatrist investigating types of activity and levels of flow. One client had most flow when manicuring her nails. They suggested she had training in this craft and report that she went on to use this in employment. Forms of art and craft are, of course, employed in various types of therapy; we are suggesting here that art in itself is beneficial and perhaps in ways we have not yet fully appreciated or researched.

Orientation to values and purpose

It is, of course, not our aim to influence the philosophical or religious orientations of clients. These issues, however, in diverse ways can arise, and may then become a direct part of the therapy itself. In general, we try to think with clients within their own frames of reference.

Religious and spiritual meanings, we believe, can make both negative and positive contributions to how clients interpret their situations and subsequently how they live. One possible striking and negative consequence of religion, for example, is that some clients come to believe that they are damned, as did Jack in Chapter 4, or they fear that the god they believe in must have sent the illness as a punishment. In general, it can be useful to ask such clients to discuss this with an appropriate, sympathetic, and non-pathologising expert in that religion. For example, most knowledgeable Christians would argue, we believe, that suffering on earth is not in any way linked to one's moral status, so the fact that one is ill does not show the person has transgressed the tenets of the religion.

If a client clearly has a certain commitment to a religious belief system, be it Christian, Islam, Buddhist, Hindu, then it can be useful, if appropriate, to invoke the positive aspects of these systems, indicated by the clients themselves perhaps at other times, to emphasise that life has purpose in spite of suffering and setbacks. For those without a religious framework, the theme of punishment as sent by a deity does not usually arise, though the problem of purpose in the face of suffering can arise in the same way as it does for the religious. The simplest response in dialogue with the non-religious is often to point out that the contribution such persons make to the lives of others is seen as having distinct value and purpose, and that the clients themselves have indicated values and purpose in their lives and might experience these again when in better times. Again it can be useful here to list areas of success or intrinsic value that the client has indicated in solution focused work or in the development of a narrative.

Clients with psychosis, like everyone else, want value and purpose in their lives. Finding and maintaining a sense of 'worth' is a central challenge for clients with long-term difficulties (Barham and Hayward, 1998). It is very difficult, as Estroff (1999) argued, for clients to take up the position of 'I have schizophrenia' as opposed to 'I am schizophrenic'.

It can be very useful to discuss with clients their values, what they care about (Frankfurt, 1988), what sort of things they would appreciate in their lives in the future. This process is often begun in the solution focused phase when asking clients to describe a hypothetical future. This question can, however, reveal glaring gaps for a person; for example, they have never considered how they would like life to be.

The process of constructing with clients a life narrative also helps in clarifying values and how a person wishes to live. By strongly remembering times before psychosis colonised their lives, clients can remember interests and aspirations. Having a sense of who one was can help construct a future narrative of who one might be. Great caution and realism must, however, be practised in any discussions in these areas. Many clients have experienced enormous losses over the years, and do find it extremely difficult to be accepted by the conventional world. Perceptions of 'stigma', lack of opportunity, and hostile rejection are not 'paranoid', persecutory ideas.

The despair of clients concerning their lives can emerge spontaneously in a session. That is, we have found such topics emerging without explicit questioning. Our basic approach has been to listen, to allow the clients to fully express themselves without our making any facile attempts at saying, 'but you have X, Y, and Z'. Knowing a client, one can, however, usually find some area where they matter for others or for something, where their presence is appreciated. We also believe strongly that 'success' cannot just be found in conventional paid employment and conventional family arrangements, and certainly not in having expensive material possessions. We might at least offer to clients these considerations, and might wonder with clients whether there is both meaning and pleasure in appreciation of simple everyday beauty of, say, the sky outside the office window and in the simple appreciation of being alive itself.

ENDING REGULAR THERAPY

The structure of ending

When the therapist feels that treatment is coming towards the end phase it is important to discuss this with the client and to come to a collaborative decision about how this will be managed. Our realisation of the importance of these factors was heightened by the case of a man we saw at the beginning of our work with psychotic clients. We worked with him on a weekly basis for an 18-month period. He continually heard voices telling him that he was to be killed and tortured. He avoided going out on the street as much as possible due to this and he had virtually no social or family contacts. At follow-up he told us that the experience of ending therapy had been particularly traumatic. He had had weekly sessions with his therapist and had had the opportunity to discuss his problems at length. Some of the sessions had been held in local cafes and the behavioural experiments had involved trips to art museums and other locations, so that therapy had involved a considerable amount of interpersonal contact. After the end of therapy he had continuing contact with a busy case manager but on a less frequent basis. These meetings had largely focused on issues of medication compliance. As the therapist had left the service in this case it was not possible to offer any further contact at the end of treatment.

A planned end is therefore advisable. One should raise the issue of ending some time prior to the end of treatment, that is, some months in the case of a long-term therapy. It is important to have a conversation with the client about this issue so that they are included in the process. One can be clear that the therapy cannot go on forever but ask the client how long they feel it would be good to have to round up the therapy. This process of negotiation can be important in giving the client a sense of control. Therapy for some clients with psychosis could probably usefully be continued indefinitely. Deciding when to end usually is a balance between having completed the work described in the body of this book and service availability.

The meaning of the ending and interpersonal beliefs

The attempt to review the person's narrative of their life, or their dysfunctional interpersonal core beliefs, continues until the very last session. The ending phase is a useful opportunity to revisit issues discussed during the core beliefs stage of the therapy that relate to previous endings in the client's life. Indeed, during this phase of the treatment certain core beliefs may be activated which have not been active at previous stages of the therapy. For example, the person may have a core belief concerning abandonment, and see themselves as unlovable and others as abandoning. This could become activated in the therapy: the client feeling abandoned and the therapist being perceived as abandoning and uncaring. Sometimes clients will defensively minimise the importance of the therapy. These schemas can be described and worked with in the manner described in the chapter on working with core beliefs (Chapter 5). In addition to attempts to modify these core beliefs it can be particularly useful to simply describe and discuss how the client is interpreting the current ending. Often the client will need to be prompted to talk about these issues. It is a useful strategy to look out for spontaneous opportunities to discuss these topics. Examples of this include the client discussing other issues that have themes of loss or abandonment or ending. The meaning should be explored, when the opportunity arises, in terms of its meaning in the present but the client can also be asked if it brings back previous endings or losses. On the other hand, some clients with psychotic symptoms have a great deal of difficulty in forming attachments to others and their experience of the therapy will have been very different (that is, they formed very little attachment to the therapist). This is, of course, also an opportunity, if thought useful, to explore the client's core beliefs.

The particular meaning of the ending for the client should be identified rather than making one-size-fits-all assumptions. The importance of addressing negative features of the therapy is illustrated by the following case.

Bill: case illustration

Bill had largely negative and unresolved feelings about his father. His father had been critical and harsh: Bill engaged in a similar process with himself and this produced negative feelings concerning his self-worth. In terms of core beliefs he had two alternating schemas of himself in relation to others. The first was of himself as an inadequate failure and others as harsh critics. The second was of himself as a victim and others as persecutors. Preoccupation with the second belief seemed to have the effect of avoiding the first belief. These core beliefs or schemas had not been manifest in our therapy relationship, which had been almost exclusively positively coloured. There was a strong sense that the client wanted to maintain an idealised relationship with the therapist. As negative roles had not been enacted in the therapy it did not seem appropriate to directly address them at the end. Here we dealt with the ending by emphasising the progress he had made and avoiding any suggestions that the therapy had been anything other than helpful. Although he improved during treatment and this continued for over a year, he later had a further breakdown and did not contact the therapist. We hypothesised that this could have been because he was afraid to report that he had not continued to do so well. If we had addressed aspects of the therapy that had been less than perfect this might have allowed him to return after his breakdown.

The therapist should be guided by the client's responses in this area. The idea here is not to suggest to the client that they were more attached to the therapist than they were aware of. Rather, the point is to acknowledge the potential importance of the relationship. This can involve a discussion of why the therapy was not ideal or why it might not have changed all that the client had wished for.

If the client's responses indicate that they are unaware of the importance of their relationship to the therapist, how one responds will depend upon a number of factors. First, if the therapy has been short it may not be important to pursue this matter. If, however, one has seen the client for a considerable period of time it can be helpful to indicate the possibility of the importance of such a relationship, rather than insisting that the relationship was important. It can be useful for the client to be aware that the therapist is thinking about the importance of the relationship even if clients are unaware of it themselves. So, for example, with a client who seems oblivious to any importance in the relationship, one can note that the client and therapist have met for some time and wonder why the client is not going to miss the opportunity to talk. This can lead back to a discussion about core beliefs. This needs to be judged on the individual case. The core beliefs that are likely to arise include those relating to trust, intimacy, commitment, care, abandonment, autonomy, and connection versus isolation. At its best, therapy will have helped a client to change their social world such that there are now opportunities to interact, be with others, and therefore find within their own social lives replacements for the interactions of therapy.

Expression of feelings concerning the ending

In addition to exploring the meaning of the ending of the relationship by looking at core beliefs or narratives it is also important to allow time and space for clients to express their feelings about the ending. The degree to which this happens varies considerably. Many clients find it difficult to express or even acknowledge their feelings. It is useful to talk about this process in a way that connects with the experience of the client. Some clients, as stated, do not feel particularly sad or distressed about the ending and will have experienced little attachment to the therapist. On the other hand, sometimes clients will appear not to be distressed, as they want to avoid their feelings. Exploring why this is difficult can be a productive line of inquiry in this situation.

Difficult endings

A number of factors can lead to difficult endings in therapy. For example, the client may drop out of therapy early, or fail to engage very early in treatment, or the client may drop out because of difficulties in their relationship with the wider team. Alternatively the client may be very resistant to ending therapy.

Early dropout

Clients drop out for a number of reasons. The client may develop paranoid ideas about the therapist, or may have little interest in engaging with the therapist, or may lose interest in working with the therapist. It is important in these cases to handle the disengagement in the most constructive way possible. It is useful to consider that the work might be the first attempt to engage the client in therapy in what may turn out to be a number of attempts. If clients are left with a positive feeling about the end of treatment they may be more likely to re-engage at a later stage (see the case described below). It is important to regard the decision about whether to continue treatment or not as the client's decision, but also to be positive about potential benefits.

Losing interest in treatment

The various difficulties people with psychosis suffer make it hard for them to form relationships with other people, as stated, and can make contact with others aversive. It is probable that many clients never enter into psychological treatment for these reasons or drop out very early. Some clients will not attend any therapy at all, but most clients once they have begun treatment will want to continue in therapy. Therefore if the client begins to lose interest it is important to investigate why this is the case. The issue of a basic difficulty in relating to another person can emerge after therapy has proceeded for some time. It can, for example, be difficult to engage with the material that the client brings, or the client talks very little, or the client talks around the point of real concern and listens little. It is important to be as aware of these issues in clients who are dropping out later in therapy as it is in the engagement phase. If one feels it hard to respond to the clients empathically this may signal a difficulty of the clients in relating to others in general or that there may be a specific difficulty in the interaction of the specific therapist/client pair.

Paranoid reactions

Some clients become suspicious or develop frankly paranoid ideas about the therapist. Sometimes the therapist is incorporated into the client's delusions. It is most useful, in these cases, to think about this as an example of the difficulty that the client has in relating to other people. It is an example of what goes wrong in the interpersonal life of the client.

William

William was a 50-year-old man who believed that there was a long-standing conspiracy against him, involving continual surveillance by the health service. He had worked for a health authority many years before but had been sacked due to an assault on a client. He was currently working, had a partner and children, so in many ways he functioned at a high level, but he had few close relationships, and interpreted most of what happened to him through the glasses of his delusion. Shortly after he began therapy he interpreted a comment made during an evening class as indicating that the therapist had communicated information he had discussed in the previous session to the teacher, and that this indicated that the therapist was involved in the conspiracy to monitor him. Here the therapist is in the unfortunate position of falling into the category of suspected persons before the therapy had really got under way. This reaction, which led him to abandon therapy, despite our best efforts to keep him in, was simply an example of what occurred for him all the time in relationships with others. He was fortunate in that it did not generalise to all his relationships.

In this case the therapist stated that he had not communicated with the evening class teacher and spent the rest of the session encouraging the client to talk and empathising with his distress. Even if clients drop out it is important to convey that one would be happy to have them return to therapy in the future. The point here is to leave clients with the idea of a therapist who has not responded with hostility or defensiveness to their accusations or decision to drop out of therapy, and which may allow them to return. It is one of the most important reasons for not having a dual role with a client of being a case manager and psychiatrist.

Deterioration in the relation with the wider team

A particularly difficult, although fortunately rare, problem occurs when clients' relationship with the wider team deteriorates to the extent that they disengage from the wider service. Again it is useful to see such deterioration as a reflection of clients' difficulties in maintaining interpersonal relationships, and as an example in the therapy of what probably goes on all the time outside of the therapy. If it is possible to rescue the therapy relationship this may have implications for clients' wider relationships. In such cases of conflict with a team and when the client wishes to remain in therapy there is a dilemma for the therapist. The client has developed trust in the therapist, engaged in the therapy, and perhaps in some way finds it helpful. However, if the client decides not to see the rest of the team this puts the therapist in a difficult position. If the client only sees the therapist then the responsibilities of the mental health service will default to the therapist. The therapist will be the primary person responsible for ensuring that the client is safe. This, of course, radically changes the nature of the contact with the therapist. It is important to consider whether it is possible to continue with the client under these circumstances. If the therapist feels it is not possible to continue seeing a client, then it is best to openly explain one's concerns to all involved and hope therapy can be restarted after some time in better circumstances.

Letters of farewell

Towards the very end of therapy in many cases we write a simple letter saying goodbye. The letter can be written in many ways but usually includes the following: a summary of the presenting problem and a summary of the changes that have occurred and steps taken. It can also include details of how the person might continue to take steps in the near and distant future. If not done already, we might put in details, where genuine, of how we have appreciated our time with the client.

Connecting to the future

In the final sessions of treatment it is important to revisit clients' goals for the future. A good way to do this is to ask clients what are the most important things that they have achieved in therapy. After one has a list of the most important achievements one can think with the client about how these achievements can be maintained and taken forward. What would the client like to have achieved in a year's time? What are the steps in making that achievement? The aim here is to draw out a detailed plan that the client could follow to achieve these goals. If the client suggests an unrealistic goal we tend to focus on the first few steps of achieving the goal. Obviously clients have to generate their own goals but it is helpful if they can include the continuation of some type of constructive activity and some type of social activity as we discussed earlier. We prompt the client to check if these types of goals should be included in their future plan.

Relapse prevention

If not done already in therapy, in the ending phase it can be useful to consider a simple relapse prevention plan. The best is where the client takes complete responsibility for developing this and keeping it available for use. A good plan might include a simple listing of any changes that have occurred with some regularity in the past and which have usually occurred before a resurgence of symptoms. The plan also needs to include what might be done in such a situation; for example, it might suggest that the client seeks out a particular friend or relative who is good to talk to in such situations. It might suggest that the client takes a 'break' from stressful activities and increases activities such as relaxation and exercise.

Intermittent therapy

There can be many patterns of therapy over time. For some clients, the work begins, proceeds, and ends; follow-ups are rare and only occasional. However, for some clients, therapy might have to start several times before there can be a long period of sustained engagement. For other clients, the main body of work might occur during the beginning period, but there is a pattern of intermittent therapy, that is, there may be many months, if not years, between periods of work. Intermittent work of this kind was particularly useful with Richard (Chapter 8). The main body of work was the second time the client had been referred. The client's symptoms became bothersome when there had been a major change in his residential situation. The latter booster sessions simply aimed to reinstate the previous useful arrangements and as described, worked quickly and well. When symptoms have been stable for long periods of time, and then flare up again, it is always worth checking carefully the living arrangements of the client, particularly those in residential settings where the turnover of staff can have a serious impact upon the well-being of the clients.

Substantial work followed by intermittent booster sessions as required can be a very useful and satisfying way of working for both the client and therapist. It is, of course, only possible if the therapist has stayed a long time in one post and if the organisational structures allow such intermittent work.

CONCLUDING COMMENTS

Clients with psychosis can be difficult to work with for many reasons; however, they can also be as cooperative as any other type of client and can often be fascinating individuals. Many therapists approaching this area for the first time might profit from an honest consideration of their own stereotypes and prejudices concerning persons with psychosis. Many therapists, we suspect from occasional comments, assume that all psychotic clients have extreme symptoms all the time, cannot communicate, and are similar to the clients seen on the streets engaging in disturbed behaviour such as shouting at strangers. This is a highly distorted picture of the nature of psychosis. These states do occur, but not for most clients most of the time. Clients with psychosis are also responsible partners, continue with a range of responsible jobs, and make contributions in many ways just like everyone else.

Working with psychosis: initial assessment guidelines

Pre-assessment issues

Be prepared to have a series of meetings with a vague agenda, or no agenda at all, if this helps to develop rapport.

- Did the client understand the referral? Was it properly discussed with the client?
  Are they coming against their will?
- Does the patient have an 'agenda' so at variance with 'therapy' that the meeting should stop?

Note: one must be professional, considerate, respectful, attempting to put the person at ease, yet also very flexible, e.g. to have a very short meeting if necessary.

Possible areas to explore:

- What problems, concerns, do they have now? (Explore events, thoughts, emotions, motives, and needs. Check for any other problems.)
- What would they like to change in their life?
  Obtain a full description of any phenomena. (Try not to make assumptions, e.g. what words mean, what concepts involve.)
- What happens in the problem situation (before, during, after)?
- When did it start?
- What was happening before?
- What relationships did the person have in his or her family, school, or at work?
- What intimate relationships have there been? Any now?
- Who is in the person's world?
- How hopeful is the client? (About change, about solving the problem.)
- What are the person's strengths, values, resources?
- What have they managed to cope with and survive?
- What is the person doing most of the time?

- What is the client's education and work history?
- How did the client experience school and the peer group?
- In very general terms, what was their childhood like?
- When X occurs, how do they feel?
- When else have they felt like this?

Explain what a metaphor is: how would you describe your feelings?

Note any spontaneous metaphors used to describe problems, goals, etc.

Review results of any tests, e.g. on depression, anxiety, self-esteem.

Consider symptom-specific measurements (e.g. see Chadwick, Birchwood, and Trower, 1996).

Therapeutic alliance

- What is it like being with this client?
- What does the client look like?
- Write down in detail how the session began, from meeting the client in the waiting room. How do they behave?
- What does the client spontaneously talk about, ask you, etc.?
- How do you feel with the client? Are you e.g. interested, on edge, find it difficult to understand what is happening?
- How does the client communicate with you?
- What are you like with this client?
- How does the client talk/behave?
- What interaction patterns occur between you and the client?
- How does the client see you?
- Are there several states-of-the-person which manifest themselves? Can you describe these? What seems to be his/her attitude to you?
- Are any cultural/sociological expectations influencing how you perceive this client?
- Do you get through what you plan to do?
- If not, why not?
- Do you think you understand the background of the client?
- Are tasks agreed and done?
- If not, why not?

Appendix B

Interview schedule for problematic beliefs

(There are four sections: questions should be used flexibly and varied according to the language and attitudes of the participant.
NB. Questions with an asterisk are the most important.)

A Problematic beliefs

1* (In some cases where the therapist knows the client, a possible question might be . . .)
    We have sometimes discussed your belief that X, could you summarise your ideas again for me about X in as much detail as possible, concentrating on what is happening at the present time?
    (In other cases the therapist will know there may be a problematic belief from case notes or other comments by others. A possible question might be . . .)
    I have been told by your key worker that you are very concerned about X, could you tell me as much as possible about this?
2   (Often an important feature or object is mentioned, e.g. insects. Try to explore the connotations of this object O.) Can you describe this object? Anything else?
3   What effect is the O having upon you?
4   How is it (are they) doing that?
5   What do you think this O is trying to achieve?
6   With regard to X, how will it turn out in future?

B Belief formation

1* When exactly did the above events and changes first begin? What was happening?
    How did you come to realise that this was going on?
    And what happened next? (And next etc., i.e. trace out the exact perceptions and thinking of the person.)

Was anything making you unhappy at that time? (Review the year before onset.)

2   In general, what was going on in your life?
3   When you came to believe X, what did this tell you about the world?
4   When you came to believe X, what did this tell you about yourself?

C Personal life

1   What experiences or thinking has occurred recently to make you think that X is still true? (Try to find out exactly what the person experiences.)
2   Because of X, have you had to change the way you live in any way and what are those changes? (For example, in the way you behave, or think or feel, or what you do during the day.)
3   When do you tend to think about X most?

D Personal goals and difficulties

1* What do you consider to be the main problems/difficulties in your life now?
2   What problems/difficulties have you had over long periods of your life? (Probe: others?)
3   (This question should summarise what state/goal the person is trying to achieve or would like.) How would you like your life to be?
4   What would you like to change about yourself?
5   What blocks or gets in the way of you achieving these goals/activities?
6   How was your childhood; in particular, what were your mother and father like?
7   What were your teenage years like?
8   What good feature or strength do you consider yourself to have?

Rating scales for delusions

(Adapted from scales originally developed by Chadwick, Birchwood, and Trower, 1996)

Conviction scale (in words)

Belief

1	2	3	4	5	6	7	8	9
Absolutely certain it is false	Almost certain it is false	Doubt a lot	Doubt a little	No idea if true or false	Believe a little	Believe a lot	Almost certain it is true	Absolutely certain it is true

Preoccupation

Please state which of the following best fits the way you thought during the last week.

1   Over the past week I did not think about my belief.
2   Over the past week I thought about my belief a few times.
3   Over the past week I thought about my belief once a day.
4   Over the past week I thought about my belief more than once a day.
5   Over the past week I thought about my belief almost all the time.

Emotional distress

Please state which of the following best fits the way you felt during the last week.

1   Thinking about my belief does not make me emotionally distressed.
2   Thinking about my belief I get a little emotionally distressed.
3   Thinking about my belief I get fairly emotionally distressed.
4   Thinking about my belief I get very emotionally distressed.
5   Thinking about my belief I get extremely emotionally distressed.

Examples of solution focused questions

Goals

- How will you know when the problem is finally over?
- Who will be the first to notice that you have moved towards your goal?
- How will (your partner) know when the jealousy problem is solved? What will be the first small sign that the problem has been resolved?

Exceptions

- Is there a time when (the complaint) does not occur, or occurs less than at other times?
- Does anything work to stop this problem (or make it bearable, or shortens the time)?
- How do you cope?
- When does your daughter/partner/friend listen to you?
- Have you noticed a time when Fred is able to play with other children without fighting?

This can be followed by:

- What's different about these times?
- What do you do differently?
- Who else is involved and notices these differences?
- How could more of that happen? How do you explain these differences?
- How did you get that to happen?
- Have you ever solved a problem like this in the past?
- Was there a time when X didn't happen when you expected it to happen?

Rating scales

If 1 is equivalent to when your voices are at their worse, and 10 would be life without this problem:

- Where are you now?
- What needs to happen so that you move from 4 to 5?
- How confident are you that you can stay at 5?
- What would increase your confidence?

Hypothetical solutions

- Suppose one day you woke up after a good night's sleep and the problems were solved, how would you know they were solved?
- Who would notice first?
- Have any of these things happened already to you?
- Is any of this happening now?

Key tasks

- Between now and the next session please notice when you overcome the urge to . . .
- Between now and the next time, please notice what you would like to continue in your family life/work/partnership, etc.
- The problems seemed to stop when you were doing X. Can you do more of X, or see what happens if you do X?

Metaphors and language

One patient said 'I am in control of the steering wheel'.
   Later with this patient I asked:

- Can you give me more examples of you being at the steering wheel this week?
- How do you manage to keep hold of the steering wheel?
- Is this a new experience in your life?
- What can help to make sure you stay in control of the wheel?

Resources

- Are there areas of your life not taken over by 'depression', 'fear', etc.?
- Tell me about any of your interests or hobbies, etc.
- What do you value about your self, life, relationships?

SOLUTION FOCUSED HYPOTHESISING FOR THERAPISTS

Worksheet for overall planning/hypothesising outside sessions

- What is the problem?
- What is the goal?
- Are there exceptions?
- Are these chance/under control/routine/surprising?
- Why are the exceptions not realised/put into action already? Does something block them?
- How could the exceptions be done differently?
- What hypothetical future was described? (goals/solutions)
- Is the future description clear, vague, behavioural, feasible to do? What is the client doing differently in the hypothetical future picture?
- What might stop the client putting the hypothetical future into action?
- What would make a difference?
- Is there a repeating fixed problem pattern? Can you describe it? Why is it not changing?
- What aspects could be changed? What could the client change? What would make sense to the client?

Exploring meaning

Padesky's core belief work assessment

Ask the client to complete the following:

- I am . . .
- Other people are . . .
- The world is . . .
- Other people think I am . . .

Ask the client then to complete:

- I prefer that I am . . .
- I prefer that other people are . . .
- I prefer that the world is . . .
  (I prefer that other people think I am . . .)

Discovering meaning

What does the client say about the problem or the self? Make a list.
Explore implications: If I am X, then it means I'm . . .
Ask for open writing/diary.
Collect automatic thought records. What did you think/believe about this situation?
What would be another way of looking at this situation?
If the client reports dreams ask for details and what the events in the dream remind the person of.
Consider using tests for cognition.
Ask for visual images, a piece of music, drama that express how the person feels, or how the difficulty seems.
What metaphor, analogy, complex image captures the problem? e.g. When I experience this problem, I feel like I am a . . .; others seem like . . .; the situation seems like . . .
Consider role-playing the problem situation.

Go through a distressing situation in imagery and ask for the 'meaning' of particular experiences.

Explore 'rules', e.g. If I don't do X, then Y will happen; if I do X, then Z happens.

What metaphors/images recur?

You said you wanted to be 'thin' and not 'fat'? What does 'fat' mean to you?

- What is your picture, your stereotype of a fat person? What happens to such people?
- How do you imagine this?
- Where do these ideas come from?
- What do you believe about such people?

Emotion and context

- Have you had a sudden change of mood or feeling? What was happening?
- Can you describe the emotion or emotions?
- What did you believe was happening or what did you believe about the situation? (Yourself, the others, the events, etc.)
- Were there any specific thoughts or images you had before your feelings were strong (or as they became strong)?
- If you were trying to do something in the situation, what was that?
- Do your feelings reveal anything you might have needed or wanted (in the short term or long term)?
- Has this event or situation or reaction got a history in your life? What is it?
- Have situations like this happened before? Can you describe these?

Narrative focused questions

- What major difficulties or traumas have happened in your life?
- How did these influence a change in the way you view yourself and/or others? How did others view and experience these events (family, friends, teachers, etc.)? What was it like being in your family as a child (as a teenager)?
- What made you adopt this view of yourself?
- You mentioned (e.g. a death, separation), can you tell me more about that?
- When X events happened, how did you feel?
- How did you manage to keep going, keep your sense of worth?
- How did you develop your sense of values, of right and wrong?
- What were the strengths, the good points of your childhood?
- Who was on your side? Who stood by you? What did they contribute to your life? How did your being in that person's life contribute to their life?
- How did you manage to (study, have a relationship, a friend)?
- Did anyone recognise you, reach out, and try to help?
- Knowing what you know now about life, what would you have liked to tell your young suffering self?
- What did you know, or what did you value then that could be of use to you now?
- You have mentioned certain strengths and certain values you have had in your life. If you took steps now in line with these, what might you do differently, what steps might you take?

Appendix H

Alternative perspectives

Advantages and disadvantages

- Given the situation X (i.e. what is claimed to be the case in the delusion), what advantages are there, good aspects etc., what disadvantages?
- If X turns out to be not true, what advantages would there be and what disadvantages?

Alternatives

- You believe X, but what just does not fit in with your opinion?
- When does X not happen?
- What puzzles or baffles you about X happening?
- Do you have any doubts? What are these?
- What would be another way of looking at what has happened?
- If X is happening, then it implies that Y (e.g. if everyone has a 'device', it would cost millions of pounds). What do you think about these consequences?
- When X occurs, how do you feel? When else in your life have you felt like that?
- What does your doctor, friend, partner, say about what is happening to you?
- Is it possible they are right?
- Of course I could easily have got this wrong but I wonder if another way of explaining that (piece of evidence or delusional account) might be Y, what do you think?
- How does X (delusion) fit with Y (a proposition assented to and inconsistent with Y)?
- How could we test out your belief? (Obtain a very specific account of the prediction.)
- In the past you thought that several things would happen because of X, and they didn't happen. What does this say about X?

- Does feeling certain about something mean that it is true? (Followed by examples of having been mistaken oneself.)
- I think that you have said that X has the following consequences for you (list negative consequences of the belief). Now if it turned out that you weren't completely correct about this you would be having these consequences for no reason. Would it be worth checking this out?

Voices onset sequence

NAME:
DATE:

	Before the voice(s) started	During the voice(s)	After
What was happening?			
Any thoughts or images			
Emotion			
Wants and needs			
Voice content and how behaving			

References

Allport, G.W. (1955). *Becoming: Basic Considerations for a Psychology of Personality*. New Haven: Yale University Press.

Barham, P. and Hayward, R. (1998). In sickness and in health: dilemmas of the person with severe mental illness. *Psychiatry*, 61(2), 163–170.

Barker, P. and Buchanan-Barker, P. (2005). *The Tidal Model*. Hove: Routledge.

Barrowclough, C., Tarrier, N., Humphreys, L., Ward, J., Gregg, L., and Andrews, B. (2003). Self-esteem in schizophrenia: relationships between self-evaluation, family attitudes and symptomology. *Journal of Abnormal Psychology*, 112(1), 92–99.

Bartlett, F.C. (1932). *Remembering*. Cambridge: Cambridge University Press.

Baumeister, R.F. (2005). *The Cultural Animal: Human Nature, Meaning and Social Life*. Oxford: Oxford University Press.

Bebbington, P. and Kuipers, L. (1994). The predictive utility of expressed emotion in schizophrenia: an aggregate analysis. *Psychological Medicine*, 24(3), 707–718.

Bebbington, P., Wilkins, S., Sham, P., and Jones, P. (1996). Life events before psychotic episodes: do clinical and social variables affect the relationship? *Social Psychiatry and Psychiatric Epidemiology*, 31(3–4), 122–128.

Beck, A.T., Rush A.J., Shaw, B.F., and Emery, G. (1979). *Cognitive Therapy of Depression*. Chichester: Wiley.

Bell, V., Halligan, P.W., and Ellis, H.D. (2008). Are anomalous perceptual experiences necessary for delusions? *Journal of Nervous and Mental Disease*, 196(1), 3–8.

Bentall, R.P. (1994). Cognitive biases and abnormal beliefs. In A.S. David and J.C. Cutling (Eds.), *The Neuropsychology of Schizophrenia*. Hove: Lawrence Erlbaum Associates.

Bentall, R.P. (2003). *Madness Explained*. London: Allen Lane.

Bentall, R.P. Jackson, H.F., and Pilgrim, D. (1988). Abandoning the concept of schizophrenia: some implications of validity arguments for psychological research into psychotic phenomena. *British Journal of Clinical Psychology*, 27(4), 303–324.

Bhaskar, R. (1989). *Reclaiming Reality*. London: Verso.

Birchwood, M., Iqbal, Z., Chadwick, P., and Trower, P. (2000). Cognitive approach to depression and suicidal thinking in psychosis. *British Journal of Psychiatry*, 177, 516–528.

Birchwood, M., Meaden, A., Trower, P., and Gilbert, P. (2002). Shame, humiliation, and entrapment in psychosis: a social rank theory approach to cognitive intervention with voices and delusions. In A.P. Morrison (Ed.), *A Casebook of Cognitive Theory for Psychosis*. Hove: Brunner-Routledge.

Bizub, A.L., Joy, A., and Davidson, L. (2003). 'It's like being in another world': demonstrating the benefits of therapeutic horseback riding for individuals with psychiatric disability. *Psychiatric Rehabilitation Journal*, 26(4), 377–384.

Blakemore, S.J., Smith, J., Steel, R., Johnstone, E.C., and Frith, D. (2000). The perception of self-produced sensory stimuli in patients with auditory hallucinations and passivity experiences: evidence for a breakdown in self-monitoring. *Psychological Medicine*, 30(5), 1131–1139.

Bolton, D. and Hill, J. (1997). On the causal role of meaning. In M. Power and C. Brewin (Eds.), *The Transformation of Meaning in Psychological Therapies*. Chichester: Wiley.

Boscolo, L., Cecchin, G., Hoffman, L., and Penn, P. (1997). *Milan Systemic Family Therapy*. New York: Basic Books.

Bourdieu, P. (1990). *The Logic of Practice*. Cambridge: Polity Press.

Bovet, P. and Parnas, J. (1993). Schizophrenic delusions: a phenomenological approach. *Schizophrenia Bulletin*, 19(3), 579–597.

Boyle, M. (1990). *Schizophrenia – a Scientific Delusion?* London: Routledge.

Brewin, C.R. (2003). *Post-Traumatic Stress Disorder: Malady or Myth?* New Haven: Yale University Press.

Brewin, C.R. (2006). Understanding cognitive behaviour therapy: a retrieval competition account. *Behaviour Research and Therapy*, 44(6), 765–784.

Brown, G.W., Adler, Z., and Bifulco, A. (1988). Live events, difficulties and recovery from chronic depression. *British Journal of Psychiatry*, 152, 487–498.

Bruner, J. (1986). *Actual Minds, Possible Worlds*. Cambridge, MA: Harvard University Press.

Bruner, J. (1987). Life as narrative. *Social Research*, 54(1), 11–32.

Burnham, J.B. (1986). *Family Therapy*. London: Routledge.

Byrne, S., Trower, P., Birchwood, M., and Meaden, A. (2006). *Cognitive Therapy for Command Hallucinations*. London: Brunner-Routledge.

Cameron, N. (1959). The paranoid pseudo-community revisited. *American Journal of Sociology*, 65(1), 52–58.

Carpenter, W.T. Jr and Kirkpatrick, B. (1988). The heterogeneity of the long-term course of schizophrenia. *Schizophrenia Bulletin*, 14(4), 645–652.

Casper, E.S. and Fishbein, S. (2002). Job satisfaction and job success as moderators of the self-esteem of people with mental illness. *Psychiatric Rehabilitation Journal*, 26(1), 33–42.

Cecchin, G. (1987). Hypothesizing, circularity, and neutrality revisited: an invitation to curiosity. *Family Process*, 26(4), 405–413.

Chadwick, P.D.J. and Lowe, F. (1990). Measurement and modification of delusions. *Journal of Clinical and Consulting Psychology*, 58(2), 225–233.

Chadwick, P.K. (1993). The stepladder to the impossible: a first hand phenomenological account of a schizoaffective psychotic crisis. *Journal of Mental Health*, 2(3), 239–250.

Chadwick, P. (2006). *Person-Based Cognitive Therapy for Distressing Psychosis*. Chichester: Wiley.

Chadwick, P. and Birchwood, M. (1994). The omnipotence of voices I: a cognitive approach to auditory hallucinations. *British Journal of Psychiatry*, 164(2), 190–201.

Chadwick, P., Birchwood, M., and Trower, P. (1996). *Cognitive Therapy for Delusions, Voices, and Paranoia*. Chichester: Wiley.

Cienfuegos, J. and Monelli, C. (1983). The testimony of political repression as a therapeutic instrument. *American Journal of Othopsychiatry*, 53(1), 43–51.

Cohen, S. and McKay, G. (1985). Stress, social support, and the buffering hypothesis. *Psychological Bulletin*, 98(2), 310–357.

Corin, E. (1998). The thickness of being: intentional worlds, strategies of identity, and experience arising schizophrenics. *Psychiatry*, 61(2), 133–146.

Corin, E. and Lauzon, G. (1992). Positive withdrawal and the quest for meaning: the reconstruction of experience among schizophrenics. *Psychiatry*, 55(3), 266–278.

Cosoff, S.J. and Hafner, R.J. (1998). The prevalence of comorbid anxiety in schizophrenia, schizoaffective disorder and bipolar disorder. *Australian and New Zealand Journal of Psychiatry*, 32(1), 67–72.

Coursey, R.D., Keller, A., and Farrell, E.W. (1995). Individual psychotherapy and persons with serious mental illness: the clients' perspective. *Schizophrenia Bulletin*, 21(2), 283–301.

Cox, M. and Theilgaard, A. (1987). *Mutative Metaphors in Psychology*. London: Tavistock Publications.

Cromby, J. and Harper, D. (2005). Paranoia and social inequality. *Clinical Psychology Forum*, 153, 17–21.

Csikszentmihalyi, M. (1997). *Finding Flow: The Psychology of Engagement with Everyday Life*. New York: Basic Books.

D'Andrade, R.E. (1992). Schemas and motivation. In R.G. D'Andrade and C. Strauss (Eds.), *Human Motives and Cultural Models*. Cambridge: Cambridge University Press.

D'Ardenne, P. and McCann, E. (1997). The sexual and relationship needs of people with psychosis – a neglected topic. *Sexual and Marital Therapy*, 12(4), 301–303.

Davidson, D. (1980). *Essays on Actions and Events*. Oxford: Oxford University Press.

Davidson, L. (2003). *Living Outside Mental Illness: Qualitative Studies of Rrecovery in Schizophrenia*. New York and London: New York University Press.

Deegan, P.E. (1988). Recovery: the lived experience of rehabilitation. *Psychosocial Rehabilitation Journal*, 11(4), 11–19.

de Shazer, S. (1985). *Keys to Solution in Brief Therapy*. New York: Norton.

de Shazer, S. (1988). *Clues: Investigating Solutions in Brief Therapy*. New York: Norton.

de Shazer, S. (1991). *Putting Difference to Work*. New York: Norton.

de Shazer, S., Dolan, Y., Korman, H., Trepper, T., McCollum, E., and Berg, I.K. (2007). *More than Miracles: The State of the Art of Solution-Focused Brief Therapy*. New York: Haworth Press.

Diaz, E., Fergusson, A., and Strauss, J. (2004). Innovative care for the homeless mentally ill in Bogota, Colombia. In J.H. Jenkins and R.J. Barrett (Eds.), *Schizophrenia, Culture, and Subjectivity: The Edge of Experience*. Cambridge: Cambridge University Press.

Eakes, G., Walsh, S., Markowski, M., Cain, H., and Swanson, M. (1997). Family centred brief solution-focused therapy with chronic schizophrenia: a pilot study. *Journal of family Therapy*, 19(2), 145–158.

Edelman, G.M. and Tononi, G. (2000). *Consciousness: How Matter becomes Imagination*. London: Penguin.

Edwards, D. and Potter, J. (1992). *Discursive Psychology*. London: Sage.

Ehlers, A., Clark, D.M., Hackmann, A., McManus, F., and Fennell, M. (2005). Cognitive therapy for post-traumatic stress disorder: development and evaluation. *Behaviour Research and Therapy*, 43(4), 413–431.

Ellis, N., Crone, D., Davey, R., and Grogan, S. (2007). Exercise interventions as an adjunct therapy for psychosis: a critical review. *British Journal of Clinical Psychology*, 46(1), 95–111.

Eron, J.B. and Lund, T.W. (1996). *Narrative Solutions in Brief Therapy*. New York: Guilford Press.

Estroff, S.E. (1999). Self, identity, and subjective experiences of schizophrenia: in search of the subject. *Schizophrenia Bulletin*, 15(2), 189–196.

Evenson, E., Rhodes, J., Feigenbaum, J., and Solly, A. (in press). The experiences of fathers with psychosis. *Journal of Mental Health*.

Fauconnier, G. and Turner, M. (2002). *The Way We Think: Conceptual Blending and the Mind's Hidden Complexities*. New York: Basic Books.

Fava, G.A., Rafanelli, C., Cazzaro, M., Conti, S., and Grandi, S. (1998). Well-being therapy: a novel psychotherapeutic approach for residual symptoms of affective disorders. *Psychological Medicine*, 28(2), 475–480.

Fodor, J.A. (1987). *Psychosemantics*. Cambridge, MA: MIT Press.

Foucault, M. (1965). *Madness and Civilization: A History of Insanity in the Age of Reason*. New York: Random House.

Fowler, D., Garety, P., and Kuipers, E. (1995). *Cognitive Behaviour Therapy for Psychosis: Theory and Practice*. Chichester: Wiley.

Fowler, D., Freeman, D., Steel, C., Hardy, A., Smith, B., Hackman, C., Kuipers, E., and Bebbington, P. (2006). The catastrophic interaction hypothesis. In W. Larkin and A.P. Morrison (Eds.), *Trauma and Psychosis*. Hove: Routledge.

France, C.M. and Uhlin, B.D. (2006). Narrative as an outcome domain in psychosis. *Psychology and Psychotherapy: Theory, Research and Practice*, 79(1), 53–67.

Frankfurt, H.G. (1988). *The Importance of What We Care About*. Cambridge: Cambridge University Press.

Freeman, D. and Garety, P.A. (2003). Connecting neurosis and psychosis: the direct influence of emotions on delusions and hallucinations. *Behaviour Research and Therapy*, 41(8), 923–947.

Freeman, D. and Garety, P.A. (2004). *Paranoia: The Psychology of Persecutory Delusions*. Hove: Psychology Press.

Freeman, D., Pugh, K., Antley, A., Slater, M., Bebbinton, P., Gittins, M., Dunn, G., Kuipers, E., Fowler, D., and Garety, P. (2008). Virtual reality study of paranoid thinking in the general population. *British Journal of Psychiatry*, 192(4), 258–263.

Freeman, W.J. (1995). *Societies of Brains: A Study in the Neuroscience of Love and Hate*. Hillside, NJ: Lawrence Erlbaum Associates.

Freud, S. (1900). *The Interpretation of Dreams*. Aylesbury: Pelican Books.

Friston, K.J. and Frith, C.D. (1995). Schizophrenia: a disconnection syndrome? *Clinical Neuroscience*, 3(2), 89–97.

Frith, C.D. (1992). *The Cognitive Neuropsychology of Schizophrenia*. Hove: Lawrence Erlbaum Associates.

Furman, B. and Ahola, T. (1992). *Solution Talk: Hosting Therapeutic Conversations*. New York: Norton.

Garety, P.A. and Freeman, D. (1999). Cognitive approaches to delusions: a critical review of theories and evidence. *British Journal of Clinical Psychology*, 38(2), 113–154.

Garety, P.A. and Hemsley, D.R. (1994). *Delusions*. Oxford: Oxford University Press.

Garety, P.A., Fowler, D., Kuipers, E., Freeman, D., Dunn, G., Bebbington, P., Hadley, C., and Jones, F. (1997). London–East Anglia randomised controlled trial of cognitive-behavioural therapy for psychosis. *British Journal of Psychiatry*, 171, 420–426.

Georgaca, E. (2000). Reality and discourse: a critical analysis of the category of 'delusions'. *British Journal of Medical Psychology*, 73(2), 227–242.

Georgieff, N. and Jeannerod, M. (1998). Beyond consciousness of external reality: a 'who' system for consciousness of action and self-consciousness. *Consciousness and Cognition*, 7(3), 465–477.

Gilbert, P. (1989). *Human Nature and Suffering*. Hove: Lawrence Erlbaum Associates.

Gilbert, P. (Ed.) (2005). *Compassion: Conceptualisation, Research and Use in Psychotherapy*. Hove: Routledge.

Gilbert, P., Birchwood, M., Gilbert, J., Trower, P., Hay, J., Murray, B., Meaden, A., Olsen, K., and Miles, J.N.V. (2001). An exploration of evolved mechanisms for dominant and subordinate behaviour in relation to auditory hallucinations in schizophrenia and critical thoughts in depression. *Psychological Medicine*, 31(6), 1117–1127.

Gingerich, W.J. and Eisengart, S. (2000). Solution-focused brief therapy: a review of the outcome research. *Family Process*, 39(4), 477–498.

Goffman, E. (1974). *Frame Analysis*. New York: Harper & Row.

Goldie, P. (2000). *The Emotions: A Philosophical Exploration*. Oxford: Oxford University Press.

Goldie, P. (2004). *On Personality*. London: Routledge.

Gonçalves, O.F. (1994). Cognitive narrative psychotherapy: the hermeneutic construction of alternative meanings. *Journal of Cognitive Psychotherapy*, 8(2), 105–125.

Green, L. (2003). *Living with Psychosis: Family Perspectives on Giving and Receiving Support*. Dissertation, University College London.

Greenberg, L.S. (2002). *Emotion-Focused Therapy*. Washington: APA.

Greenberg, L.S. and Pascual-Leone, J. (1997). Emotion in the creation of personal meaning. In M. Power and C. Brewin (Eds.), *The Transformation of Meaning in Psychological Therapies*. Chichester: Wiley.

Greenberger, D. and Padesky, C.A. (1995). *Mind over Mood: A Cognitive Therapy Treatment Manual for Clients*. New York: Guilford Press.

Greenwood, J.D. (1994). *Realism, Identity and Emotion*. London: Sage.

Grey, N. and Young, K. (2008). Cognitive behaviour therapy with refugees and asylum seekers experiencing traumatic stress symptoms. *Behavioural and Cognitive Psychotherapy*, 36(1), 3–19.

Grey, N., Young, K., and Holmes, E. (2002). Cognitive restructuring within reliving: a treatment for peritraumatic emotional 'hotspots' in posttraumatic stress disorder. *Behavioural and Cognitive Psychotherapy*, 30(1), 37–56.

Guidano, V.F. (1991). *The Self in Process*. New York: Guilford Press.

Gumley, A. and Schwannauer, M. (2006). *Staying Well After Psychosis: A Cognitive Interpersonal Approach to Recover and Relapse Prevention*. Chichester: Wiley.

Hackman, A. (2005). Compassionate imagery in the treatment of early memories in Axis I anxiety disorders. In P. Gilbert (Ed.), *Compassion: Conceptualisations, Research and Use in Psychotherapy*. Hove: Routledge.

Hall, P.L. and Tarrier, N. (2003). The cognitive-behavioural treatment of low self-esteem in psychotic patients: a pilot study. *Behaviour, Research, and Therapy*, 41(3), 317–332.

Hallahan, B. and Garland, M.R. (2005). Essential fatty acids and mental health. *British Journal of Psychiatry*, 186, 275–277.

Hardy, A., Fowler, D., Freeman, D., Smith, B., Steele, C., Evans, J., Garety, P., Kuipers, E., Bebbington, P., and Dunn, G. (2005). Trauma and hallucinatory experience in psychosis. *Journal of Nervous and Mental Disease*, 193(8), 501–507.

Harper, D.J. (2004). Delusions and discourse: moving beyond the constraints of the modernist paradigm. *Philosophy, Psychiatry, and Psychology*, 11(1), 55–64.

Harrow, M., Rattenbury, F., and Stoll, F. (1988). Schizophrenic delusions: an analysis of their persistence, of related premorbid ideas, and of three major dimensions. In T.F. Oltmanns and B.A. Maher (Eds.), *Delusional Beliefs*. New York: Wiley.

Hawton, K. and Kirk, J. (1989). Problem-solving. In K. Hawton, P.M. Salkovskis, J. Kirk, and D.M. Clark (Eds.), *Cognitive Behaviour Therapy for Psychiatric Problems: A Practical Guide*. Oxford: Oxford University Press.

Hawton, K., Salkovskis, P.M., Kirk, J., and Clark, D.M. (Eds.) (1989). *Cognitive Behaviour Therapy for Psychiatric Problems: A Practical Guide*. Oxford: Oxford University Press.

Hedges, F. (2005). *An Introduction to Systemic Therapy with Individuals: A Social Constructionist Approach*. Basingstoke: Palgrave Macmillan.

Hemsley, D.R. (1998). The disruption of the 'sense of self' in schizophrenia: potential links with disturbances of information processing. *British Journal of Medical Psychology*, 71(2), 115–124.

Hemsley, D.R. (2005). The schizophrenic experience: taken out of context? *Schizophrenia Bulletin*, 31(1), 43–53.

Henriques, G. (2003). The tree of knowledge system and the theoretical unification of psychology. *Review of General Psychology*, 7(2), 150–182.

Herman, J. (1992). *Trauma and Recovery*. New York: Basic Books.

Holma, J. and Aaltonen, J. (1998). The experience of time in acute psychosis and schizophrenia. *Contemporary Family Therapy*, 20(3), 265–276.

Hurlburt, R.T. (1990). *Sampling Normal and Schizophrenic Inner Experience*. New York: Plenum Press.

Hustig, H.H. and Hafner, R.J. (1990). Persistent auditory hallucinations and their relationship to delusions of mood. *Journal of Nervous and Mental Disease*, 178(4), 264–267.

Hutto, D.D. (2008). *Folk Psychological Narratives: The Sociocultural Basis of Understanding Reasons*. Cambridge, MA: Bradford.

Isenwater, W., Lanham, W., and Thornhill, H. (2002). The college link programme: evaluation of a supported education initiative in Great Britain. *Psychiatric Rehabilitation Journal*, 26(1), 43–50.

Jacobson, N. and Curtis, L. (2000). Recovery as policy in mental health services: strategies emerging from the states. *Psychiatric Rehabilitation Journal*, 23(4), 333–341.

Jakes, S. and Rhodes, J. (2003). The effect of different components of psychological therapy on people with delusions: five experimental single cases. *Clinical Psychology and Psychotherapy*, 10(5), 302–315.

Jakes, S., Rhodes, J., and Turner, T. (1999). Effectiveness of cognitive therapy for delusions in routine practice. *British Journal of Psychiatry*, 175, 331–335.

Jakes, S., Rhodes, J., and Issa, S. (2004). Are the themes of delusional beliefs related to the themes of life-problems and goals? *Journal of Mental Health*, 13(6), 611–619.

James, I.A. (2001). Schema therapy: the next generation, but should it carry a health warning? *Behavioural and Cognitive Psychotherapy*, 29, 401–407.

Jaspers, K. (1959). *General Psychopathology* (trans. Hoenig, J. and Hamilton, M.W., 1963). Manchester: Manchester University Press.

Johnson, J., Godding, P., and Tarrier, N. (2008). Suicide risk in schizophrenia: explanatory models and clinical implications, The Schematic Appraisal Model of Suicide (SAMS). *Psychology and Psychotherapy: Theory, Research and Practice*, 81(1), 55–77.

Johnson, M. (1987). *The Body in the Mind*. Chicago: Chicago University Press.

Jung, C.G. (1907). The psychology of dementia praecox. In *The Psychogenesis of Mental Disease. Collected Works of Carl Jung, Vol. 3* (1960). London: Routledge and Kegan Paul.

Kashima, J. (1997). Culture, narrative, and human motivation. In D. Munro, J. Schumaker, and S.C. Carr (Eds.), *Motivation and Culture*. New York: Routledge.

Keen, E. (1986). Paranoia and cataclysmic narrative. In T.R. Sarbin (Ed.), *Narrative Psychology: The Storied Nature of Human Conduct*. New York: Praeger.

Kelly, G.A. (1955). *The Psychology of Personal Constructs, Vols 1 and 2*. New York: Norton.

Kingdon, D.G. and Turkington, D. (1994). *Cognitive Behaviour Therapy of Schizophrenia*. Hove: Lawrence Erlbaum Associates.

Kingdon, D.G. and Turkington, D. (2004). *Cognitive Therapy of Schizophrenia*. New York: Guilford Press.

Knudson, B. and Coyle, A. (2002). The experience of hearing voices: an interpretative phenomenological analysis. *Existential Analysis*, 13(1), 117–134.

Kövecses, Z. (1990). *Emotion Concepts*. New York: Springer-Verlag.

Laing, R.D. (1960). *The Divided Self*. Harmondsworth: Penguin.

Lakoff, G. (1987). *Women, Fire, and Dangerous Things: What Categories Reveal about the Mind*. Chicago: University of Chicago Press.

Lakoff, G. and Johnson, M. (1980). *Metaphors We Live By*. Chicago: University of Chicago Press.

Larkin, W. and Morrison, A.P. (Eds.) (2006). *Trauma and Psychosis*. Hove: Routledge.

Lee, D.A. (2005). The perfect nurturer: a model to develop a compassionate mind within the context of cognitive therapy. In P. Gilbert (Ed.), *Compassion: Conceptualisations, Research, and Use in Psychotherapy*. Hove: Routledge.

Linehan, M.M. (1993). *Cognitive-Behavioral Treatment of Borderline Personality Disorder*. New York: Guilford Press.

Lipchick, E. (2002). *Beyond Technique in Solution Focused Therapy*. New York: Guilford Press.

Lyons, W.E. (1995). *Approaches to Intentionality*. Oxford: Oxford University Press.

Lysaker, P.H. and Lysaker, J.T. (2001). Psychosis and the disintegration of dialogical self-structure: problems posed by schizophrenia for the maintenance of dialogue. *British Journal of Medical Psychology*, 74, 23–33.

Lysaker, R.S., Lancaster, R.S., and Lysaker, J.T. (2003). Narrative transformation as an outcome in the psychotherapy of schizophrenia. *Psychology and Psychotherapy: Theory, Research and Practice*, 76(3), 285–299.

MacBeth, A., Schwannauer, M., and Gumley, A. (2008). The association between attachment style, social mentalities, and paranoid ideation: an analogue study. *Psychology and Psychotherapy: Theory, Research, and Practice*, 81(1), 79–93.

MacIntyre, A. (1981). *After Virtue: A Study in Moral Theory*. London: Duckworth.

MacLeod, A.K. and Moore, R. (2000). Positive thinking revisited: positive cognitions, well-being, and mental health. *Clinical Psychology and Psychotherapy*, 7(1), 1–10.

Maher, B. (1988). Anomalous experience and delusional thinking: the logic of explanations. In T.F. Oltmanns and B.A. Maher (Eds.), *Delusional Beliefs*, pp. 15–33. New York: Wiley.

Mahoney, M.J. (1991). *Human Change Processes*. New York: Plenum Press.

Mahoney, M.J. (2003). *Constructive Psychotherapy: A Practical Guide*. New York: Guilford Press.

Martell, C.R., Addis, M.E., and Jacobson, N.S. (2001). *Depression in Context: Strategies for Guided Action*. New York: Norton.

Matussek, P. (1987/1952). Studies in delusional perception. In J. Cutting and M. Shepard (Eds.), *The Clinical Roots of the Schizophrenic Concept*. Cambridge: Cambridge University Press.

McAdams, D. (1993). *Stories We Live By: Personal Myths and the Making of the Self*. New York: Marrow.

McCann, E. (2000). The expression of sexuality in people with psychosis: breaking the taboos. *Journal of Advanced Nursing*, 32(1), 132–138.

McGinn, C. (1999). *The Mysterious Flame*. New York: Basic Books.

Mead, G.H. (1934). *Mind, Self and Society*. Chicago: University of Chicago Press.

Meaden, A. and Van Marle, S. (2008). When the going gets tougher: the importance of long-term supportive psychotherapy in psychosis. *Advances in Psychiatric Treatment*, 14, 42–49.

Meltzer, B.N., Petras, J.W., and Reynolds, L.T. (1975). *Symbolic Interactionism: Genesis, Varieties and Criticism*. Boston: Routledge and Kegan Paul.

Mirowsky, J. and Ross, C.E. (1983). Paranoia and the structure of powerlessness. *American Sociological Review*, 48(2), 228–239.

Moorhead, S. and Turkington, D. (2001). The CBT of delusional disorder: the relationship between schema vulnerability and psychotic content. *British Journal of Medical Psychology*, 74, 419–430.

Moran, D. (2000). *Introduction to Phenomenology*. London: Routledge.

Moritz, S. and Woodward, T.S. (2004). Plausibility judgment in schizophrenic patients: evidence of a liberal acceptance bias. *German Journal of Psychiatry*, 7, 66–74.

Moritz, S., Woodward, T.S., and Lambert, M. (2007). Under what circumstances do patients with schizophrenia jump to conclusions? A liberal acceptance account. *British Journal of Clinical Psychology*, 46, 127–137.

Morrison, A.P. (Ed). (2002). A *Casebook of Cognitive Therapy for Psychosis*. Hove: Brunner-Routledge.

Morrison, A.P., Frame, L., and Larkin, W. (2003). Relation between trauma and psychosis: a review and integration. *British Journal of Clinical Psychology*, 42(4), 331–353.

Morrison, A.P., Renton, J.C., Dunn, H., Williams, S., and Bentall, R.P. (2004). *Cognitive Therapy for Psychosis*. Hove: Brunner-Routledge.

Mueser, K.T., Salyers, M.P., Rosenberg, S.D., Goodman, L.A., Essock, S.M., Osher, F.C. et al. (2004). Interpersonal trauma and posttraumatic stress in patients with severe mental illness: demographic clinical and health correlates. *Schizophrenia Bulletin*, 30(1), 45–57.

Nagel, T. (1979). *Mortal Questions*. Cambridge: Cambridge University Press.

Nayani, T.H. and David, A.S. (1996). The auditory hallucination: a phenomenological survey. *Psychological Medicine*, 26(1), 177–189.

Neimeyer, R.A. (1993). An appraisal of constructivist psychotherapies. *Journal of Consulting and Clinical Psychology*, 61(2), 221–234.

Nelson, H. (1997). *Cognitive-Behavioural Therapy with Schizophrenia: A Practice Manual*. Cheltenham: Stanley Thornes.

Nelson, H. (2005). *Cognitive-Behavioural Therapy with Delusions and Hallucinations: A Practical Manual* (2nd edition). Bath: Nelson Jones.

Neuner, F., Schauer, M., Roth, W.T., and Elbert, T. (2002). A narrative exposure treatment as intervention in a refugee camp: a case report. *Behavioural and Cognitive Psychotherapy*, 30, 205–209.

Oberst, U.E. and Stewart, A.E. (2003). *Adlerian Psychotherapy*. Hove: Brunner-Routledge.

O'Hanlon, W.H. and Weiner-Davis, M. (1989). *In Search of Solutions: A New Direction in Psychotherapy*. New York: Norton.

O'Nell, T.D. (1999). 'Coming Home' among Northern Plains Vietnam veterans: psychological transformations in pragmatic perspective. *Ethos*, 27(4), 441–465.

Padesky, C.A. (1994). Schema change processes in cognitive therapy. *Clinical Psychology and Psychotherapy*, 1(5), 267–278.

Padesky, C.A. (2000). *Transforming Personality*. (Workshop materials). Newport Beach: Center for Cognitive Therapy.

Padesky, C.A. (2002). *Cognitive Therapy Unplugged*. (Workshop materials). Newport Beach: Center for Cognitive Therapy.

Padesky, C.A. and Greenberger, D. (1995). *Clinician's Guide to Mind Over Mood.* New York: Guilford Press.

Parnas, J. and Sass, L.A. (2002). Self, solipsism, and schizophrenic delusions. *Philosophy, Psychiatry, Psychology*, 8(2–3), 101–120.

Penn, D.L., Mueser, K.T., Tarrier, N., Gloege, A., Cather, C., Serrano, D., and Otto, M.W. (2004). Supportive therapy for schizophrenia: possible mechanisms and implications for adjunctive psychosocial treatments. *Schizophrenia Bulletin*, 30(1), 101–122.

Pennebaker, J.W. (1990). *Opening Up: The Healing Power of Confiding in Others.* New York: Guilford Press.

Potter, J. and Wetherell, M. (1987). *Discourse and Social Psychology.* London: Sage.

Read, J., Perry, B.D., Moskowitz, A., and Connolly, J. (2001). The contribution of early traumatic events to schizophrenia in some patients: a traumagenic neuro-developmental model. *Psychiatry: Interpersonal and Biological Processes*, 64(4), 319–345.

Read, J., Mosher, L.R., and Bentall, R.P. (Eds.) (2004). *Models of Madness.* Hove: Brunner-Routledge.

Resick, P.A. (2001). *Stress and Trauma.* Hove: Pyschology Press.

Rhodes, J.E. and Gipps, R. (in press). Delusion, certainty, and the Background. *Philosophy, Psychiatry, and Psychology.*

Rhodes, J.E. and Jakes, S. (2000). Correspondence between delusions and personal goals: a qualitative analysis. *British Journal of Medical Psychology*, 73(2), 211–225.

Rhodes, J.E. and Jakes, S. (2002). Using solution focused therapy during a psychotic crisis: a case study. *Clinical Psychology and Psychotherapy*, 9, 139–148.

Rhodes, J.E. and Jakes, S. (2004a). The contribution of metaphor and metonymy to delusions. *Psychology and Psychotherapy: Theory, Research, and Practice*, 77(1), 1–17.

Rhodes, J.E. and Jakes, S. (2004b). Evidence given for delusions during cognitive behaviour therapy. *Clinical Psychology and Psychotherapy*, 11, 207–218.

Rhodes, J.E. and Jakes, S. (in press). *Perspectives on the onset of delusions.* Manuscript submitted for publication.

Rhodes, J., Jakes, S., and Robinson, J. (2005). A qualitative analysis of delusional content. *Journal of Mental Health*, 14(4), 383–398.

Roberts, G. (1992). The origins of delusion. *British Journal of Psychiatry*, 161, 298–308.

Roberts, G. (1999). Healing stories. In G. Roberts and J. Holmes (Eds.), *Narrative in Psychiatry and Psychotherapy.* Oxford: Oxford University Press.

Romme, M. and Escher, S. (Eds.) (1993). *Accepting Voices.* London: Mind Publications.

Russell, R.L. (1991). Narrative in views of humanity, science, and action: lessons for cognitive therapy. *Journal of Cognitive Psychotherapy: An International Quarterly*, 5(4), 241–256.

Schomerus, G., Heider, D., Angermeyer, M.C., Bebbington, P.E., Azorin, J.M., Brugha, T., and Touni, M. (2008). Urban residence, victimhood and the appraisal of personal safety in people with schizophrenia: results from the European Schizophrenia Cohort (EuroSC). *Psychological Medicine*, 38(4), 591–597.

Searle, J.R. (1983). *Intentionality: An Essay in the Philosophy of Mind*. Cambridge: Cambridge University Press.

Searle, J.R. (1992). *The Rediscovery of the Mind*. Cambridge, MA: MIT Press.

Searle, J.R. (2001). *Rationality in Action*. Cambridge, MA: MIT Press.

Searle, J.R. (2004). *Mind: A Brief Introduction*. Oxford: Oxford University Press.

Seikkula, J., Alakare, B., and Aaltonen, J. (2001). Open dialogue in psychosis 1: an introduction and case illustration. *Journal of Constructivist Psychology*, 14, 247–265.

Seligman, M.E.P., Steen, T.A., Park, N., and Peterson, C. (2005). Positive psychology progress: empirical validation of interventions. *American Psychologist*, July–August, 410–421.

Sensky, T., Turkington, D., Kingdon, K., Scott, J.L., Scott, J., Siddle, R., O'Carroll, M., and Barnes, T.R.E. (2000). A randomised controlled trial of cognitive-behavioural therapy for persistent symptoms in schizophrenia resistant to medication. *Archives of General Psychiatry*, 57(2), 165–712.

Shapiro, M.B. (1961). A method of measuring psychological changes specific to the individual psychiatric patient. *British Journal of Medical Psychology*, 34, 151–155.

Shapiro, M.B. and Ravenette, A. (1959). A preliminary experiment on paranoid delusions. *Journal of Mental Science*, 105, 295–312.

Sharpley, M., Hutchinson, G., McKenzie, K., and Murray, R.M. (2001). Understanding the excess of psychosis among the African-Caribbean population in England. *British Journal of Psychiatry*, 178(Suppl. 40), 60–68.

Shepherd, G., Boardman, J., and Slade, M. (2008). *Making Recovery a Reality*. London: Sainsbury Centre for Mental Health.

Sims, A. (1995). *Symptoms in the Mind: An Introduction to Descriptive Psychopathology* (2nd edition). London: Saunders.

Sims, P.A. and Whynot, C.A. (1997). Hearing metaphor: an approach to working with family-generated metaphor. *Family Process*, 36(4), 341–355.

Slade, P.D. and Bentall, R.P. (1988). *Sensory Deception: A Scientific Analysis of Hallucinations*. London: Croom Helm.

Sluzki, C.E. (1992). Transformations: a blueprint for narrative changes in therapy. *Family Process*, 31(3), 217–230.

Smith, B., Steel, C., Rollinson, R., Freeman, D., Hardy, A., Kuipers, E., Bebbington, P., Garey, P., and Fowler, D. (2006). The importance of traumatic events in formulations and intervention in cognitive behavioural therapy for psychosis: three case examples. In W. Larkin and A.P. Morrison (Eds.), *Trauma and Psychosis*. Hove: Routledge.

Smith, J.A. (2004). Reflecting on the development of interpretative phenomenological analysis and its contribution to qualitative research in psychology. *Qualitative Research in Psychology*, 1(1), 39–54.

Smith, J.A. and Osborn, M. (2003). Interpretative phenomenological analysis. In J.A. Smith (Ed.), *Qualitative Psychology: A Practical Guide to Research Methods*. London: Sage.

Snaith, R.P. and Zigmond, A.S. (1994). *The Hospital and Anxiety Scale*. Windsor: NFER-Nelson.

Stahl, S.M. and Buckley, P.E. (2007). Negative symptoms of schizophrenia: a problem that will not go away. *Acta Psychiatrica Scandinavica*, 115(1), 4–11.

Steel, C., Fowler, D., and Holmes, E.A. (2005). Trauma-related intrusions and psychosis: an information processing account. *Behavioural and Cognitive Psychotherapy*, 33(2), 139–152.

Sundquist, K., Frank, G., and Sundquist, J. (2004). Urbanisation and incidence of psychosis and depression. *British Journal of Psychiatry*, 184, 293–298.

Szechtman, H., Woody, E., Bowers, K.S., and Nahmias, C. (1998). Where the imaginal appears real: a positron emission topography study of auditory hallucination. *Proceedings of the National Academy of Sciences*, 95(4), 1956–1960.

Talvitie, V. and Tiitinen, H. (2006). From the repression of contents to the rules of the (narrative) self: a present-day cognitive view of the 'Freudian phenomenon' of repressed contents. *Psychology and Psychotherapy: Theory, Research and Practice*, 79(2), 164–181.

Tarrier, N. (2002). The use of coping strategies and self-regulation in the treatment of psychosis. In A.P. Morrison (Ed.), *A Casebook of Cognitive Therapy for Psychosis*. Hove: Brunner-Routledge.

Thornhill, H., Clare, L., and May, R. (2004). Escape, enlightenment, and endurance. *Anthropology and Medicine*, 11(2), 181–199.

Tienari, P., Wynne, L.C., Sorri, A., Lahti, I., Laksy, K., Morirg, J., Naarala, M., Nieminen, P., and Wahlberg, K. (2004). Genotype–environment interaction in schizophrenia: long-term follow-up study of Finnish adoptees. *British Journal of Psychiatry*, 184, 216–222.

Tolton, J.C. (2004). First person account: how insight poetry helped me to overcome my illness. *Schizophrenia Bulletin*, 30(2), 469–472.

Tononi, G. and Edelman, E.M. (2000). Schizophrenia and the mechanisms of conscious integration. *Brain Research Reviews*, 31(2–3), 391–400.

Toolan, M.J. (1988). *Narrative: A Critical Linguistic Introduction*. London: Routledge.

Turner, M. (1996). *The Literary Mind: The Origins of Thought and Language*. New York: Oxford University Press.

Watts, F.N., Powell, E.G., and Austin, S.V. (1973). Modification of abnormal beliefs. *British Journal of Medical Psychology*, 46(4), 359–363.

Watzlawick, P., Weakland, J.H., and Fisch, R. (1974). *Change*. New York: Norton.

Weine, S.M., Kulenovic, A.D., Pavkovic, I., and Gibbons, R. (1998). Testimony psychotherapy in Bosnian refugees: a pilot study. *American Journal of Psychiatry*, 155(12), 1720–1726.

White, M. (1989). *Selected Papers*. Adelaide: Dulwich Centre Publications.

White, M. (1995). *Re-authoring Lives: Interviews and Essays*. Adelaide: Dulwich Centre Publications.

White, M. (2004). *Narrative Practice and Exotic Lives: Resurrecting Diversity in Everyday Life*. Adelaide: Dulwich Centre Publications.

White, M. (2007). *Maps of Narrative Practice*. New York: Norton.

White, M. and Epston, D. (1990). *Narrative Means to Therapeutic Ends*. New York: Norton.

White, R.G., McCleery, M., Gumley, A.I., and Mulholland, C. (2007). Hopelessness in schizophrenia: the impact of symptoms and beliefs about illness. *Journal of Nervous and Mental Disease*, 195(12), 968–975.

Winter, D.A. and Viney, L.L. (Eds.) (2005). *Personal Construct Psychotherapy: Advances in Theory, Practice and Research*. London: Whurr.

Wittgenstein, L. (1953). *Philosophical Investigations*. Oxford: Basil Blackwell.

Wittgenstein, L. (1969). *On Certainty*. Oxford: Blackwell Publishers.

Wolpe, J. (1990). *The Practice of Behavior Therapy* (4th edition). New York: Pergamon Press.

Young, E., Klosko, J.S., and Weishaar, M.E. (2003). *Schema Therapy: A Practitioner's Guide*. New York: Guilford Press.

Zahavi, D. (2000). *Exploring the Self: Philosophical and Psychopathological Perspectives on Self-Experience*. Amsterdam: Benjamins.

Zubin, J. and Spring, B. (1977). Vulnerability: a new view on schizophrenia. *Journal of Abnormal Psychology*, 86(2), 103–126.

Index